Reserve Law Enforcement
in the United States
(The Re-Issue)

A National Study of State, County and City Standards
Concerning the Training & Numbers of
Non-full-time Police and Sheriff's Personnel

First Edition

Manufactured in the United States of America

ISBN: 978-0-9828697-3-4
(8 1/2 X 11 US trade paperback)

www.TheCopDoc.com

B

Reserve Law Enforcement
in the United States
(The Re-Issue)

A National Study of State, County and City Standards
Concerning the Training & Numbers of
Non-full-time Police and Sheriff's Personnel

By

Dr. Richard Weinblatt

Also by

Dr. Richard Weinblatt

Books

Reserve Law Enforcement in the United States:
A National Study of State, County, and City Standards Concerning the Training & Numbers of Non-full-time Police and Sheriff's Personnel (1993)

The Cop Doc's Classic Writings on
Police Media Relations (2010)

The Cop Doc's Classic Writings on
Police Careers (2010)

Cops and College:
Lessons in Professionalism (2010)

The Cop Doc's Classic Writings on
Police Reserves (2011)

D

Also by

Dr. Richard Weinblatt

Columns

Law and Order:
The Magazine for Police Management
"Reserve Reports"
(1991-2001)

Officer.com
"Reserve Power" and "Career Corner"
(2005-2006)

PoliceLink.com
"Law Enforcement Career Expert"
(2007-Present)

PoliceOne.com
"Weinblatt's Tips" and "Police and the Press"
(2004-Present)

Websites

www.PoliceReserveOfficer.com

www.PoliceChiefJobs411.com

F

Reserve Law Enforcement in the United States... THE RE-ISSUE

When I originally researched and wrote <u>Reserve Law Enforcement in the United States</u> over the course of a full year in 1993, little did I realize the impact the book would continue to have some 20 years later. Noted reserve leader Frank Rizzo, as well as other colleagues involved in supporting me with the original project, also underestimated the long lasting effect the book has had on dedicated and community-minded folks whose titles include reserve, auxiliary, and special. People are still actively referring to the book that has been sitting on their shelf for years.

Many of the issues that law enforcement executives and reserves grappled with then are the same ones vexing them today. Agencies are still tasked with the need for excellence in police services and community relations within tight fiscal constraints. If anything, with the downturn in the economy, the issues are even more pronounced in 2011 than they were in 1993.

All of the original copies printed in 1993 were sold within days and it is listed by booksellers as being "out of print." Since I still get regular requests for the book from full-time law enforcers, reservists, and criminal justice scholars, I decided to have it reprinted and reissued now, in 2011, in its entirety. I have included the original front and back covers within the newly re-issued version's covers.

Much like the material contained in my The Cop Doc's Classic Writings series books, the information contained in this book reflects some yesteryear concepts that still have validity to this day. Also, some of the facts and figures may seem less than ideal, but they should be viewed in the context of the date they were originally researched and printed. Many of the contact people, addresses, and phone numbers listed in the book have changed since 1993, so be aware of that if attempting contact. Obviously, my address is no longer in New Jersey (as it was in 1993) at the address printed in the original book. Rather than trying to make contact with a person that is no longer there, please feel free to contact me via the 2011 modern method: my website www.TheCopDoc.com. I hope the re-issue of what many have called the most comprehensive study on reserve law enforcement to date helps you in your quest for reserve excellence.

Dr. Richard Weinblatt
The Cop Doc
Orlando, FL

www.TheCopDoc.com

About the Author

Dr. Richard Weinblatt, The Cop Doc, is a law enforcement expert, consultant, writer, radio show host, and media commentator, who has served as a police chief, criminal justice professor, and police academy director.

Dr. Weinblatt has worked in several regions of the United States in reserve and full-time sworn positions ranging from Auxiliary Police Lieutenant in New Jersey to Patrol Division Deputy Sheriff in New Mexico to Police Chief in North Carolina. A certified instructor for Taser, pepper spray, firearms, vehicle operations, and defensive tactics, he instructed and oversaw criminal justice degree programs and/or police academies in Florida, New Mexico, North Carolina, and Ohio.

With over two decades of concept research and practical experience regarding law enforcement reserves, Dr. Weinblatt is a sought after speaker and writer on the volunteer and part-time law enforcement officer topic. He has authored several regular columns on reserves. Those include "Reserve Reports," which ran for a decade in Law and Order: The Magazine for Police Management, and "Reserve Power" for Officer.com. He wrote the Reserve Law Enforcement in the United States book.

Dr. Weinblatt is the former president of the Center for Reserve Law Enforcement, as well as the New Jersey Auxiliary Police Officers Association (NJAPOA – New Jersey's association for auxiliary and special law enforcement officers) which included its NJAPOA Training Academy and The Shield magazine. He is the creator of the website PoliceReserveOfficer.com. He is experienced with all facets of reserve operations. In addition to serving as a full-time law enforcer, he has served as a reservist on the street, a reserve administrator, a reserve liaison, and as a police chief who created and operated active police reserve and police explorer (for teenagers) programs.

A well-known police issues commentator for local and national media, Dr. Weinblatt has been interviewed by the Associated Press, CBS News, CNN, HLN, MSNBC, and The Washington Post among others. He has authored hundreds of articles on law enforcement topics for magazines and websites

Dr. Weinblatt earned a bachelor's degree in Administration of Justice, A Master of Public Administration in Criminal Justice, an Education Specialist degree, and a Doctor of Education.

Dr. Weinblatt resides in the greater Orlando, FL, area with his wife, Anne, and son, Michael. Further information is available at www.TheCopDoc.com and www.PoliceReserveOfficer.com.

J

Dr. Richard Weinblatt

Reserve Law Enforcement in the United States (The Re-Issue)

L

RESERVE LAW ENFORCEMENT IN THE UNITED STATES

A National Study of State, County and City Standards
Concerning the Training & Numbers of
Non-full-time Police and Sheriff's Personnel

By Richard B. Weinblatt

with a foreward by James C. Lombardi
Reserve Officer in Charge of Los Angeles Police Reserve Corps.

In this book, find out...

What local department has their reserve officers police academy trained for 768 hours?

What local county department's individual reserves donate an average of 43 hours each month?

What state has a minimum training requirement of only ten hours for their auxiliary officers?

What state has 589 armed auxiliary state troopers?

What local reserve unit donated $13,220,900 in equipment and manpower last year?

What state does not have any minimum standards set for their full-time, part-time and volunteer law enforcement officers?

What local police department's reserve officers worked 40,000 hours last year?

What state has more then twice as many part-timers than full-timers?

What state can part-time officers receive state certification through a correspondance course?

What state abolished their volunteer police in 1988?

What state does a citizen have a 50% chance, depending on the time and day of week, of having a reserve officer respond to their call for police service?

What state changed their minimum academy training standards in one shot from zero to 400 hours in July of 1992?

What local city has the most volunteer officers with 4,402 uniforms hitting the streets?

What local agency's field training officer (FTO) program consists of 15 stints on each of the three shifts (within two years) for a total of 360 hours?

(For answers, please turn to page 249.)

RESERVE LAW ENFORCEMENT IN THE UNITED STATES

A National Study of State, County and City Standards
Concerning the Training & Numbers of
Non-full-time Police and Sheriff's Personnel

By Richard B. Weinblatt

Copyright ©1993 by Richard B. Weinblatt

Richard B. Weinblatt

About the author

Richard B. Weinblatt, president of the Center for Reserve Law Enforcement, Inc. and the New Jersey Auxiliary Police Officers Association, Inc., writes and speaks extensively on the topic of volunteer and part-time police and has been recognized by President George Bush for his leadership role. A nationally known expert, he has a regular column, "Reserve Reports," in one of the country's largest police publications, *LAW and ORDER* Magazine. The veteran of many years of policing holds a bachelors degree in administration of justice and is pursuing his master's in criminal justice.

Advisory Board
New Jersey Auxiliary Police Officers Association, Inc.

Reserve Law Enforcement in the United States

Advisory Board
Center for Reserve Law Enforcement, Inc.

Daniel Brandt
    Secretary/Treasurer
    Iowa State Reserve Law Officers
        Association
    Marshalltown, IA

    Reserve Captain
    Marshalltown Police Department
    Marshalltown, IA

Timothy B. Burgess
    Reserve Inspector
    Metropolitan Police
    Washington, DC

Harold L. Butterfield
    Auxiliary Colonel
    Florida Highway Patrol
    Port St. Lucie, FL

Richard H. Davis
    Major/Chief Deputy of Reserves
    Fulton County Sheriff's Office
    Atlanta, GA

Mel Kalkowski
    Reserve Captain
    Anchorage Police Department
    Anchorage, AK

James C. Lombardi
    President
    California Reserve Peace Officers
        Association
    San Jose, CA

    Reserve Officer in Charge
    Los Angeles Police Department
    Los Angeles, CA

Bill Martin
    President
    Texas Reserve Law Officers
        Association
    Dallas, TX

E.F. Maybanks, OBE, QPM
    Chief Commandant
    Metropolitan Special Constabulary
    London, England

John S. O'Brien
    President
    Oregon Reserve Peace Officers
        Association
    Redmond, OR

L. Ray Vickers
    Chief of Reserves
    Harris County Sheriff's Office
    Houston, TX

Note

1.) The term "reserve" has been used in the *Reserve Law Enforcement in the United States* book generically to connote any individual who is serving law enforcement in a part-time capacity for little or no compensation. A few other terms for the non-full-time category of law enforcer are auxiliary, special, supernumerary, part-timer and volunteer.

Some states and local jurisdictions have exact titles and corresponding duties codified. The integrity of officer classification titles within the text covering specific states, cities and counties has been preserved.

2.) Civilian volunteers and Explorers (a junior police program operated by the Boy Scouts of America) are not considered to be part of the reserve component of law enforcement, thus they were not included in this book.

3.) All information was gathered directly from the states or local jurisdictions in question. Since the book's goal was to break out the numbers concerning full-time and non-full-time law enforcement personnel, no data was utilized from the FBI's Uniform Crime Report (UCR). The figures reported in the UCR may or may not include lumped in figures regarding reserves depending on the reporting agency's parameters.

4.) While every effort to assure accuracy regarding the large amount of information contained in *Reserve Law Enforcement in the United States* was undertaken, errors or omissions may have occurred. Corrections, correspondence and other information should be sent in care of the author:

Richard B. Weinblatt, President
Center for Reserve Law Enforcement, Inc.
New Jersey Auxiliary Police Officers Association, Inc.
7 Deer Park Drive
Building 2, Suite A2
Monmouth Jct., NJ 08852-9689

TEL: 908/329-8924
FAX: 908/329-0479

Acknowledgement

Reserve Law Enforcement in the United States took hundreds of hours to research and write, much of which was done during late evenings and countless weekends. The book could not have been done without the assistance and cooperation of many people.

The design work was undertaken by KenMar Graphics and its president, Ken Markowitz. Expert printing guidance was given by NJAPOA Board Member and Paramus, NJ, Police reserve lieutenant Frank Rizzo, a decorated volunteer officer.

Highly motivated South Brunswick, NJ, auxiliary police officer Ryan T. Kane, an NJAPOA Board Member and certified Monadnock PR-24 instructor, undertook the proof reading and offered suggestions. Michael Tota, a Class II. special law enforcement officer from Cliffside Park, NJ, who is studying for his master's degree in criminal justice at Jersey City State College, provided assistance with some of the statistical elements of the book.

A good deal of feedback was derived from the various state reserve associations and much credit is given to these dedicated regional leaders who are blazing new reserve trails everyday. The lord of leaders is, of course, James C. Lombardi who for quite some time has been shepherding both the high profile California Reserve Peace Officers Association and the Los Angeles Police Department's well-respected reserve corps. We are honored to include his foreword in this book.

Appreciation is extended to the administration and officers of the South Brunswick Township, NJ, Police Department for supporting our efforts here, as well as for facilitating the creation of a tightly knit and highly trained group of auxiliary officers who serve with a sense of pride and espirit de corps. Particular thanks are addressed to Captain Michael D. Paquette, Captain Frederick A. Thompson and Sergeant Scott N. Hoover.

Also displaying a high degree of interest and encouragement were Essex County, NJ, Sheriff Armando B. Fontoura, along with Captain Edward H. Malia, Director Eric A. Mayer and Captain Peter J. Corbo.

Additionally, we'd also like to thank the many people whose contributions have made our work here possible.

Lastly, this book is dedicated to the quarter of a million men and women who pin on a badge and protect strangers for little or no money. It is because of them that the reserve law enforcement phenomenon is thriving.

Preface

This study was undertaken in response to requests for information from both criminal justice administrators and part-time/volunteer law enforcers. With few exceptions, individuals endeavoring to create a reserve, auxiliary or special officer program from scratch, or expand an existing unit, have had to operate in a knowledge vacuum.

The utilization of part-time paid and volunteer officers by municipal, county and state law enforcement organizations is a longstanding, widespread and rapidly growing tradition in the United States, as well as overseas.

Reserves can be found discharging the same diverse duties as those attached to their full-time counterparts. In addition to uniformed patrol, long the backbone of policing, reservists are deployed with titles in a plethora of areas including undercover narcotics operatives, homicide detectives, juvenile investigators, SWAT team members, K-9 officers, dive team members, search and rescue mountaineers, aviation pilots, evidence technicians and mounted horse officers. In today's litigious age in which police and sheriff's agencies operate, the proper selection and training of officers is vitally important.

Implementation of enhanced entrance and training standards is the key to true professionalism within the reserve ranks. The move can only be fueled through acquisition of knowledge concerning the many progressive programs which dot the nation. Interestingly, it is the reserve officers themselves who have been the most vocal in their drive for professionalism through strict standards.

The book profiles the law enforcement training and entrance standards set forth by all of the country's state regulatory bodies. A sampling of some major city and county programs is included in another section.

Demonstrated in quantifiable terms is the theory that a "hard line" on standards actually serves to increase the quality and quantity of people seeking to put their lives on the line for strangers in exchange for little or no compensation. States with more detailed regulations concerning this unique category of law officer in turn seem to have local programs that are even stricter and more challenging.

Reserve Law Enforcement in the United States is designed to enable full-time, part-time and volunteer decision makers to more easily get a handle on information, thereby making an informed judgment concerning the role non-full-time law enforcement personnel should play in their jurisdiction. The material in this book is clear evidence that reserve law enforcement is limited only by the tenacity, ability and professionalism of the reserves and their departments.

Foreword

One of the first projects on which I worked with Richard Weinblatt was put together in 1989. Richard, in addressing the graduates of an auxiliary police academy, put together a book of letters from reserve police leaders which was distributed to the officers and their families at the ceremony.

That endeavor sparked a large amount of dedicated pro-reserve work which includes his widely read articles in our California Reserve Peace Officer Association's magazine, *THE BACKUP*. Among his other related activities were articles in *LAW and ORDER* and other national magazines, his work with the New Jersey Auxiliary Police Officers Association and *THE SHIELD* magazine, and a meeting with the President in the White House. His efforts both in his home state, New Jersey, and nationwide have gained momentum and has proved to be a boon to an important segment of the law enforcement community. Richard's book paints a powerful and compelling picture of a national movement towards the use of professional reserves.

An experienced and highly trained reserve officer himself, Richard, a former auxiliary police officer in New York City, works in New Jersey as an auxiliary lieutenant with the South Brunswick Police and as a volunteer deputy sheriff in the City of Newark with the Essex County Sheriff's Office. The knowledge, research and training opportunities he shares with his fellow reserves comes from his personal understanding of what is needed to continue the professionalism of reserves.

This book is a clear signal that reserve law enforcement officers are an important part of the law enforcement community. The goal of these officers is to assist and supplement regular officers in controlling crime throughout the nation.

To my knowledge, this book is the first time a comprehensive national reference source has been provided for those contemplating the startup or expansion of a reserve unit. Much information is presented in a reader friendly format. The charts and graphs help give the reader a clearer picture of what is described in the writing.

I was interested to find out the variety of different ways reserves are regulated by their states and their local departments.

James C. Lombardi
Reserve Officer in Charge
Los Angeles Police Department
and
President
California Reserve Peace Officers Association

Contents

Section V.

Section VI.

Section VII.

Section VIII.

Section IX.

*   HAWAII is the only state which does not have statewide minimum training standards set for full-time, part-time and volunteer law enforcement officers. Minimum standards for all categories are set by the local employing agency. The Aloha State also does not track the numbers of officers.

SECTION

I

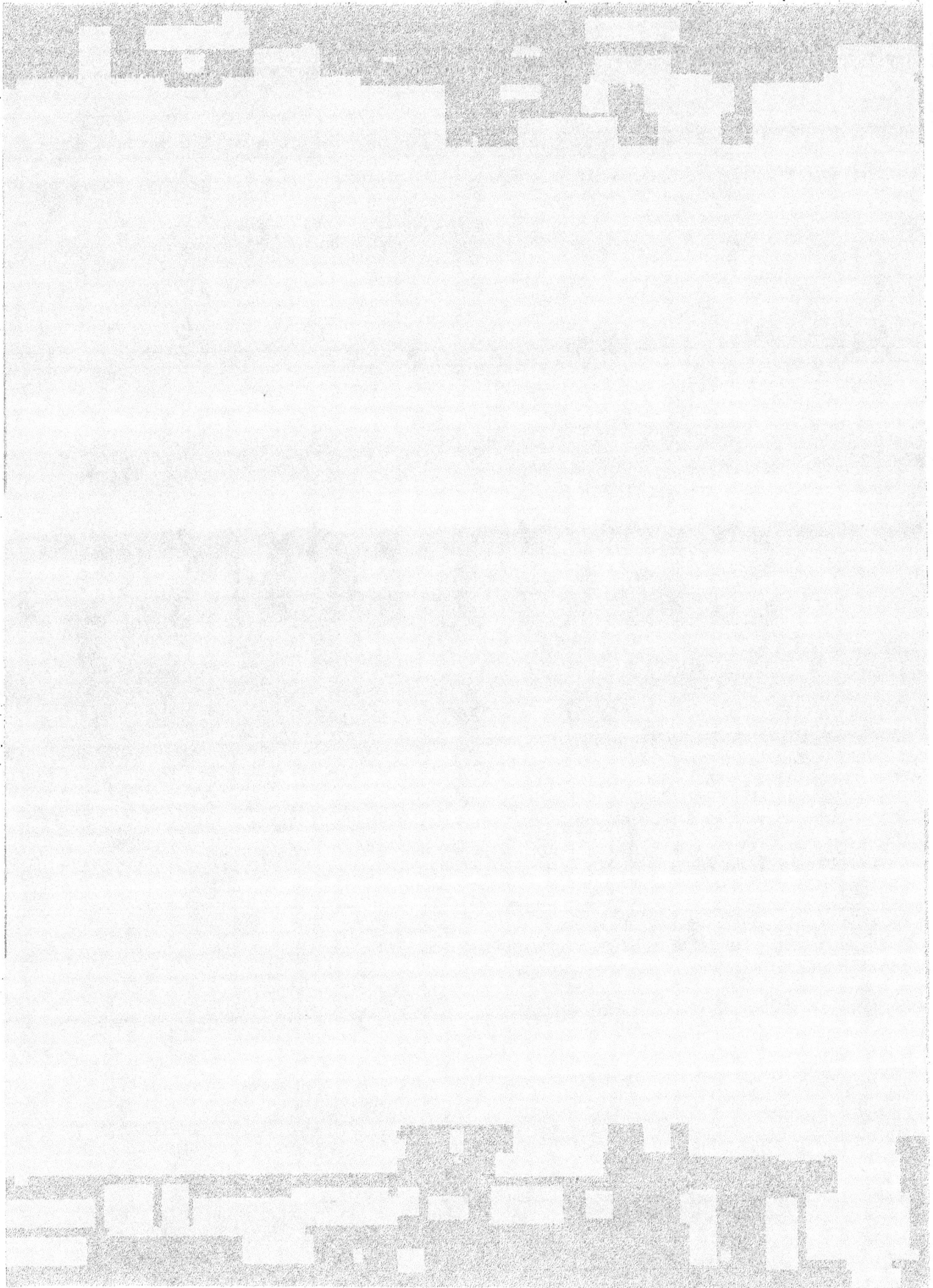

Section I.
International

An examination of reserve law enforcement in the U.S. would be incomplete without an acknowledging and touching on the work done by the many men and women in other countries who perform essentially the same duties as their Yankee counterparts.

Perhaps the most well known volunteer police are the special constables of England which trace their roots back to 1829. British police, volunteer and full-time, do not carry firearms.

Nationwide, there are 25,000 specials in 43 forces. London's Metropolitan Special Constabulary has 1,400 members to back up the 28,000 full-time bobbies. Uniforms are provided by the city. Training for the specials takes place on a weekend day each week for 20 weeks for a total of 160 hours. They have authority off duty provided they have their warrant card, the equivalent of a U.S. ID card.

The Royal Hong Kong Auxiliary Police has 5,400 reservists. Among their duties are guarding the boat people at the Vietnamese refugee camps. Young people in France do service in the Gendarmerie, the national police force, after which they serve for one year in the reserve. The Israeli Ministry of Police utilizes 40,000 people in its civil guard.

WHEN HE'S ON DUTY - as a Metropolitan Special Constable

Specials are volunteers, people with regular day-to-day occupations, prepared to put in some of their spare time each week working in support of their local police in the London area.

In their ranks you'll find everyone from housewives to taxi drivers, from teachers to sales reps, from opticians to travel agents.

They're men and women, aged between 18 and 55 (although 50 is the upper age limit for joining). They look like their regular police colleagues and have the same powers. They perform tasks such as street patrolling, traffic duty and crowd control at football grounds. They often deal with trickier situations such as disturbances, burglaries or road accidents.

As a Special you'll be thoroughly trained, on Saturdays or Sundays over a 20-week period, to deal with any situation as it arises. Your duties will teach you a lot about human nature, boosting your self-confidence in the process. You'll learn to look at life and its situations in a different and more fascinating light. And, as part of a team, you'll forge lasting friendships.

To find out more about how you could make a real contribution to the quality of life in your community - telephone 0345 300101 or fill in the coupon below and send it to: SC FREEPOST (BS528/71), BRISTOL BS3 3YY.

WHEN DOES A CARPET FITTER EVER WORK IN THE GARDEN?

LONDON'S VOLUNTEER POLICE SERVICE

Please send me more information about the Metropolitan Special Constabulary.
Name:
Address and Postcode:
Age: _____ LWA03

Recruitment advertisement for the London Metropolitan Police's Special Constable program

An emphasis on emergency response, rather than routine police work, is the guiding concept behind the volunteer forces in Australia, Norway, Sweden, and Switzerland. Most of these reserves are former regular officers.

Bermuda's Reserve Constabulary, founded in 1951, is a small 84 member force comprised of four senior officers, six inspectors, 14 sergeants and 60 constables who must work at least 150 hours annually. They attend the Bermuda Police Training School for two evenings a week over the course of eight weeks. The reservists are actively engaged in assisting the 450 full-time officers who serve the 20 square mile island chain 600 miles off the coast. The Marine Section of the reserve has two sergeants and six constables who worked 560 hours last year.

In the Netherlands, the 170 reserve officers in Amsterdam are armed, go through a two year training stretch (two evenings a week) and work closely with a regular officer in one of the eight districts. They must pass the same rigorous exams given to full-timers.

The United States' neighbor to the north, Canada, makes extensive use of volunteer auxiliary constables. The people of Vancouver in British Columbia are used to seeing the auxiliaries who work for the famous Royal Canadian Mounted Police. Armed with .38 revolvers and uniforms like their full-time counterparts, the only difference involves the yellow band on the hat.

The Metropolitan Toronto Police Department celebrated the 30th anniversary of its 400 plus officer auxiliary force in 1986, a year which saw 75,000 hours donated. Under the direction of staff superintendent James G. Carnegie, who works full-time as general manager of the Ontario Chamber of Commerce, members of the volunteer organization serving the largest municipal police service in Canada must work at least 20 hours per month and participate in in-service training the second Tuesday of each month.

Successful applicants must be a Canadian citizen age 21 or older. They must be physically and mentally fit and have completed at least four years of secondary school. Recruitment is typically conducted in August and September. The department goes through some 600 applicants to come up with the 85 candidates who are enrolled in the training program.

Training is held one evening per week for 32 weeks with two Sundays for first aid qualification. Among the topics covered are introduction to law, powers of arrest, criminal code, police driving techniques, traffic direction, tonfa training (similar to the U.S. version of a PR-24 sidehandle baton), and firearms training.

Firearms training is also continued twice a year and a special advanced training course is given to selected personnel at the range at C.O. Bick Police College each year.

Auxiliary officers may be assigned to one of five districts, the marine unit (which patrols Toronto Harbour and the Lake Ontario shoreline) or in one of the headquarters unit. HQ assignments include administration, inspections, public affairs, special events, and training.

Also available are assignments in one of the support units. The motorcycle unit's auxiliary personnel is comprised of an inspector, a staff sergeant, three sergeants and 24 constables. Among their activities are support to all the districts and crowd and traffic control at Blue Jay baseball games and Argonaut football games. Other units are the drill squad, the identifications bureau and communications.

James G. Carnegie
Staff Superintendent
Commanding
Metropolitan Toronto Auxiliary Police

SECTION

II

Reserve Law Enforcement in the United States

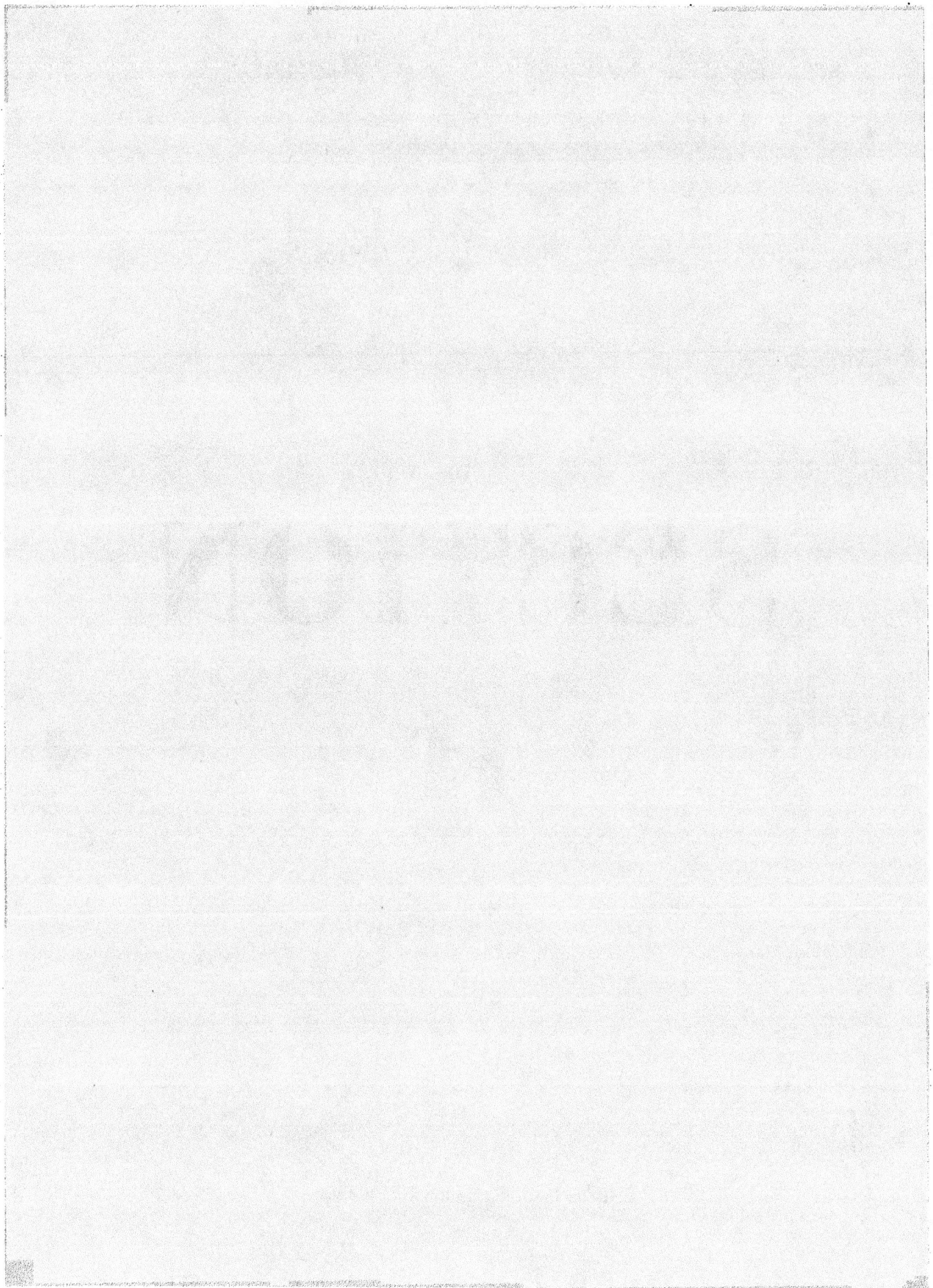

Section II.
Previous Surveys

Previous studies concerning the number of personnel utilized, as well as training and entrance standards, in reserve law enforcement has been scant at best. The reserve information categories in criminal justice libraries are for the most part void, a phenomenon which is unusual in a field which studies itself extensively. The law enforcement community seems to acknowledge the presence and need for qualified men and women who can support full-time law enforcers in the discharge of their duties, as demonstrated by the widespread promulgation of reserve units or the expanding of existing programs.

Some attribute the lack of earlier fanfare, and even public awareness, surrounding the non-full-time law enforcers in our midst as a testament to the quiet and efficient manner in which they discharge their duties. As the world of policing becomes ever more complex and sophisticated, so too does the reservist, thus eliminating negative actions and the predictable headlines which would long ago have called for a slanted investigation of the reserve component of policing.

In this book, and the speeches and magazine articles that have preceded it, the underlying concept is the positive strides reserves have made to earn the respect of their full-time counterparts.

In 1969, the Arlington County, VA, Police Department conducted a reserve police survey of 57 departments (city populations over 250,000) with 48 agencies responding. According to the Arlington County survey, out of the 48 queried, 34 jurisdictions said they had reserves for a total number of 10,414 reservists. Interestingly, the survey confirmed that departments with the most successful programs, in terms of hours donated, "imposed the strictest conditions for recruitment, training, both classroom and range, and maintained a set number of hours" the reserve must serve.

The Arlington County study cited two earlier studies: one in 1960 by Philadelphia and another in 1965 by St. Louis. The increase of recruitment and training standards clearly shows a positive trend through the three studies. Training hours and other quantifiable elements in this book have greatly advanced thereby continuing on the upward professionalism in reserve policing noted in Arlington County's document.

"Consideration of a Charlottesville Police Auxiliary", a February 1976 staff study prepared by then Charlottesville, VA, patrolman Richard R.E. Kania, revealed an interest even back in the

'70s in creating programs that were thoughtfully executed with highly trained and motivated individuals. Kania, who has since earned his Ph.D. and is currently an associate professor of justice and policy studies at Guilford College in Greensboro, NC, proposed that the city adopt a volunteer officer program, minus a rank structure, which would be trained, uniformed and armed in a comparable manner to the full-time officers.

Kania examined three other programs, Virginia Beach, VA, Portsmouth, VA, and Dallas, and found them to exemplify high standards for the 1970s. His study found that in 1974 the approximately 85 Virginia Beach volunteer officers, with a 20 hour per month minimum commitment, received 200 hours of training and that they donated 28,155 hours of service with an additional 5,760 hours in in-service training.

Dr. Richard R. E. Kania

Kania found that Portsmouth's 80 officer version begins with a four hour "crash course" on police basics with the rookie officer required to complete a 140 hour training program within one year. Wearing identical uniforms, provided by the city, and bearing full police powers, the reservists were obligated to serve at least 16 hours per month. Some officers with 200 hours of training worked independently in such areas as K-9, youth bureau, homicide, or crime scene investigation. Kania reported that the organization, which had a rank structure, gave the City of Portsmouth 23,000 hours of service in 1974.

Information on the Dallas, TX, Police Reserve Battalion of 1976, compiled by Kania's study, showed a strength of 250 officers, who had to be nominated by a full-time or volunteer Dallas police officer, trained at recruitment for 72 hours.

In 1987, Peter Horne, a former Compton, CA, police officer and Ballwin, MO, reserve officer, wrote his City University of New York criminal justice Ph.D. thesis on "The Creation of Standards for Special Police in New Jersey: A Case Study of the Legislative Process." Horne, currently a professor and coordinator with the criminal justice program at Mercer County Community College in Trenton, NJ, chronicled the creation and implementation of New Jersey Special Law Enforcement Officers (SLEO) Act of 1986.

He cited two extensive studies conducted in 1969 and 1975 by New Jersey's Police Training Commission (PTC) which indicate that the use of specials at the time was widespread and that they were, unfortunately, poorly trained. His research revealed that 6,000 special police officers and 17,000 regular officers were serving 482 municipalities. Regarding the use of SLEOs as seasonal officers during the summer, he further revealed that 35 resort communities in four Jersey shore counties (Atlantic, Cape May, Monmouth, and Ocean) employed about 600 specials a season prior to the summer of 1987.

Another study was conducted in Colorado in 1987. Sergeant Michael L. Maudlin, of the Lakewood, CO, Police Department, conducted the survey as part of his master's degree in management thesis "A Study of Managerial Considerations in the Use of Reserve Police Officers in Colorado." His research revealed that 61% of the 152 Colorado police and sheriffs agencies that responded do utilize reserves and that "those officers are deployed in nearly every area of service routinely performed by regular officers."

An interesting and vital document on the subject is Bernard E. Nash's August 1988 dissertation for his doctorate in public administration from the University of Southern California. "Volunteerism in Law Enforcement" revealed that less than 130 background literature titles existed on the topic of volunteers in law enforcement. That figure would no doubt be greatly reduced if the the non-uniformed, civilian aid volunteer classification was excised from the list. He further stated that "little guidance or research was available to aid administrators in making decisions about whether and how to use volunteers or how to train them."

Nash, who works full-time for the American Association for Retired People (AARP) in Washington, DC, cited information gleaned in 1983 from Otto Vehle, executive director of the now defunct San Antonio, TX-based Reserve Law Officers Association of America, which put the number of reserves across the United States at 175,000 in 1967, 350,000 in 1977, and 400,000 in 1978. Nash also called attention to a 1974 survey of 78 Arizona agencies. That survey had 72 respondents and 34 (or 47 percent) said they had reserve officers. Two were in the midst of forming a program.

More recently, in 1992, a master's portfolio was prepared by U.S. Air Force Security Police Captain Richard N. Wright proposing that a reserve officer program be implemented by the Columbia, SC, Police Department. The hefty piece of paper details, among other items, the thirty year history of volunteer police in South Carolina.

Wright's survey, as support to his contention that Columbia utilize reserves, had 45 South Carolina departments contacted with 15 responses received and nine out.of state agencies with six responses generated. Among the findings were that all departments had their reserves carrying firearms. Also indicated were the requirements that all reserves adhere to the same rules and policies governing regular officers. All had identical or similar uniforms with the only differences, if any, being manifested in the badge and/or shoulder patch.

Wright concluded from the survey that states with high minimum standards, such as California and North Carolina, had reserve programs of proportional quality in their individual departments, whereas states with "minimal and rudimentary" standards, such as South Carolina, were evident in the lesser quality reserve officers units.

Also conducted in 1992, was a survey of Georgia reserve programs by the Fulton County Sheriff's Office in the City of Atlanta, GA. Major Richard H. Davis, the overseer of the county's sophisticated reserve operation, found that 40 agencies in Georgia had reserves. An earlier 1988 survey by Davis found that 34 agencies in the state used reserves at that time.

Much like the surveys and academic materials, the law enforcement trade press has had but a few articles on the reserve topic. Certainly among the most prolific writers has been Martin A. Greenberg. Chairman and assistant professor of criminal justice at Ulster County Community College in Stone Ridge, NY, Greenberg is a former New York City court officer and an ex-auxiliary deputy inspector with the New York City Police.

Armed with a New York Law School law degree and a John Jay College of Criminal Justice master's degree in criminal justice, the former coordinator/instructor of the police science program at Hawaii Community College at the University of Hawaii at Hilo has been writing on the subject of auxiliary policing for many years. His plethora of articles started appearing in the '70s, and include his rather detailed analysis of the history and function of the auxiliary police force in New York City in the "Journal of Police Science and Administration," a respected periodical.

Georgia Agencies which use Reserves

COUNTY SHERIFFS

Chatham
Chatsworth
Cherokee
Clinch
Cobb
Floyd
Fulton
Forsyth
Gwinnett
Henry
Liberty
Madison
Oglethorpe
Rockdale
Telfair
Thomas
Whitfield

MUNICIPAL POLICE

Bremen
Chatsworth
Clayton State College P.D.
College Park
Conyers
Cornelia
Duluth
Fayetteville
Forest Park
Griffin
Lake City
Locust Grove
Monroe
Peachtree City
Pine Lake
Rome
Sylvania
Tyrone
Union City
Valdosta
Warner Robins
Woodstock

Source: 1992 Georgia survey by Fulton County, GA, Sheriff's Reserve, courtesy of Major Richard H. Davis.

SECTION
III

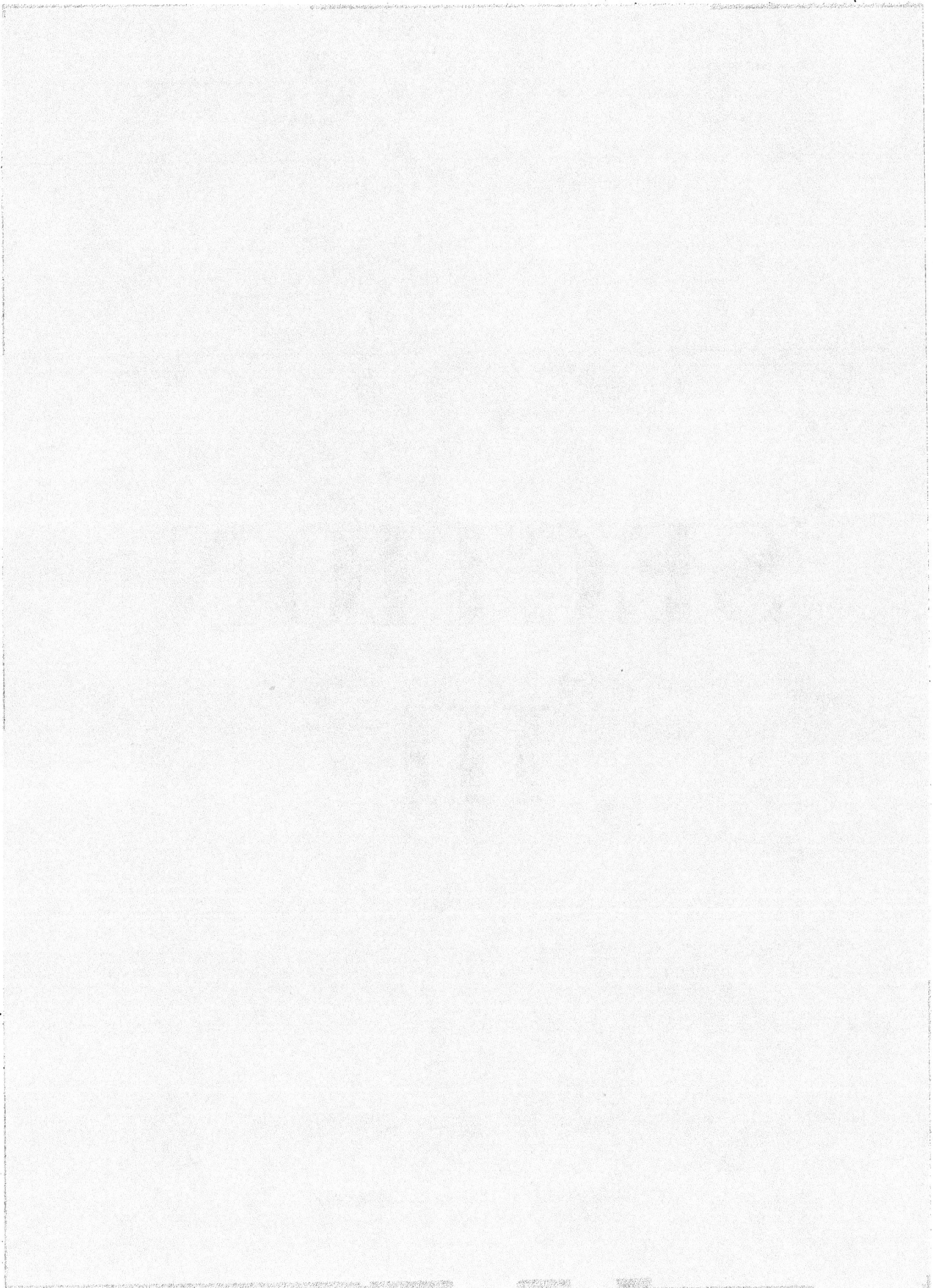

Section III.
States: Overview

Top five eastern states for non-full time officers

Rank	State	Number
1.	New York	9,930
2.	Florida	5333
3.	Massachusetts	5000
4	Pennsylvania	3825
5.	Connecticut	3000

Top 10 states by percentage of non-full-time officers

Rank	State	Percent
1.	Vermont	65
2.	Maine	44
3.	New Hampshire	43
4.	Ohio	55
5.	Mississippi	35
6	Indiana/Wisconsin	26
7.	Tennessee/Washington	25
8.	Montana	23
9.	Oregon/North Carolina/Kansas	22
10.	Iowa	21

Top 10 states which have the most training time (minimum required hours) involved for full time officers and non-full time officers

Full time officers

Rank	State	Number
1.	New Jersey	669
2.	Missouri	600(a)
2.	Vermont	600
3.	California	560
4.	Nevada	540
4.	Montana	540
5.	Florida	520
5.	Pennsylvania	520
6.	Nebraska	500
6.	Rhode Island	500
7.	West Virginia	498
7.	Delaware	498
8.	Indiana	480
8.	Maine	480
9.	New York	445
10.	Washington	440
10.	Utah	440
10.	Michigan	440
10.	Arizona	440

Non-full time officers

Rank	State	Number
1.	Missouri	600(a)
2.	California	560(b)
3.	Pennsylvania	520(c)
3.	Florida	520
4.	Nebraska	500
5.	West Virginia	498
6.	Connecticut	480
6.	Indiana	480
7.	New Jersey	452(d)
8.	New York	445
9.	North Carolina	444(e)
10.	Arizona	440

(a) For !st Class Cities (pop. 100,000 and greater)
(b) For Level I designated Reserves
(c) For Certified Reserves
(d) For Class II. Special Law Enforcement Officers
(e) For Reserve and Full Time Deputy Sheriffs

What percentages make up each states full time vs. non-full time officers in the country

State	Full Time	Non Full Time	State Regulated	Non-regulated Non-certified
Alabama	88	12	94	6
Alaska	92	8	92	8
Arizona	92	8	100	0
Arkansas	8081	N/A	100	0
California	83	17	100	0
Colorado	89	11	100	0
Connecticut	80	20	97	3
Delaware	98	2	100	0
Florida	86	14	100	0
Georgia	19286	N/A	N/A	N/A
Hawaii	N/A	N/A	N/A	N/A
Idaho	3000	N/A	N/A	N/A
Illinois	85	15	85	15
Indiana	74	26	75	25
Iowa	79	21	100	0
Kansas	78	22	78	22
Kentucky	92	8	100	0
Louisiana	18000	N/A	N/A	N/A
Maine	56	44	100	0
Maryland	92	8	92	8
Massachusetts	N/A	5000	N/A	N/A
Michigan	93	7	93	7
Minnesota	90	10	100	0
Mississippi	65	35	65	35
Missouri	95	5	97	3
Montana	77	23	100	0
Nebraska	3400	N/A	100	0
Nevada	86	13	86	13
New Hampshire	57	43	100	0
New Jersey	27337	N/A	N/A	N/A
New Mexico	4215	N/A	N/A	N/A
New York	86	14	90	10
North Carolina	78	22	100	0
North Dakota	84	16	95	5
Ohio	45	55	100	0
Oklahoma	80	20	100	0
Oregon	78	22	78	22
Pennsylvania	84	16	N/A	N/A

What percentages make up each states full time vs. non-full time officers in the country (cont.)

State	Full Time	Non Full Time	State Regulated	Non-regulated Non-certified
Rhode Island	80	20	80	20
South Carolina	84	16	100	0
South Dakota	1023 (b)	N/A	100	0
Tennessee	75	25	84	16
Texas	89	11	100	0
Utah	5000 (b)	N/A	100	0
Vermont	35	65	100	0
Virginia	24400 (b)	N/A	N/A	N/A
Washington	75	25	100	N/A
West Virginia	2500 (a)	N/A	100	N/A
Wisconsin	74	26	89	11
Wyoming	93	7	100	0

Top 10 states by number of non-full-time officers in descending order

Rank	State	Number
1.	Ohio	18,000
2.	California	13,836
3.	New York	9,930
4.	Texas	5,770
5.	Florida	5,333
6.	Massachusetts	5,000
7.	North Carolina	4,617
8.	Pennsylvania	3,825
9.	Wisconsin	3,500
10.	Connecticut	3,000

Top 10 states which have the least amount of training hours

Full Time

Rank	State	Number	
1.	Pennsylvania	160	(For Full-time & Part-time Deputy Sheriffs)
2.	Louisiana	240	
2.	Georgia	280	
3.	Alabama	280	
3.	Arkansas	280	
4.	Oklahoma	300	
5.	Kansas	320	
5.	Oregon	320	
5.	South Dakota	320	
5.	Tennessee	320	
6.	South Carolina	332	
7.	Colorado	358	
8.	Mississippi	360	
8.	North Dakota	360	
9.	Idaho	390	
10.	Alaska	400	
10.	Iowa	400	
10.	Massachusetts	400	
10.	Minnesota	400	
10.	New Mexico	400	
10.	Texas	400	
10.	Wisconsin	400	

Non-full time

Rank	State	Number	
3.	New York	10	(For auxiliary)
4.	Massachusetts	96	(For part-time)
5.	Colorado	35	(For level III. reserves)
6.	Delaware	40	(For seasonal officers)
7.	California	64	(For Level III. reserves)
8.	Vermont	168	
9.	New Jersey	78	(For Class I. special law enforcement officers)
10.	Florida	97	(For Armed auxiliary)

The following 25 states have no state imposed minimum training guidelines for all or a portion of their non-full-time officers and leave the decision of whether and how to train in the hands of local authorities.

Most local agencies do conduct at least some training for their officers in spite of their state's lack of mandates to do so.

Alabama ....(1/2 are 280 hours certified)
Alaska ....(No minimum training for all non-full-time officers)
Connecticut ....(Part-timers must be 480 hour certified)
Georgia ....(714 are certified at 280 hours)
Idaho ....(No training required: limited duty Level III.)
Illinois ....(40 hours firearms training if armed)
Indiana ....(Most volunteer reserves are 480 hour certified)
Kansas ....(No minimum training required for volunteers)
Louisiana ....(Officers' agency option as to training)
Maryland ....(No minimum training for volunteer auxiliary)
Michigan ....(No minimum training required for reserves)
Minnesota ....(No minimum training for volunteer reserves)
Mississippi ....(No minimum training for non-full-time)
Missouri ....(No minimum training for non-certified reserves)
Nevada ....(No minimum training for volunteer reserves)
New Mexico ....(No minimum training for non-full-time)
North Dakota ....(No minimum training for volunteer reserve/auxiliary)
Ohio ....(No minimum training for non-commissioned officers)
Oregon ....(No minimum training for reserves)
Pennsylvania ....(No minimum training for volunteer auxiliary)
Rhode Island ....(No minimum training for part-time, volunteers)
Tennessee ....(No minimum training for non-cert vol. res/aux)
West Virginia ....(No minimum training for volunteers)
Wisconsin ....(No minimum training for non-certified volunteers)

Full-time/Part-time/Volunteer Law Enforcement Officers by State

Training standards are only minimums. Most jurisdictions far exceed minimum standards.

STATE	Full-time	Part-time/Volunteer	State Regulate Officers
ALABAMA	7,500 280 hours for all certified officers	500 certified reserves 500 non-certified reserves Training in-house	Regulate certified officer
ALASKA	1,200 400 hrs training	110 res PT/vol Training in-house	Regulate full-time officers only
ARIZONA	9,000 440 hours for all officers statewide	800 vol reserves	Regulate all officers

ARKANSAS	8,081
	280 hours
		Unknown number of reserves
		Part-time officers -
		  Part-time I. officers (work 20 to 40 hours per week)
		  280 hours
		  Part-time II. officers (work less than 20 hours per week)
		  100 hours
		Volunteer Auxiliary officers
		100 hours
			Regulate all officers

CALIFORNIA	69,455 560 hours (avg 700 hours)	13,836 reserves Level I. Designated Reserve- full statewide police powers 24 hrs./day 560 hours Level I. Non-designated Reserve- powers on duty alone 214 hours Level II. Reserve- powers on duty with partner 146 hours Level III. Reserve- powers on duty, technical duties 56 hours	Regulate all officers
COLORADO	7,658 358 hours	948 reserves Classification I. Reserve - full police powers 358 hours Classification II. Reserve 145 hours Classification III. Reserve	Regulate all officers

STATE	Full-time	Part-time/Volunteer	State Regulate Officers
COLORADO (cont.)		109 hours Classification IV. Reserve 35 hours	
CONNECTICUT	12,000 480 hours	2,500 part-time 480 hours 500 volunteers Training in-house	Regulate full, part-time officers only
DELAWARE	1,500 498 hours	37 Seasonal officers 40 hours No volunteers. Abolished in 1988	Regulate all officers
FLORIDA	32,212 520 hours for full-time and part-time/reserve. Full police powers.	2,659 Part-time/reserve 2,674 Auxiliary (powers only while under supervision) 97 hours	Regulate all officers
GEORGIA	19,286 240 hours for all certified peace officers Going up to 280 hours as of July 1, 1992	714 certified reserves Unknown number of non-certified reserves	Regulate certified officers only
HAWAII	All officer training up to employing agency		
IDAHO	3,000 390 hours	Unknown number of reserves Level I. Reserves - full police powers 160 hours reserve academy 120 hours annual in-service training Level II. Reserves- non-certified must be sup. by full-time officers 25 hours minimum in-house training Level III. Reserve- no police pwrs. Mounted/jeep posse, parades, etc. No training minimum required by state	
ILLINOIS	27,038 400 hours	2,738 Part-time 2,085 Vol. Auxiliary Training for PT/Vol officers up to local agency 40 hours firearms training if armed	Regulate full-time officers only
INDIANA	8,015 480 hours for any paid full or part-time	192 Part-time 2,688 vol reserves In house training; most are 480 hours (Goes to 40 hours minimum in July 1993	Regulate paid officers only
IOWA	5,100 400 hours for any full, part-time officer	175 part-time 1,200 vol reserve officers	Regulate all officers

STATE	Full-time	Part-time/Volunteer	State Regulate Officers
IOWA (cont.)		180 hours total training - Remaining 150 within four years	30 hours first year
KANSAS	5,200 320 hours	300 part-time 80 hours 1,200 vol reserves No minimum training	Regulate paid officers only
KENTUCKY	4,650 400 hours	411 part-time or vol No minimum training Law on July 16 will require all new part-time or vol to get 400 hours training Currently serving part-time/vol only required to get 40 hours in-service training annually	Regulate all officers
LOUISIANA	18,000 240 hours	Unknown Some reserves may be 240 hour certified but they're lumped into the 18,000 hour figure	Regulate certified officers only
MAINE	1,549 480 hours	1,274 part-time 100 hours pre-service	Regulate all officers
MARYLAND	13,473 435 hours	89 Part-time 435 hours 100 Seasonal Trained in-house 1,000 non-certified vol auxiliary Trained in-house	Regulate paid officers only
MASSACHUSETTS	400 hours	5,000 reserves/aux/specials Part-time & Special officers 96 hour Reserve/Intermitten course 30-37 hour First Responder + CPR + firearms qualification Vol. Aux. Some use res./int. course but not required to	Regulate full, part-time officers only Vol. Aux. under state x civil defense
MICHIGAN	25,000 440	2,000 Reserves trained in-house	Regulate full-time officers only
MINNESOTA	7,501 400 hours	824 part-time No training minimum vol/reserves local	Regulate full, p/t officers only
MISSISSIPPI	4,646 360 hours	2,500 trained in-house	Regulate full-time officers only

STATE	Full-time	Part-time/Volunteer	State Regulate Officers
MISSOURI	14,142 600 hours for certified officers in larger, chartered class 1 counties/cities 120 hours for certified officers in smaller 1, 2, 3, & 4 counties/cities	352 certified reserves	Regulate certified officers only
MONTANA	1,496 540 hours for full, part-time officers	400 non-certified reserves 71 part-time	Regulate all officers
NEBRASKA	3,400 certified officers State does not differentiate btwn full, part-time officers 500 hours	382 vol reserves 180 hours in-house training	Regulate all officers
NEVADA	6,000 540 hours	250 vol reserves 134 hours Must have certified officer on duty Can't work more than 100 hours per year	Regulate full-time officers only
NEW HAMPSHIRE	2,192 430 hours	1,000 vol reserves training up to agency	Regulate all officers
NEW JERSEY	27,337 669 average hours	1,654 part-time 100 hours Part-time unknown total Class II Specials 122 trained in 1990-1991 General law enforcement duties, armed, full powers on duty 452 average hours Class I Specials (Ia. and Ib.) 218 trained in 1990-1991 Crowd & traffic control, unarmed, limited powers 78 average hours 96 vol. deputy conservation officers 200 hours 1,000 volunteer auxiliary officers 42 hours minimum training: powers on duty, armed after 40 hr. firearms course	Regulate full, part-time officers only Regulated by NJ State Police/ Office of Emergency Management
NEW MEXICO	4,215	Unknown reserves	Regulate full-time officers only
NEW YORK	62,953 445 hours for full and part-time officers	2,690 part-time 7,240 vol aux 10 hours min training	Regulate full, part-time officers only NYS Emerg Mngmnt Office regulate vol auxiliary
NORTH CAROLINA	16,526	4,617 reserves	Regulate all officers

STATE	Full-time	Part-time/Volunteer	State Regulate Officers
NORTH DAKOTA	All police officers (incl reserves): minimum 432 hours of training All sheriffs (incl reserves): minimum 444 hours of training	1,564 200 part-time 360 hours for full, part-time. Correspondance course available for part-time officers 100 res/aux officers training up to agency	Regulate full, part-time officers only
OHIO	14,789 420 hours for all full, part-time, vol officers who are commisioned	18,000 part-time, vol	Regulate all commishioned officers
OKLAHOMA	7,436 300 hours	2,105 vol/paid reserves 120 hours	Regulate all officers
OREGON	4,830 320 hours	1,342 reserves Training up to agency Most are 320 hours	Regulate full-time only
PENNSYLVANIA	19,475 520 hours for full, part-time police 160 hours for full, part-time sheriffs	3,825 part-time	Regulate full, part-time officers only
RHODE ISLAND	2,400 500 hours average	605 part-time, vol no state min training State used to hold 40 hour reserve academy	Regulate full-time officers only
SOUTH CAROLINA	7,000 332 hours for full, part-time officers	500 part-time 850 Volunteer reserves 64 hours in-house training	Regulate all officers
SOUTH DAKOTA	1,023 320 hours for full, part-time officers	Part-time incl in 1,023 figure 190 volunteer reserves 100 hours	Regulate all officers
TENNESSEE	8,000 320 hours	1,000 part-time 40 hours of training during first calendar year 1,656 non-certified vol res/aux Training up to agency	Regulate full, part-time officers only
TEXAS	47,391 400 hours	5,770 reserves 400 hour total training- 145 hour pre-service basic course 131 hour within two years 124 hour within four years	Regulate all officers

STATE	Full-time	Part-time/Volunteer	State Regulate Officers
UTAH	5,000 full-time, part-time, and volunteer officers 440 hours	Part-time, vol.- Category II. Reserve Officer 160 hour reserve academy	Regulate all officers
VERMONT	600 600 hours	1,100 part-time 58 hours pre-service 50 hours in-service 60 hours FTO program (all within 1 year)	Regulate all officers
VIRGINIA	24,400 total certified officers (Includes full-time and some vol and part-time officers) 315 hours minimum 400 average hours Unkown number of non-certified officers Training up to local agency		Regulate certified officers only
WASHINGTON	7,400 440 hours	2,500 sworn vol reserves 590 graduated last year from optional 175 hour reserve academy	Regulate all officers
WEST VIRGINIA	2,500 498 hours	Unknown part-time May be included in 2,500 full-time figure Only Charleston uses volunteer officers	Regulate all officers
WISCONSIN	10,000 400 hours for all certified officers	2,000 certified part-time Part-time certified officer modular training 400 hours within 3 years Ten 40 hour blocks 3 formats for scheduling convenience 1,500 non-certified vol officers	Regulate all certified officers
WYOMING	1,460 403 hours for all officers Full-time has one year to acquire Reserve has two years to acquire	102 certified reserves	Regulate all officers

SECTION IV

Alabama

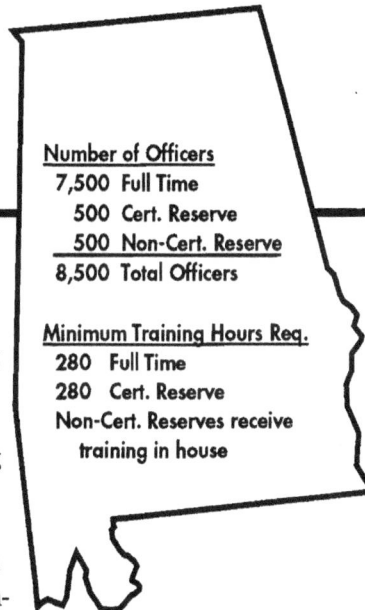

Alabama reserves, also called auxiliaries by a few departments, are alive and well in the Heart of Dixie. Wendy Jones, certification coordinator for the Alabama Peace Officers Standards Commission, said the state regulates only certified officers who must complete 280 hours of training. She emphasized that no distinction is made between 280 hour certified full-time, part-time, or volunteer officers.

According to John Anderson, executive secretary of the Commission, the state has 7,500 certified full-time officers and 500 fully certified reserves. The Commission's top administrator said the reserves can undergo their training full-time over seven weeks or take one of two part-time training routes. Option one involves weekend training until completion while the second option starts with a two week "summer camp" (for

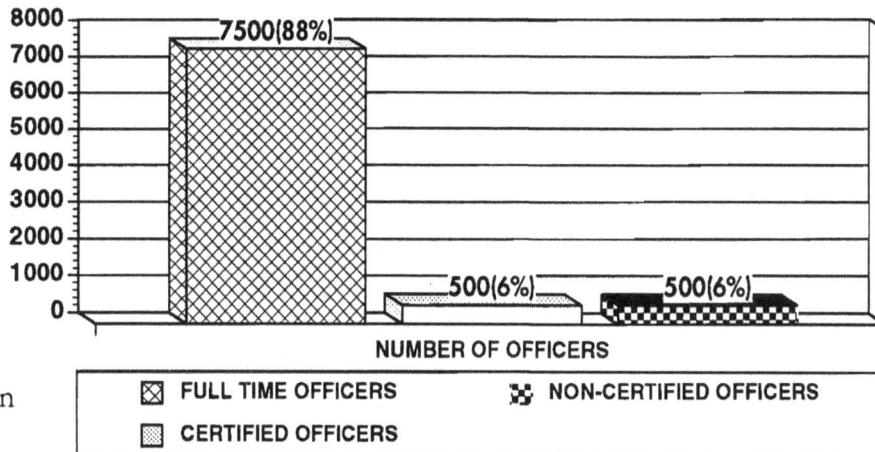

NUMBER OF OFFICERS

☒ FULL TIME OFFICERS
☐ CERTIFIED OFFICERS
⋇ NON-CERTIFIED OFFICERS

Contact:

John Anderson
Executive Secretary
or
Wendy Jones
Certification Coordinator
Alabama Peace Officer Standards and
Training Commission
472 Lawrence Street
Montgomery, AL 36104

205/242-4047

firearms, etc.) with the remaining time covered on weekends.

In keeping with the clout Southern sheriffs have, reserve deputy sheriffs have more leeway than do municipal police reserves in terms of their training. Said Anderson: "Municipal police reserves have no powers until they're fully trained. It is up to the sheriff to decide whether his (reserve) deputies have powers from day one."

Agencies are not prevented by the state from using untrained, non-certified reserves.

Anderson estimates that there are in excess of 500 officers who are not certified or are in the process of working towards their certification.

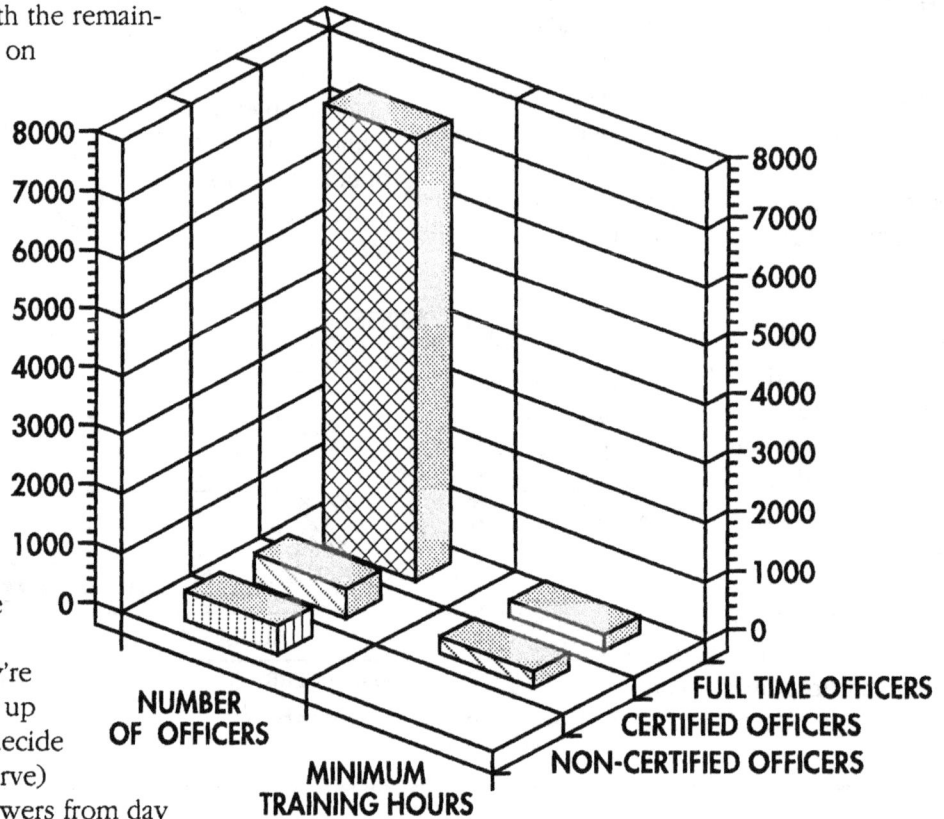

Alaska

Number of Officers
1,200 Full Time
  110 Reserve Paid/Volunteer
1,310 Total Officers

Minimum Training Hours Req.
  400 Full Time
Reserve Paid/Volunteer
  receive training in house

Alaska, the Great State, has just 1,200 full-time officers and 110 reserves to patrol 586,412 square miles. According to Jack Wray, executive director of the Alaska Police Standards Council, full-time officers must undergo a minimum of 400 hours of training. The state does not regulate volunteer or part-time paid reserve officers. Training for reserves is left up to the local agency's discretion.

Wray estimates that there are not more than 50 more reserves around the state other than those utilized by the Anchorage Police Department. With Anchorage's 60 volunteer law enforcers, that would place Alaska's total at 110 reserves. Agencies such as the Haines, AK, Police Department also have reserve officers.

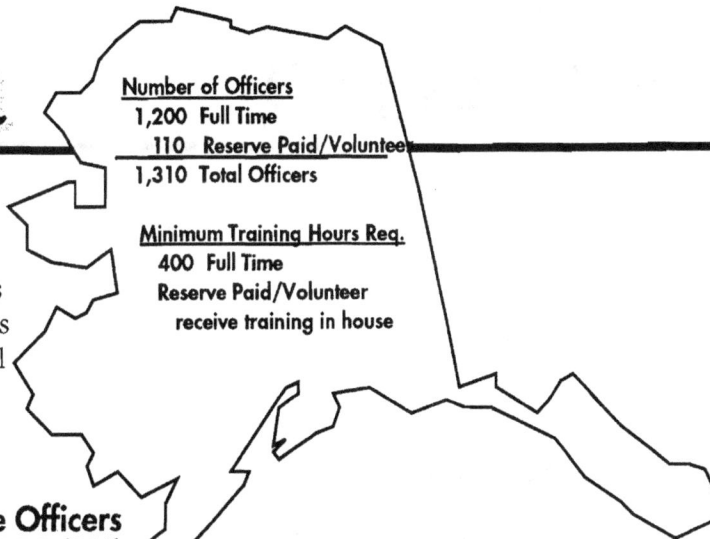

Reserve Officers
110 (8%)

Number of Officers
Alaska

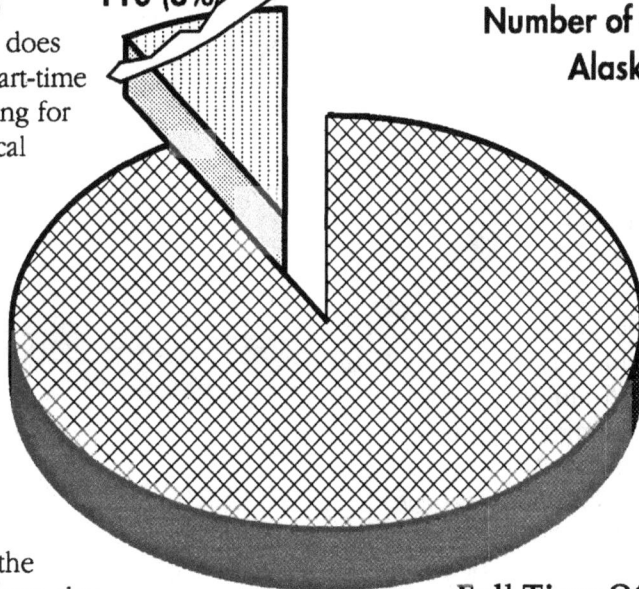

Full Time Officers
1,200 (92%)

Contact:

Jack Wray
Executive Director
Alaska Police Standards Council
Box "N"
Juneau, AK 99811

907/465-4378

Res. Capt. Mel Kalkowski
Reserve Commander
Anchorage Police Dept.
4501 South Brawaw Street
Anchorage, AK 99507-1565

Arizona

Number of Officers
9,000 Full Time
  800 Volunteer Reserves
9,800 Total Officers

Minimum Training Hours Req.
440 for all officers

Arizona, easily one of the most advanced reserve states in the nation, has a rather simple approach to the training of law enforcement officers. All officers are required to complete at least 440 hours of Arizona Law Enforcement Officer Advisory Council (ALEOAC) training.

There are 10 ALEOAC-accredited reserve academies which dot the Grand Canyon state. They are: Arizona Western College, Central Arizona Regional Law Enforcement Officer Training (Carlotta), Glendale Community College, Mesa Community College, Mohave Community College, Northland Pioneer College, Phoenix College, Phoenix Regional Police Academy, and Yavapai College.

The Council lists 9,000 full-time officers and 800 reserve officers in its records.

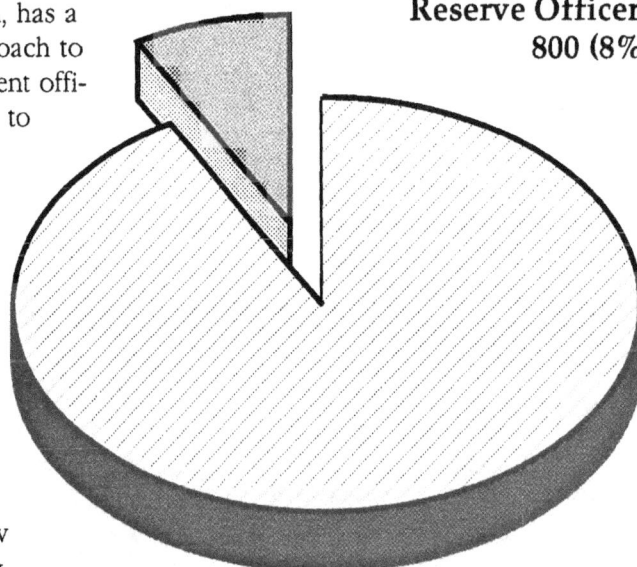

Reserve Officers
800 (8%)

Full Time Officers
9,000 (92%)

Number of Officers
Arizona

Contact:

Arizona Law Enforcement Officer Advisory Council
P.O. Box 6638
Phoenix, AZ 85005

602/223-2517

Arkansas

Number of Officers
8,081 Full Time
Unknown number of Part-time &
Auxiliaries

Minimum Training Hours Req.
280 Full Time
280 Part-time I
100 Part-time II
100 Volunteer Auxiliary

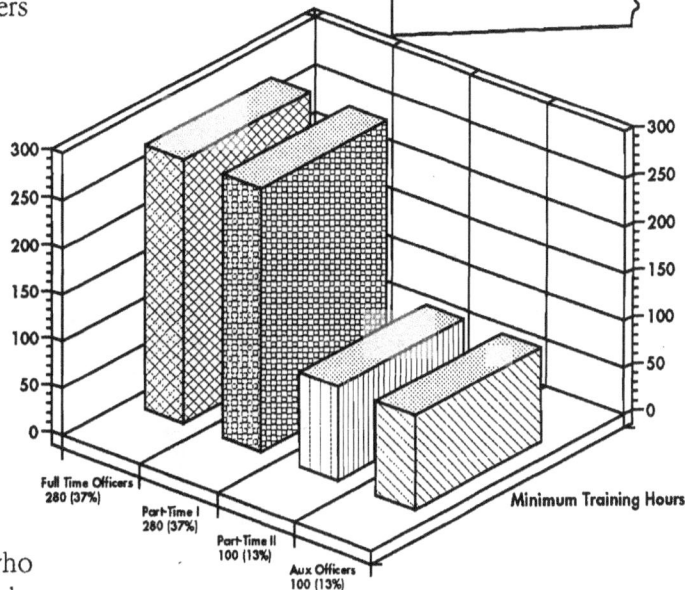

Arkansas Commission on Law Enforcement Standards and Training tracks closely their 8,081 full-time law enforcement officers trained to a 280 hour minimum standard. Municipal officers number 3,603, county sheriffs and their deputies comprise 2,659 and 1,498 state officers round out the total.

The Wonder State's citizen cops are unknown in number, but are regulated in terms of their training hours. No annual in-service training is mandated by the state.

Part-time I. officers, who work 20 to 40 hours per week, must meet the same 280 hour training requirements as their full-time counterparts. Part-time II. officers, who don a uniform less than 20 hours per week, must receive a minimum of 100 hours of training, as do volunteer auxiliary officers.

Bill Brown, deputy director of the Commission explained that, under Act 757 of 1983, volunteer auxiliary officers must be trained at the 100 hour level and work not more than 20 hours per week. Brown said the

officers must complete the 100 hours of training which could be all 100 hours in the classroom or 40 hours in the classroom and 60 hours ride-along.

Minimum Training Hours Arkansas

Chart labels: Full Time Officers 280 (37%), Part-Time I 280 (37%), Part-Time II 100 (13%), Aux Officers 100 (13%), Minimum Training Hours

Contact:

Bill Brown
Deputy Director
Arkansas Commission on Law Enforcement Standards and Training
3703 West Roosevelt Road
Little Rock, AR 72204

501/324-9209

California

California, not surprisingly, is clearly the leader in reserve law enforcement. "Depending on the time and day of the week, a citizen has a 15 to 50% chance of having a reserve respond to their call," said James C. Lombardi, president of the California Reserve Peace Officers Association. Lombardi, who also serves as the reserve officer in charge of the Los Angeles Police Reserve Corps., works closely with the California Commission on Peace Officer Standards and Training (POST) to ensure that the current level of respect via professionalism enjoyed by the reserves is continued.

Darrell L. Stewart, bureau chief in the executive office of POST, said that there are 69,455 full-time officers and 13,836 reserve officers in the state. In addition to municipal police and county sheriffs departments, reservists can be found working for the department of justice, fish and wildlife and numerous other state agencies.

Stewart said the full-time minimum training hours are 560 hours although the statewide average comes in at 700 hours. Reserves are trained to a level complementary to their duties.

Level I. Designated reserves receive 560 hours

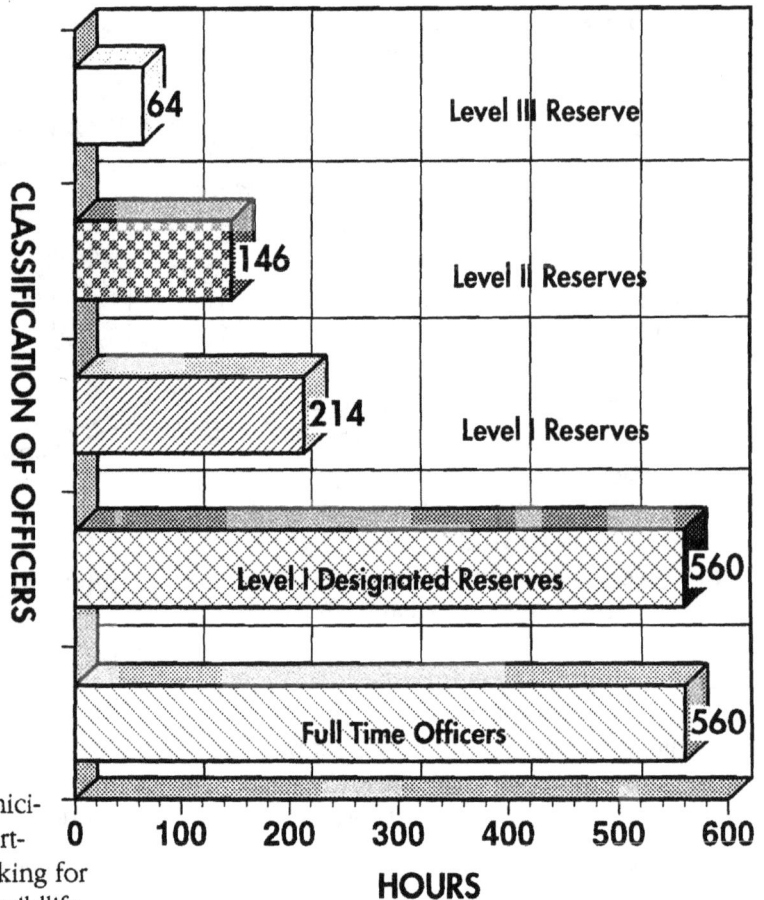

**Minimum Training Hours
California**

of training equal in quality to a full-time basic academy and undergo an extensive field training officer (FTO) program. These officers are the Tiffany reserves of the Golden State discharging their general law enforcement duties on a solo basis and possessing full police powers.

Level I. Non-designated reserves undergo 214 hours of training and discharge their solo law enforcement responsibilities only while on duty. Level II. reserves trained to the 146 hour minimum have powers while on duty with a partner only. Level III. reserves receive 64 hours of training and fulfill technical responsibilities while on duty.

Level I. Designated reserves have authority throughout the state 24 hours a day and carry a weapon off duty "on their badge." The other levels have authority only while on duty. Lombardi indicated that it is

fairly routine for agencies to issue C.C.W. permits (carry concealed weapon permits) to their non-designated reserves.

Training is available at many academies and

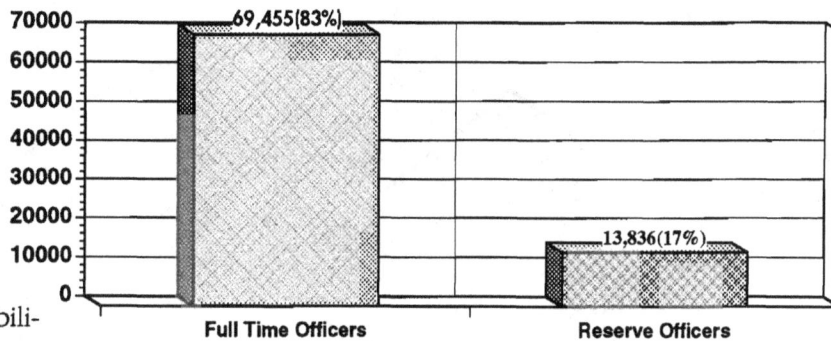

TOTAL NUMBER OF OFFICERS BY TYPE

community colleges with some individuals paying their own way to enhance their attractiveness for hire as a reserve or full-time officer.

Contact:

Darrell L. Stewart
Bureau Chief, Executive Office
California Commission on Peace
    Officer Standards and Training
1601 Alhambra Boulevard
Sacramento, CA 95816-7083

916/739-3864

James C. Lombardi
President
California Reserve Peace Officers
    Association
P.O. Box 5622
San Jose, CA 95124

408/371-8239

Colorado

L aw enforcement in Colorado, which has 7,658 full-timers and 948 reserves (as of March 31, 1992), boasts among the most advanced state imposed training guidelines in the nation. John R. Shell, director of Colorado Peace Officer Standards and Training (POST), said the feeling in his state is "whether the officer works four hours or forty hours, he still needs the same skills" for whatever duties he is discharging.

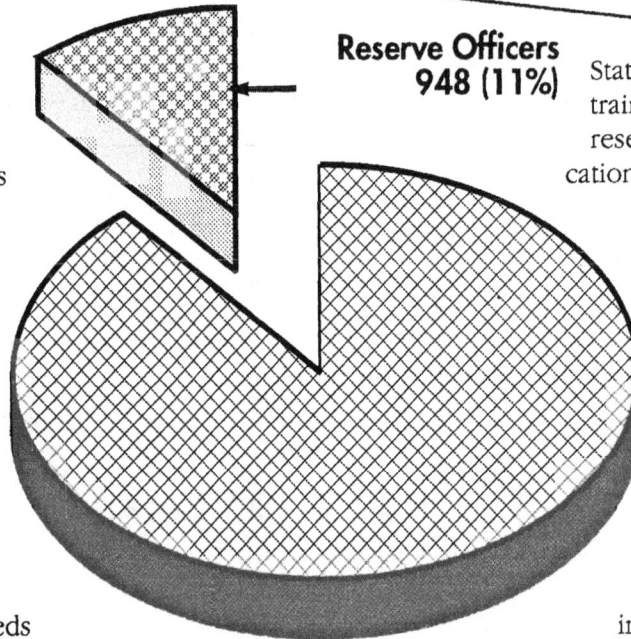

Reserve Officers 948 (11%)

Full Time Officers 7,658 (89%)

State allows agencies to train and utilize its reserves at four classifications levels. Reserves are allowed to perform varying degrees of tasks provided that their duties do not exceed their training.

Level I. reserves receive the same 358 hours of training as full-timers receive including a 38 hour firearms course and a 25 hour arrest control course. They are involved in general law enforcement duties.

Similar in concept to the Level and Module system pioneered by California, the Centennial

Contact:

John R. Shell
Director
Colorado Peace Officer Standards and Training
15000 Golden Road
Golden, CO 80401-3997

303-273-1746

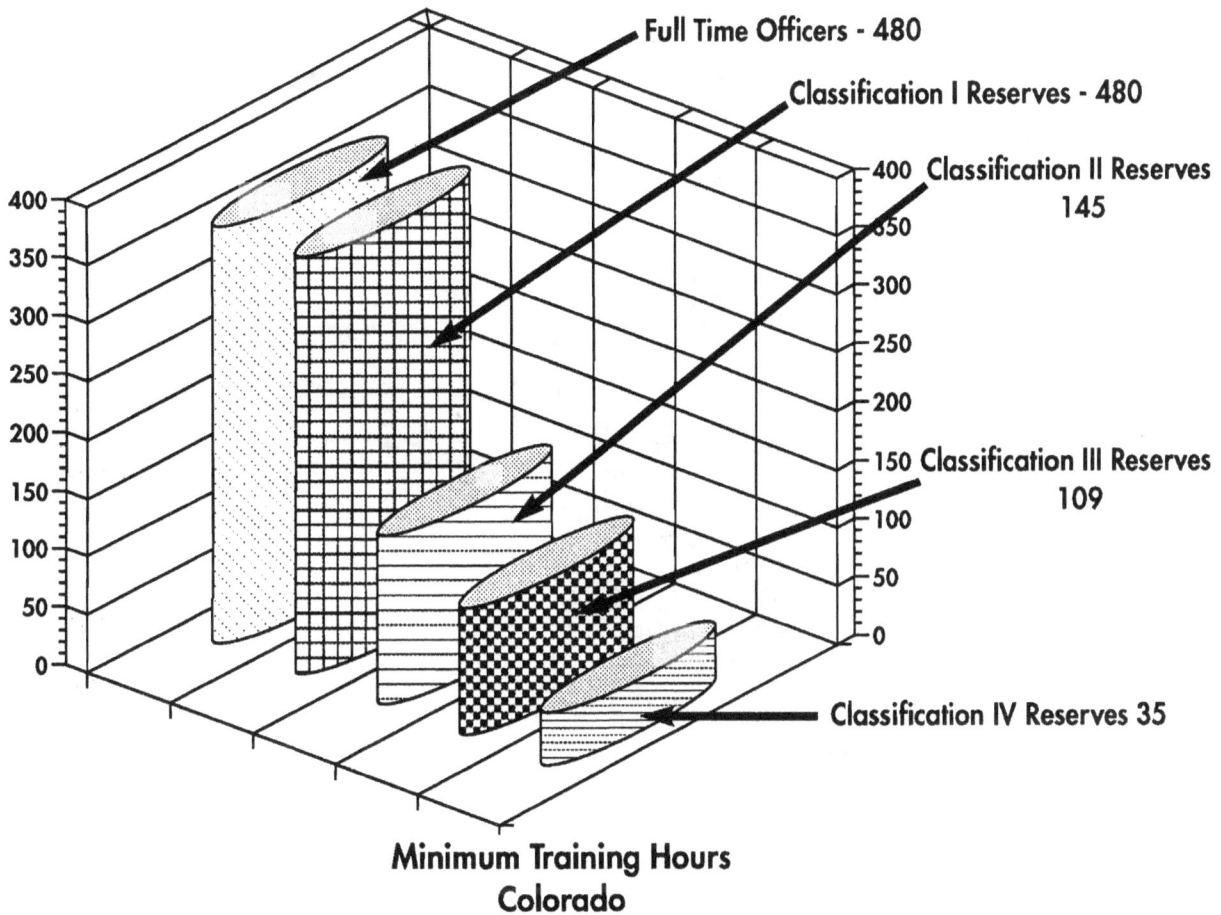

Minimum Training Hours
Colorado

- Full Time Officers - 480
- Classification I Reserves - 480
- Classification II Reserves 145
- Classification III Reserves 109
- Classification IV Reserves 35

Some reserves are not assigned to general law enforcement duties. They may be assigned to tasks involving areas such as extradition or mountain rescue. Levels II., III., and IV. do not include the two aforementioned firearms and arrest control courses which must be completed if assigned duties comprise those responsibilities and the commissioning agency wants them to be armed. A Level IV. officer completes Module A (33 hours). A Level III. officer completes Module A plus Module B (76 hours) for a total of 109 hours. A Level II. officer's training is made up of Modules A, B, and C (36 hours) which adds up to 145 hours.

A 28 hour emergency driving course is also available to officers. The Colorado Law Enforcement Training Academy course involves 4 hours of classroom and 24 hours of hands on driving on a mile and a half track complete with skid pan. Topics covered include backing and lane changes.

Connecticut

Number of Officers
12,000	Full Time
2,500	Part-time Reserves
500	Volunteer Reserves
271	Auxiliary Troopers
15,271	Total Officers

Minimum Training Hours Req.
480	Full Time
480	Part-time
207	Auxiliary Trooper
Volunteers trained in house	

Connecticut uses citizen cops empowered through statute as special constables. According to George Miller, certification officer with the Connecticut Municipal Police Training Council in Meriden, special constables must undergo the same 480 hours of minimum training that the 12,000 active full-time officers complete. Specials attend the training on weeknights and weekends.

Miller said that they do not know how many of the 2,500 trained special constables are still active but estimates place the figure at 400-500. There is also an unknown number of uncertified auxiliary/ supernumerary officers who have no training or powers.

The Connecticut State Police has a well-known auxiliary trooper program which has its own legal basis (under Connecticut General Statutes Section 29-22). Founded in 1941, the program, under the supervision of State Police Sergeant James J. Rodgers based in Meriden, boasts 271 armed, volunteer auxiliary troopers. New training planned for new auxiliary troopers will bring the training up to 207 hours (including 24 hours of firearms) from 100 hours.

Part Time Officers 2,500 (16%)

Auxiliary Trooper 271 (2%)

Volunteers 500 (3%)

Full Time Officers 12,000 (79%)

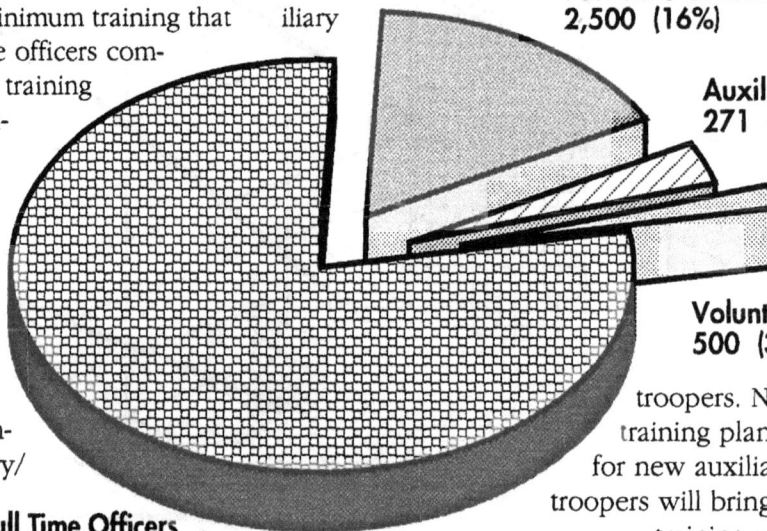

Total Officers Connecticut

Contact:

George Miller
Certification Officer
Connecticut Municipal Police Training Council
285 Preston Avenue
Meriden, CT 06450

203/238-6505

Sgt. James J. Rodgers
Auxiliary Trooper Coordinator
Connecticut State Police
294 Colony Street
Meriden, CT 06450

203/238-6018

Delaware

Number of Officers
1,500 Full Time
  37 Seasonal
1,537 Total Officers

Minimum Training Hours Req.
 498 Full Time
  40 Seasonal

Delaware's approach to part-time/ volunteer law enforcers have earned the nation's first state a unique position. According to ishing all officers fitting the classification. Captain Mergenthaler, speaking from his Dover office, indicated that there are 1500 full-time officers in the state with at least 498 hours of

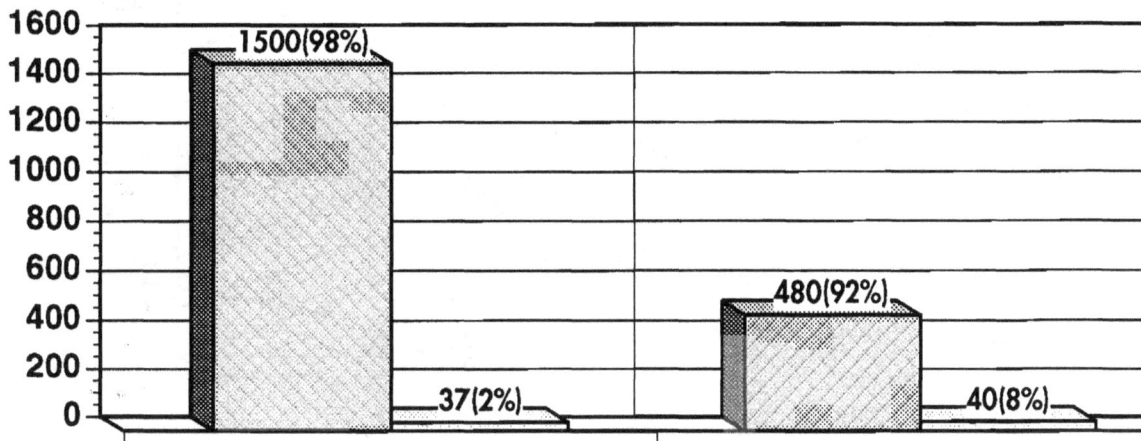

Number of Officers

Minimum Training Hours

Captain Daryl Mergenthaler, director of training for the 485 trooper Delaware State Police, there are no year-round volunteer or part-time officers. Legislation was passed in 1988 abolishing

training. He said that resort communities do hire 37 part-time seasonal officers who complete a 40 hour training period and do not carry firearms.

Contact:

Capt. Daryl Mergenthaler
Director of Training
Delaware State Police
P.O. Box 430
Dover, DE 19903

302/739-5903

Florida

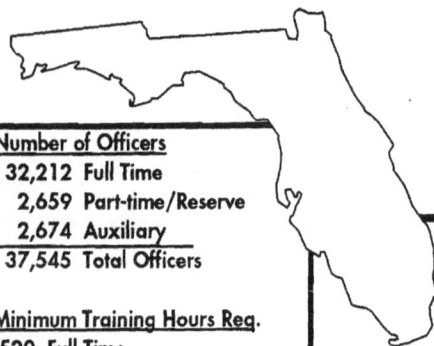

Number of Officers
32,212 Full Time
2,659 Part-time/Reserve
2,674 Auxiliary
37,545 Total Officers

Minimum Training Hours Req.
520 Full Time
520 Part-time/Reserves
97 Auxiliary

One of the more professional states when it comes to volunteer law enforcement, Florida actually has two distinct classifications codified in their state statutes (Florida State Statute FSS 943.17). Fully-certified part-time officers, or "reserves" as they are commonly called in the Sunshine State, comprise the top tier, with "auxiliary" as the lesser trained designation.

Barry E. Newman, a Jacksonville Sheriff's reserve who serves as president of the Florida Police Reserve Association, said training is the driving force behind the widespread utilization of volunteers in his state.

Volunteers are used as municipal police reserve officers, county reserve deputy sheriffs, and in state law enforcement. State reserves include state universities, Florida Highway

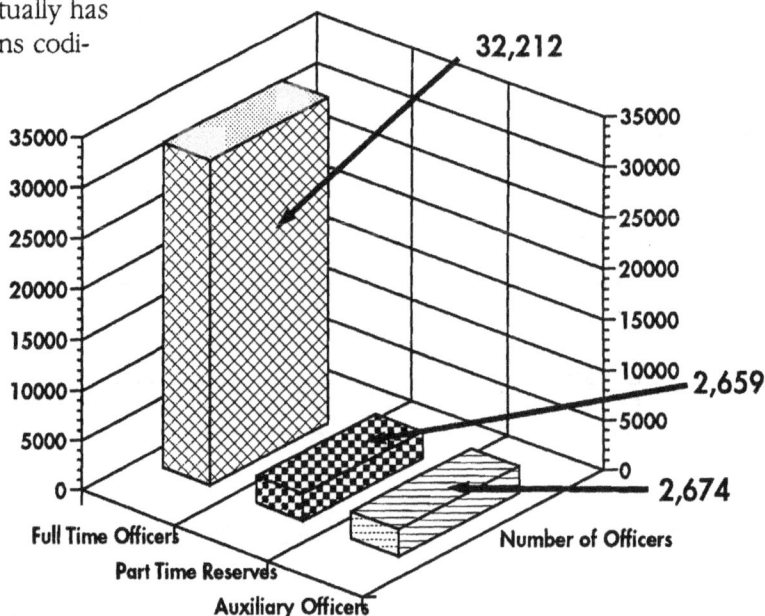

Number of Officers

Contact:

Ms. Sandra Dickey
Standards & Training Specialist
Florida Division of Criminal Justice
Standards & Training
P.O. Box 1849
Tallahassee, FL 32310

904/487-3880

Res. Off. Barry E. Newman
President
Florida Police Reserve
Association
5030 Blanding Boulevard
Jacksonville, FL 32210

904/778-4501

Patrol (FHP), Marine Patrol, Game & Fish, State Attorneys Offices, Department of Agriculture, Alcoholic Beverage Control (ABC), Department of Insurance, and the Florida Department of Law Enforcement (FDLE).The Florida Highway Patrol (FHP) has 589 volunteer auxiliary troopers, under the command of Auxiliary Colonel Harold L. Butterfield, who are armed and ride with fully-certified troopers. The auxiliary troopers donated 207,633 hours of law enforcement services in 1991. The FHP also has 12 fully-certified reserve troopers who are solo-qualified following a rigorous field training officer (FTO) program.

According to Sandra Dickey, standards and training specialist with the Florida Division of Criminal Justice Standards and Training (CJST), all full-time officers and part-time officers (they may also be paid a token one dollar a year or work on a non-compensated

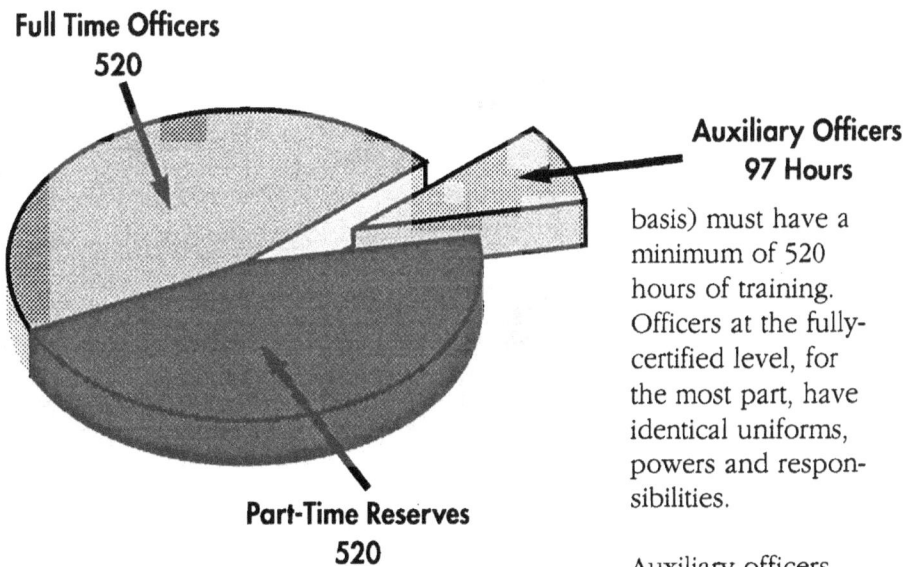

Full Time Officers
520

Auxiliary Officers
97 Hours

Part-Time Reserves
520

Minimum Training Hours

basis) must have a minimum of 520 hours of training. Officers at the fully-certified level, for the most part, have identical uniforms, powers and responsibilities.

Auxiliary officers have uniforms that are slightly distinctive and have powers only while under the supervision of certified officers. Minimum training for this

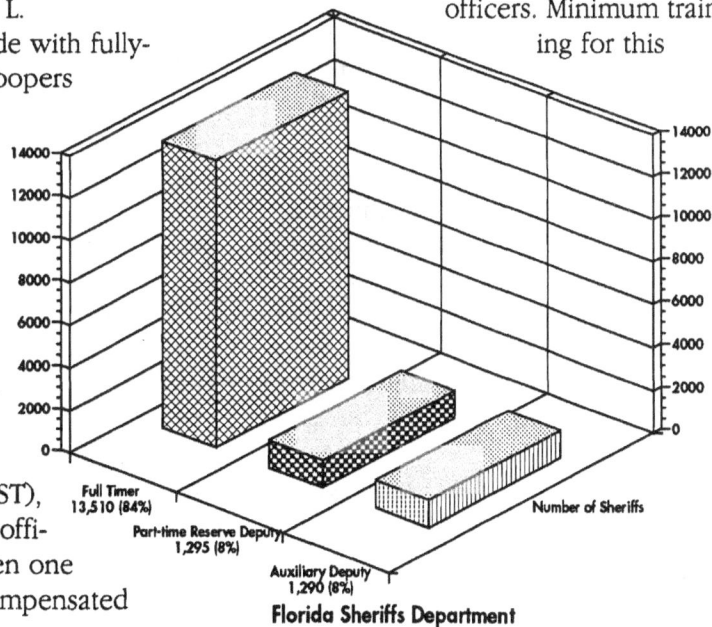

Full Timer
13,510 (84%)

Part-time Reserve Deputy
1,295 (8%)

Auxiliary Deputy
1,290 (8%)

Number of Sheriffs

Florida Sheriffs Department

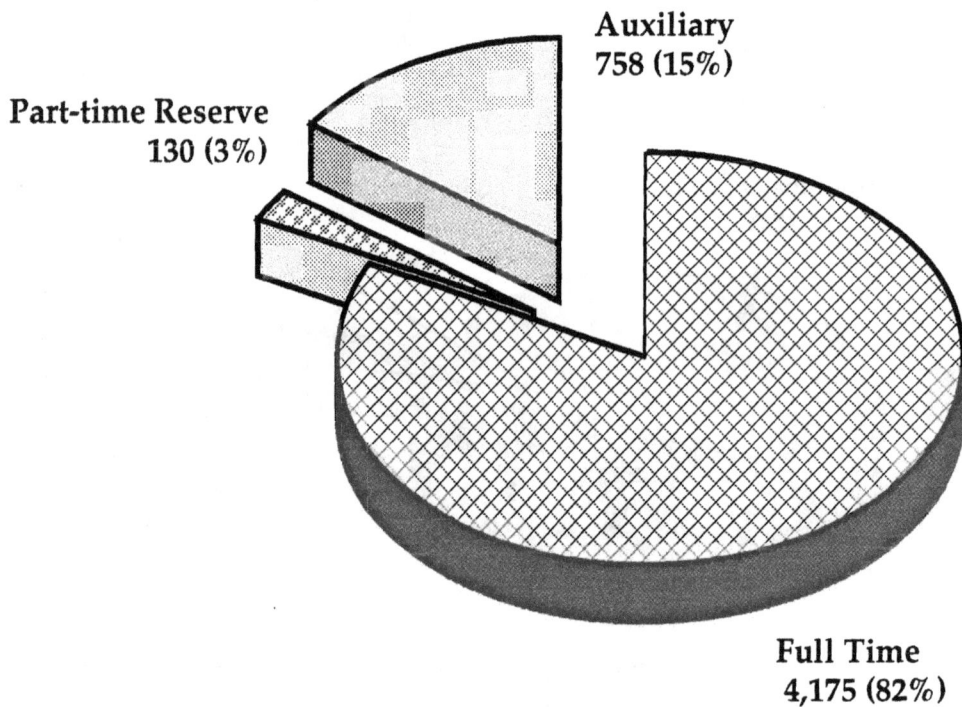

Auxiliary
758 (15%)

Part-time Reserve
130 (3%)

Full Time
4,175 (82%)

Florida State Law Enforcement Agencies

classification is 97 hours. Some agencies, such as the Florida Highway Patrol, require the supervision to be one of a visual nature, while others deem radio contact an adequate mode of supervision.

Florida's Dickey indicated that most of the 40 academies in the state far exceed the minimums required by the state. Many academies are run out of community colleges and enrollment is open to civilians after a cursory background check. Academies of this nature enable aspiring volunteers or career-oriented persons to make themselves more attractive for hire.

As of March 30, 1992, the CJST had registered

32,212 full-time officers, 2,659 part-time reserves, and 2,674 auxiliaries. Combined totals of volunteer law enforcers in the state is 5,333.

Broken down into categories, the sheriff's departments employed 13,510 full-time deputy sheriffs, 1,295 part-time reserve deputy sheriffs and 1,290 auxiliary deputy sheriffs for a sheriffs total of 16,095. Municipal police departments weigh in with 14,527 full-time police officers, 1,234 part-time reserves, and 626 auxiliary officers for a total of 16,387. State law enforcement agencies, including the FHP, had 4,175 full-timers, 130 part-time reserves, and 758 auxiliaries for a total of 5,063.

Georgia

Number of Officers
19,286 Full Time
714 Certified
20,000 Total Officers

Minimum Training Hours Req.
280 All Peace Officers

Georgia's reserves reflect the same standards applied to full-time officers. All certified officers in the Peach State must undergo 280 hours (7 weeks) of training under the auspices of the Georgia Peace Officer Standards and Training Council (POST). Jim Sims, manager of information services, said the hours were raised from 240 hours (6 weeks) as of July 1, 1992.

Sims explained that the state's attorney general makes no distinction between the training, duties, or powers of a reserve or regular officer providing that they are 280 hour POST certified. Said Sims: "The A.G. said 'If it walks like a duck, it must be a duck.'"

POST has 20,000 full-time certified officers and 714 certified reserves registered.

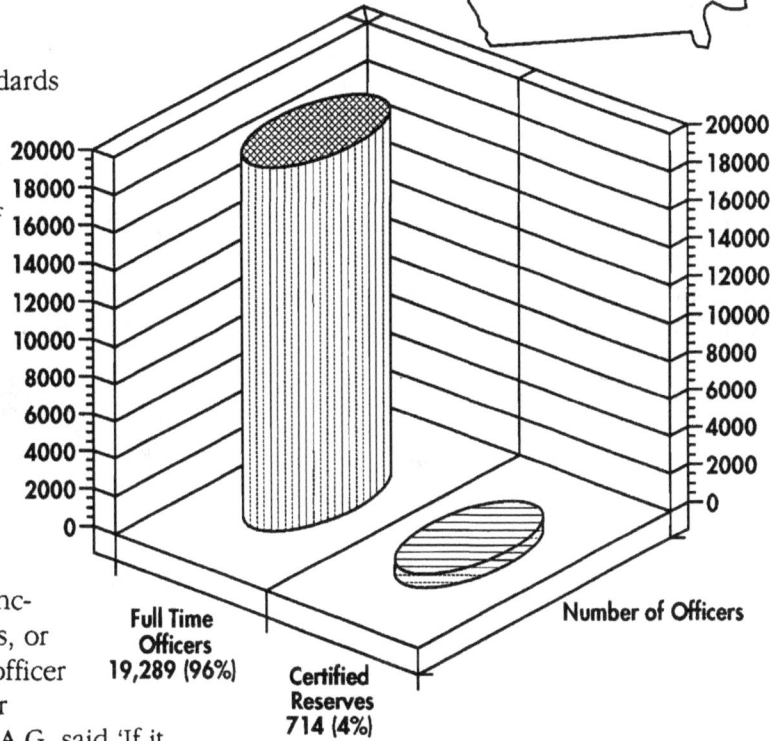

Full Time Officers 19,289 (96%)

Certified Reserves 714 (4%)

Number of Officers

Number of Officers

Contact:

Jim Sims
Manager of Information Services
Georgia Peace Officer Standards and Training Council
351 Thornton Road, Suite 119
Lithia Springs, GA 30057

404/739-5217

Idaho

Number of Officers
3,000 Full Time
Unkown number of reserves

Minimum Training Hours Req.
390 Full Time
160 Level I. Reserves
25 Level II. Reserves
No training req. for level III.

Much like California and Colorado, the State of Idaho employs a multiple training level system for their reserve officers. The state's Peace Officer Standards & Training (POST) records show 3,000 full-time officers with at least 390 hours of training.

While the number of reserves is unknown, the training process which delineates the different responsibilities they undertake is quite detailed. All reserves are armed.

Level I. Reserves are certified and have police powers. They must complete a 160 hour reserve academy and are required to partake in 120 hours of in-service training annually.

Level II. Reserves take at least 25 hours of training, are non-certified and must work under the supervision of a full-time officer. It varies from jurisdiction to jurisdiction as to whether the supervision standard of line of sight or radio contact applies.

Level III. Reserves have no training minimum and thus do not possess any law enforcement powers. They are used in specialized functions such as mounted posse, parades, and jeep posse.

Level II. Reserves
25 Hours

Level I. Reserve Officers
160 Hours Total

Full Time Officers
390 Hours

Note: Level III. Reserves
No minimum hours

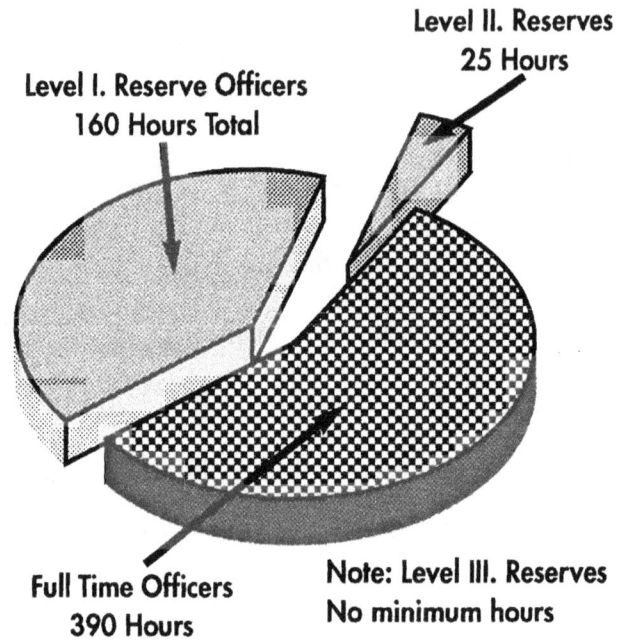

Minimum Training Hours

Contact:

Larry B. Plott
Executive Director
Idaho Peace Officer Standards and Training Academy
6115 Clinton Street
Boise, ID 83704

208/327-7150

Illinois

Volunteer and part-time law enforcement utilization and training in Illinois is left to local agency discretion. John Janssen, administrative assistant to the Illinois Local Governmental Law Enforcement Officers Training Board's executive director, Dr. Thomas J. Jurkanin, explained that part-time and volunteer officers that are armed are required to take a 40 hour firearms course. He said "the state is examining their (part-timers and auxiliaries) role and should probably make some changes in the next legislative session."

Janssen said the state requires its 27,038 full-time officers to have at least 400 hours of training. He added that are 2,738 part-time officers and 2,085 auxiliary officers in Illinois.

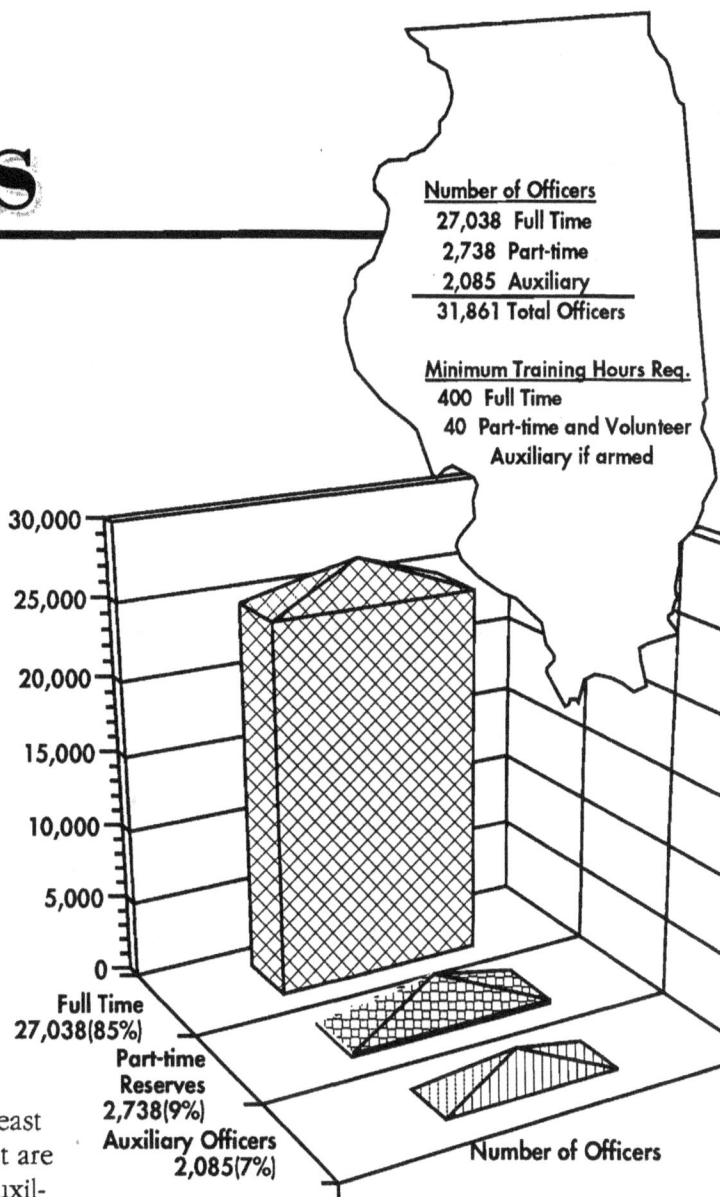

Full Time
27,038(85%)
Part-time
Reserves
2,738(9%)
Auxiliary Officers
2,085(7%)

Number of Officers

Contact:

John Janssen
Administrative Assistant to the Director
Illinois Local Governmental Law Enforcement Officers
        Training Board
600 South Second Street, Suite 300
Springfield, IL 62704-2542

217/782-4540

The metropolitan Chicago and Southern Cook County
area of **Auxiliary Officers - 40**
Illinois
follows the older
civil defense model. Volunteer
officers in the Chicago Police
Department are called "Auxiliary
Aides" and they function in an
unarmed, civilian capacity following
a 16 hour orientation course. While once
restricted to duties within the stationhouses not requiring contact with the
public, the Chicago P.D. have expanded
the auxiliary aide's role to include uniformed traffic direction and crowd
control.

Moving away from Chicago, rural agencies in
the Prairie State look to their non-full-timers to
augment thinly staffed departments in order to
maintain minimal response to calls for police
service. Chiefs in these situations do arm their
officers after completion of the mandatory 40
hour firearms course.

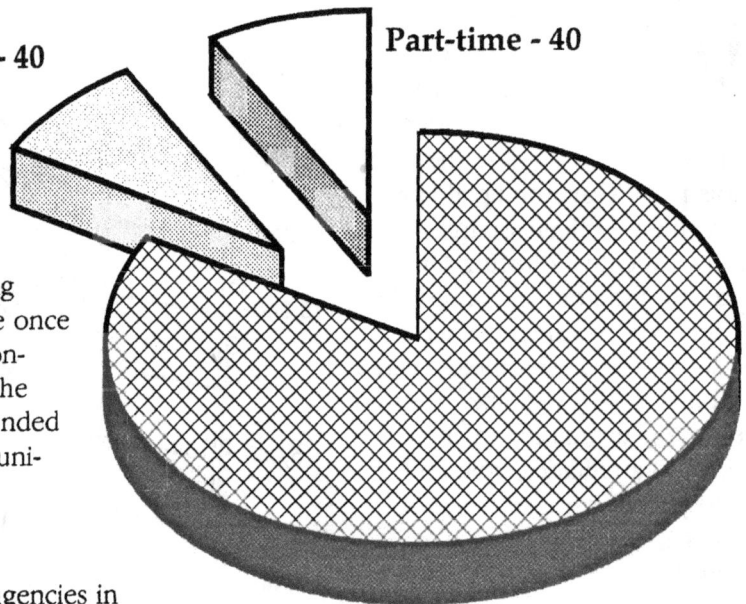

Part-time - 40

Full Time - 400

Note: 40 hours of training for part-time and
auxiliary apply only if they carry a firearm.

Minimum Training Hours Requirement

Indiana

Number of Officers
8,015 Full Time
192 Part-time
2,688 Volunteer
11,885 Total Officers

Min. Training Hrs. Req.
480 Full Time
480 Part Time
Volunteers rec've
in house training

Although only the full-time and part-time officers are required to meet the state-imposed minimum of 480 hours of training, almost all of the states volunteer officers do also. Arthur R. Raney Jr., executive director of the Indiana Law Enforcement Training Board, said his office regulates paid officers only. The state has 8,015 full-time paid officers and 192 part-time paid officers all of whom are required to have 480 hours of training.

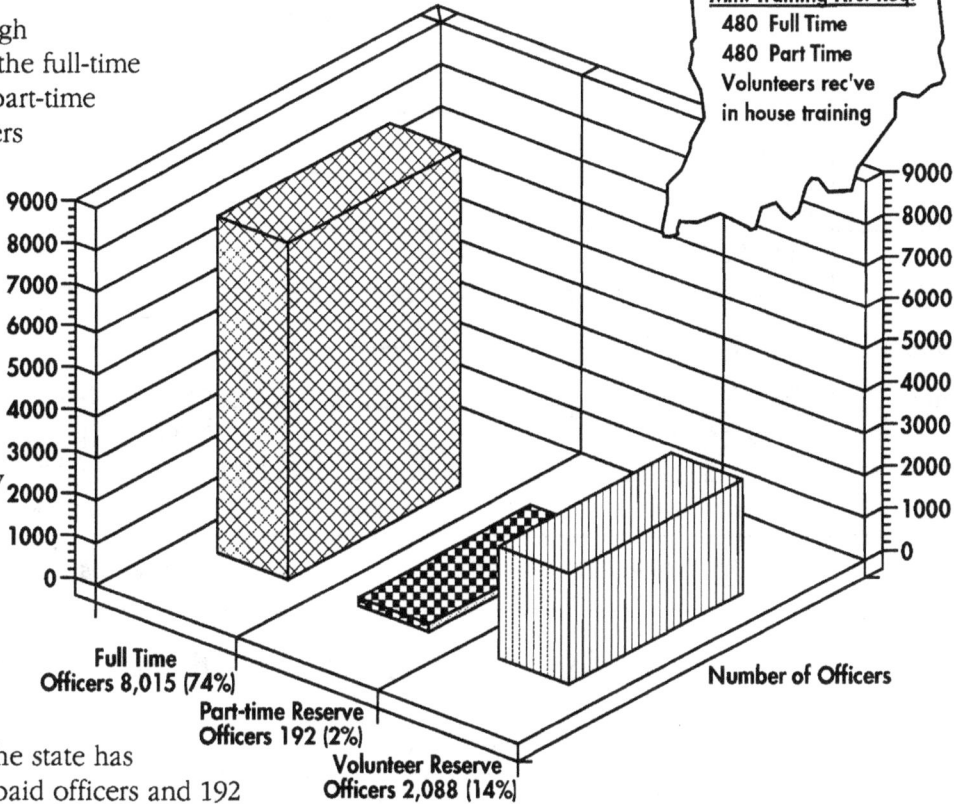

Full Time
Officers 8,015 (74%)

Part-time Reserve
Officers 192 (2%)

Volunteer Reserve
Officers 2,088 (14%)

Number of Officers

Total Number of Officers
Indiana

Contact:

Arthur R. Raney, Jr.
Executive Director
Indiana Law Enforcement Training Board
P.O. Box 313
Plainfield, IN 46168

317/839-5191

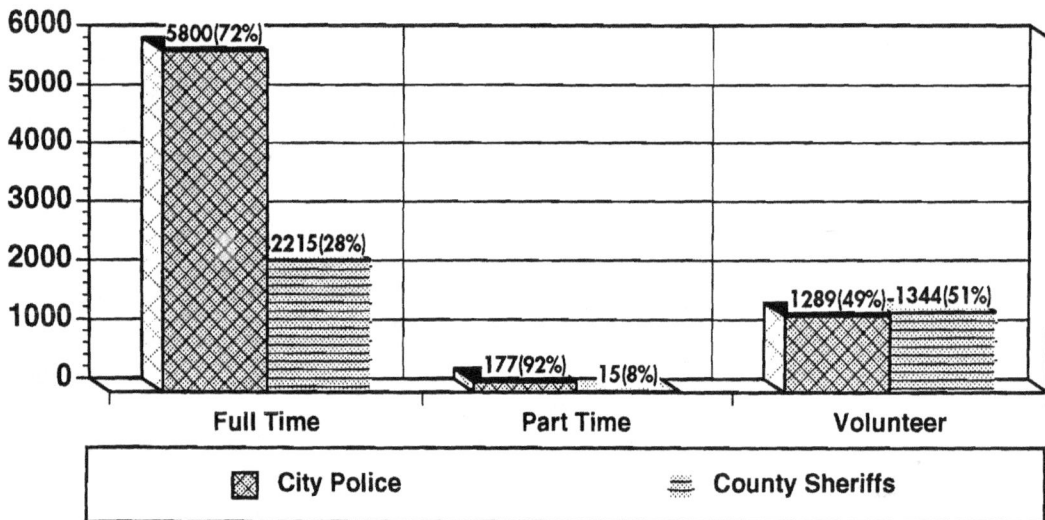

Distribution of Classification of Officers

	Full Time	Part Time	Volunteer
City Police	5800 (72%)	177 (92%)	1289 (49%)
County Sheriffs	2215 (28%)	15 (8%)	1344 (51%)

☒ City Police   ☰ County Sheriffs

The 2,688 volunteer officers are not forced to meet the same training standard, though Raney indicated that most agencies require that they do so. Most reserve academies range from the minimum 480 hours on up. Some small departments, with limited training budgets, may dictate only 40 hours of training. In July 1993, all volunteer reserve officers in the Hoosier State will find themselves under a new state statute mandating the completion of a 40 hour course.

Breaking down the jurisdictional classifications, city police departments have 5,800 full-time officers,

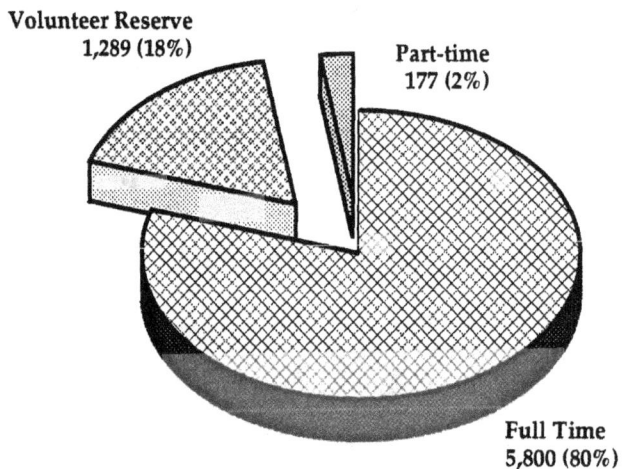

Volunteer Reserve 1,289 (18%)

Part-time 177 (2%)

Full Time 5,800 (80%)

County Deputy Sheriffs

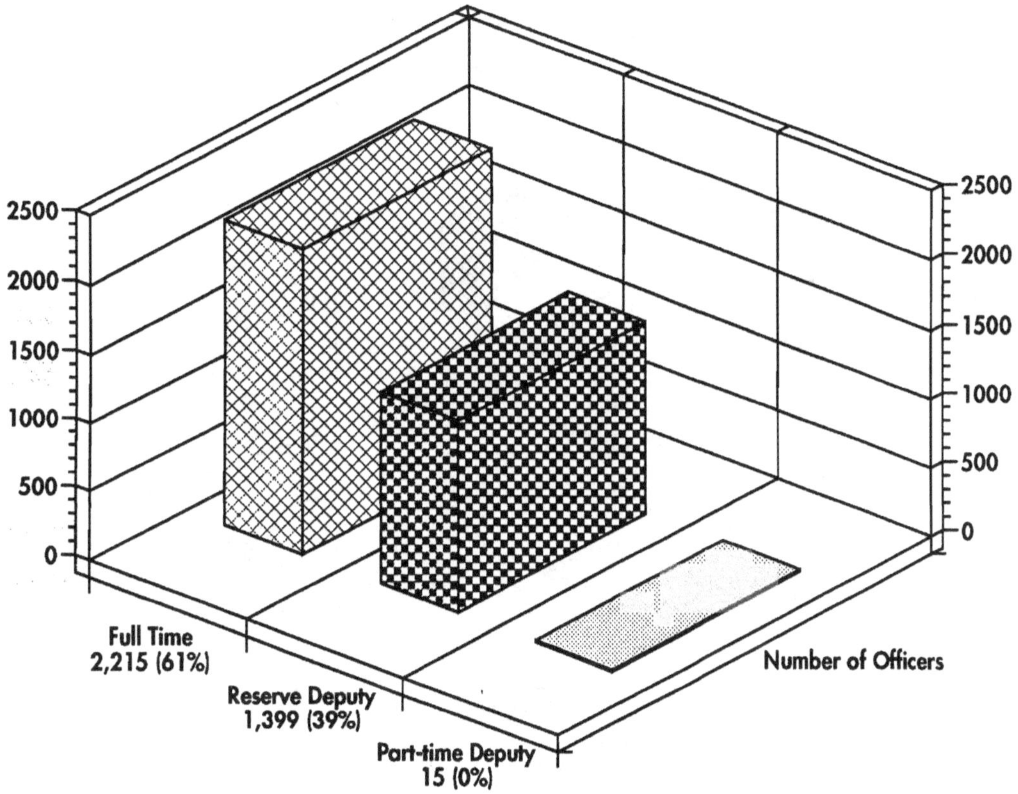
2500
2000
1500
1000
500
0
2500
2000
1500
1000
500
0
Full Time
2,215 (61%)
Reserve Deputy
1,399 (39%)
Part-time Deputy
15 (0%)
Number of Officers

Number of City Officers

177 part-time officers and 1,289 volunteer reserve officers. The county sheriffs have 2,215 deputy sheriffs, 15 part-time deputy sheriffs, and 1,399 reserve deputy sheriffs. There are 1,344 state officers with no part-time or volunteer reserves among their ranks.

Iowa

Number of Officers
5,100 Full Time
175 Part-time
1,200 Volunteer Reserves
6,475 Total Officers

Minimum Training Hours Req.
400 Full Time
400 Part-time
180 Volunteer Reserves

Reserve law enforcement in Iowa has been taking strides forward due to the joint efforts of the Iowa Law Enforcement Academy and the Iowa State Reserve Law Officer's Association. For many years the training in Iowa has been up to local law enforcement administrators.

"We want to standardize the amount and type of training received by reserve officers," said Daniel Brandt, secretary/treasurer of the Iowa reserve association. Brandt, who serves as a reserve captain with the Marshalltown, IA, Police Department,

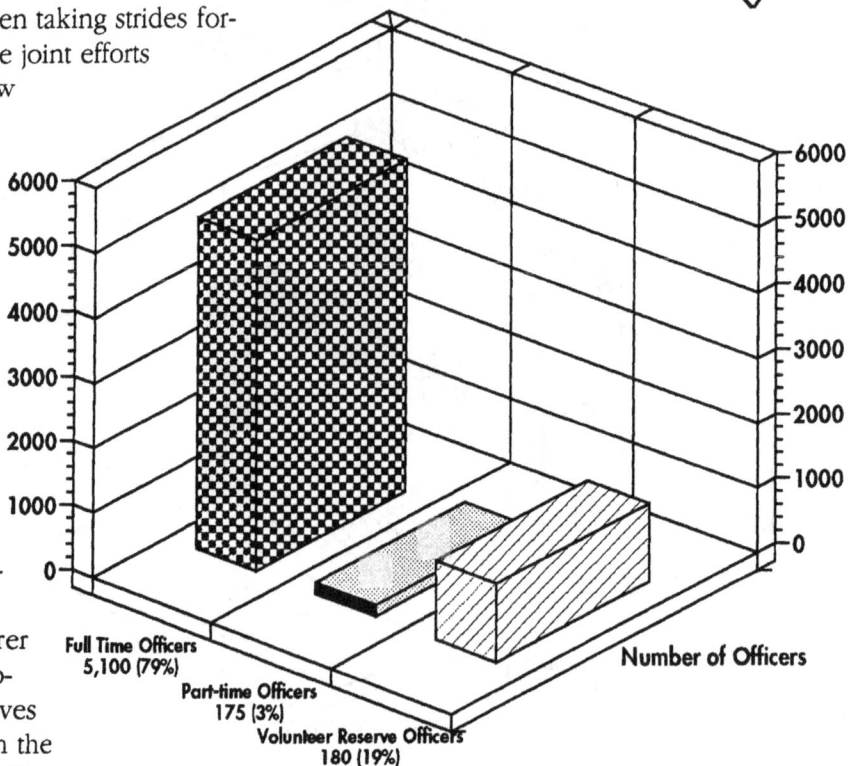

Full Time Officers
5,100 (79%)

Part-time Officers
175 (3%)

Volunteer Reserve Officers
180 (19%)

Number of Officers

Total Number of Officers

Contact:

Ben K. Yarrington
Director
Iowa Law Enforcement Academy
P.O. Box 130
Johnston, IA 50131

515/242-5357

Res. Capt. Daniel Brandt
Secretary/Treasurer
Iowa State Reserve Law Officers Association
P.O. Box 26
Marshalltown, IA 50158

Volunteer Reserve Officers
180 Total Hours
(30 hours first year
150 hours within four years)

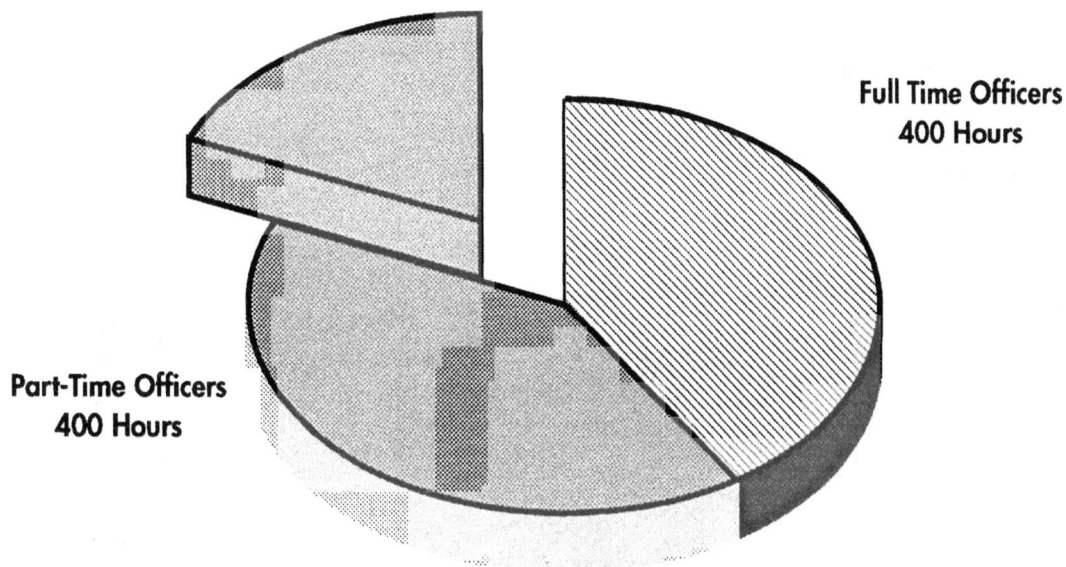

Full Time Officers
400 Hours

Part-Time Officers
400 Hours

Minimum Training Hours
Iowa

and his Association colleagues have been working closely with Ben K. Yarrington, the director of the Johnston-based Iowa Law Enforcement Academy, to establish uniform standards.

Yarrington explained that the 5,100 full-timers and 175 part-timers in the state must meet a

400 hour minimum training standard. Under a program supported by the Iowa reserves, the 1,200 volunteer police and sheriffs reserves must undergo a total of 180 hours of training. The first 30 hours are comprised of an established curriculum and must be completed within the first year. The remaining 150 hours are to be done within four years with a discretionary course content.

Kansas

Number of Officers
5,200 Full Time
300 Part-time
1,200 Volunteer Reserves
6,700 Total Officers

Minimum Training Hours Req.
320 Full Time
80 Part-time
No minimum training required for volunteers

Three levels of officers, full-time, part-time, and volunteer reserves are utilized in Kansas with the first two regulated regarding the amount of training. The state allows its three levels of law enforcement officers to possess police powers and carry firearms.

The assistant director of the Kansas Law Enforcement Center, Ed Davey, said there are 5,200 full-time officers who receive 320 hours (8 weeks) or more of training. Part-time officers (who work less than 1,000 hours per year), of which there are 300, undergo 80 hours of training. The 1,200 volunteer reserves have no state imposed minimum, but most larger agencies match the 320 hour full-time officer training requirement.

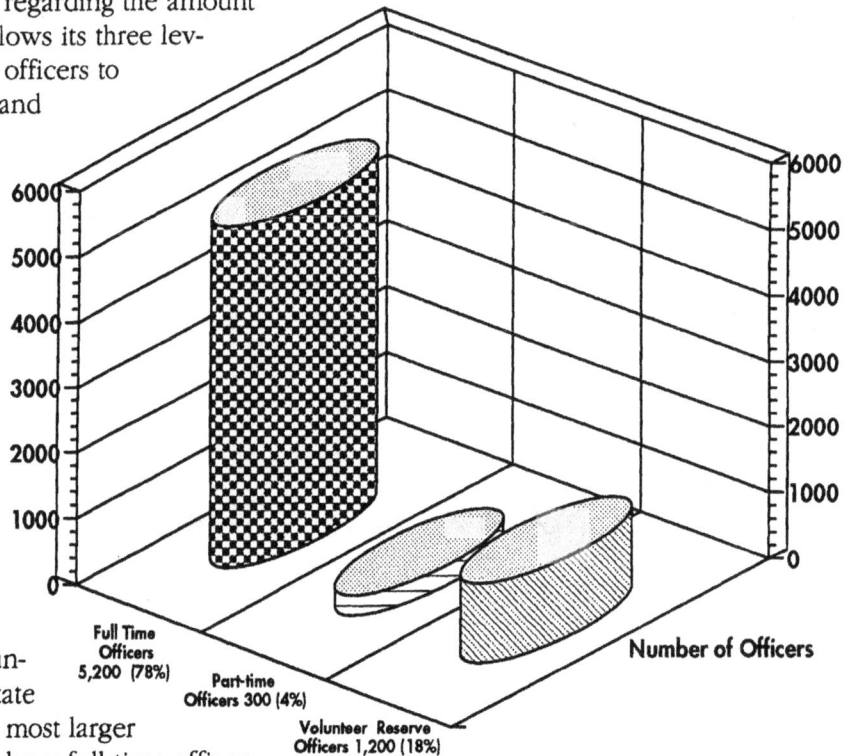

Full Time Officers 5,200 (78%)
Part-time Officers 300 (4%)
Volunteer Reserve Officers 1,200 (18%)
Number of Officers

Contact:

Ed Davey
Assistant Director
Kansas Law Enforcement Training Center
P.O. Box 647
Hutchinson, KS 67504-4720

316/662-3378

Kentucky

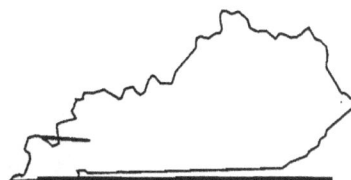

Number of Officers	
4,650	Full Time
411	Part-time/Volunteers
5,060	Total Officers

Minimum Training Hours Req.
400 All Officers

As of July 16, 1992, citizens of Kentucky became the recipients of better trained reserves. Herb Bowling, director of training for the Kentucky Department of Criminal Justice Training, said the recently enacted law required volunteer reserves to undergo the same 400 minimum hours of training as that mandated for all full and part-time officers along with an additional 40 hours of annual in-service training.

"Any officer after July 16th must receive 400 hours of basic training within their first year," said Bowling who added that part-time and volunteer officers appointed prior to July 16th are only required to get 40 hours of in-service training per annum. The Blue Grass state has 4,650 full-time officers, 750 of whom are employed by sheriff's departments, and 411 part-time or volunteer officers.

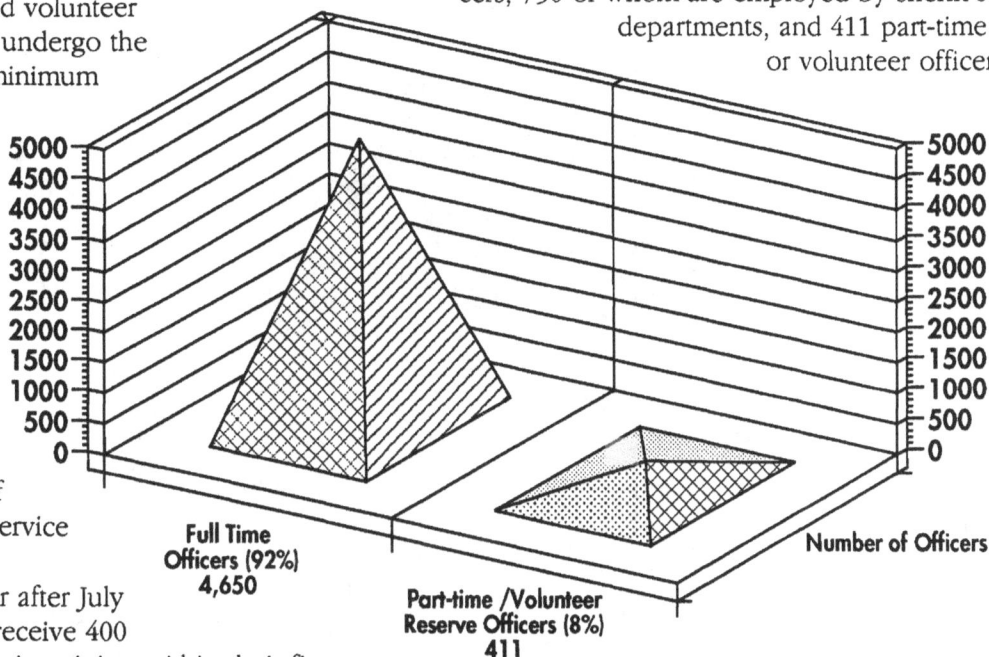

Full Time Officers (92%) 4,650

Part-time /Volunteer Reserve Officers (8%) 411

Number of Officers

Contact:

Herb Bowling
Director of Training
Kentucky Department of
**   Criminal Justice Training**
Kit Carson Drive
Richmond, KY 40475-3131

606/622-6165

Louisiana

In Louisiana, according to Nell Ishmel, POST (Police Officers Standards & Training) manager with the Louisiana Commission of Law Enforcement, the number of volunteer and part-time reserve officers is unknown. "There are no minimum standards for reserves and we don't regulate them. (We) only regulate full-time officers," she said.

The state has 18,000 officers certified at the 240 hour state minimum. Ishmel indicated that some reserves may be 240 hour certified, but that they "are lumped into the 18,000 figure."

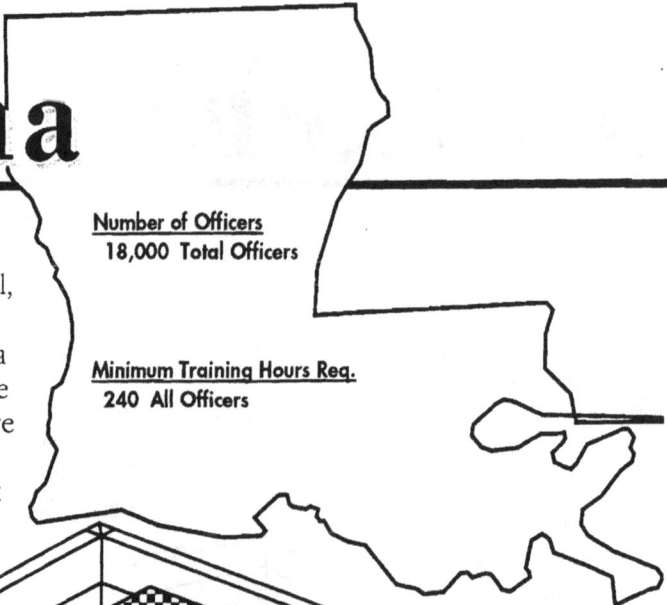

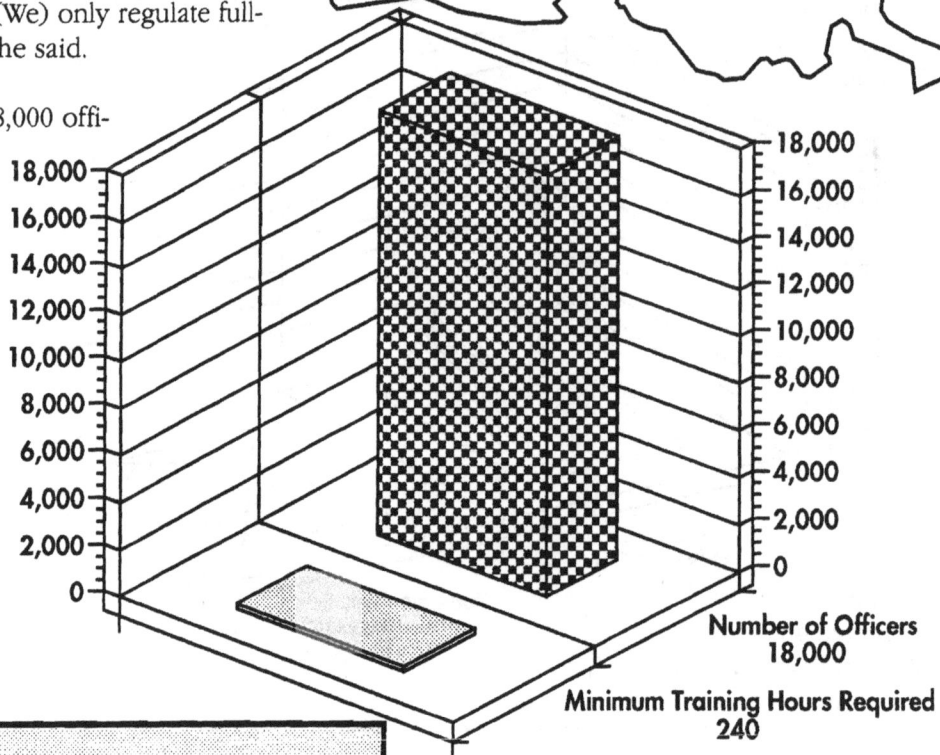

Number of Officers
18,000 Total Officers

Minimum Training Hours Req.
240 All Officers

Number of Officers
18,000

Minimum Training Hours Required
240

Contact:

**Nell Ishmel, POST Manager
Louisiana Commission of
Law Enforcement
1885 Wooddale, 7th Floor
Baton Rouge, LA 70806**

504/925-1997

Maine

Number of Officers
1,594 Full Time
1,274 Part-time
2,686 Total Officers

Minimum Training Hours Req.
480 Full Time
100 hours pre-service for
Part-time Paid
and Volunteers

In the 1992 Annual Report presented to the Maine Legislature, 1,594 full-time officers and 1,274 part-timers were noted as being trained and registered with the Maine Criminal Justice Academy. Steven R. Giorgetti, training manager for the Academy, said these officers were being utilized by the 134 organized law enforcement departments in the state. Maine also has 44 plantations and other small towns that may have part-time constables.

Full-time officers in the Pelican State receive 480 hours of training over the course of 12 weeks and part-time volunteer or paid officers have 100 hours of pre-service training. "Part-time officers have the same powers of arrest and receive the training under four regional coordinators at host departments," explained Giorgetti.

Two main scheduling options are available.

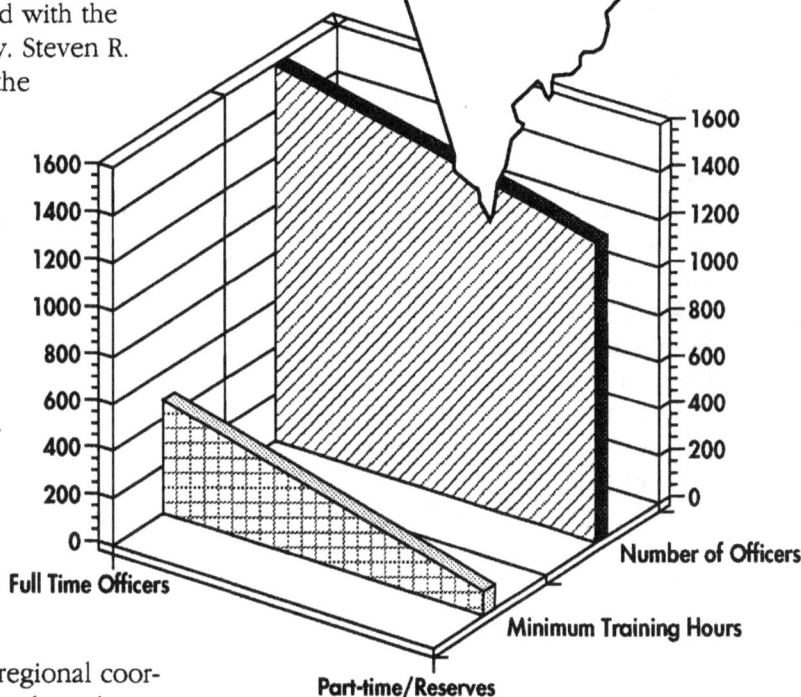

Option one involves a single three hour night per week for 33 weeks. The second available route involves two nights for three hours each

Contact:

Steven R. Giorgetti, Training Manager
Maine Criminal Justice Academy
93 Silver Street
Waterville, ME 04901

207/873-2651x

for 15 weeks. Another choice has the training taking place full-time at the Academy for two weeks.

"As of July 1, 1991, part-time officers had to have their 100 hours prior to going on the street. Previously, as of July 1, 1983, they had up to one year to get the training," said Giorgetti.

Sample 100 Hour Maine Reserve Academy Curriculum

Class	Hours
Orientation	1
Police Ethics and Moral Issues	3
Police, Power, Authority and Discretion	3
Maine Criminal Law	6
Maine Motor Vehicle Law	6
Maine Juvenile Law	1.5
Maine Liquor Law	1.5
Laws of Arrest	3
Search and Seizure	3
Use of Force	3
Introduction to the Service Weapon	3
Practical Live Fire at the Range	8
Laws of Evidence	2
Courtroom Demeanor/Conduct	1
Crisis Conflict Management/Variant Behavior	6
Child Abuse	3
Police and the Public	3
Mechanics of Arrest and Restraint Control	9
Note Taking and Report Writing	3
Traffic Law Enforcement (incl. Felony Car Stops)	6
Traffic Direction and Control	1
Accident Reporting	2
Hazardous Materials	3
Crime Scene Procedures	3
Admissions and Confessions	3
Defensive Driving/E.V.O.C.	6
Basic First Aid and C.P.R.	8

Maryland

In the state of Maryland, according to Christine Melville, certification specialist with the Maryland Police & Correctional Training Commission, full-time and part-time law enforcers serve a probationary period of one year during which time they must complete 400 hours of prescribed training. They must also complete a 35 hour firearms course prior to carrying. Melville said the ruling was put forth in the June 1, 1966 Police Training Act, Article 41, Section 4-201 of the Annotated Code of Maryland by the Maryland General Assembly.

Francis Manear, assistant director for administrative services for the Police & Correctional Commission, said that there are 13,473 full-time officers in the Old Line State.

Certified part-time officers, who must also complete the 400 hours of basic training within one year (the probationary year) and pass a 35 hour firearms course before being issued a sidearm, come in at 89, according to Maryland State Police Lt. James Bowman.

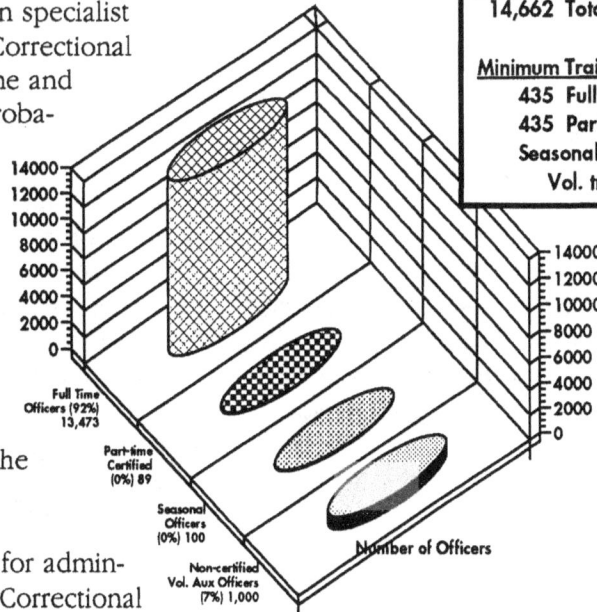

The Commission's Manear said resort area departments may employ seasonal officers who receive agency promulgated in-house training on firearms, etc. Seasonal officers may not work more than 7 months at a time and she said 100 are being used in Maryland presently. The state's 1,000 volunteer auxiliary officers are also non-certified and trained in-house.

Contact:

Christine Melville, Certification Specialist
or
Francis Manear, Assistant Director for Administrative Services
Maryland Police & Correctional Commission
3085 Hernwood Road
Woodstock, MD 21163

301/442-2700

Massachusetts

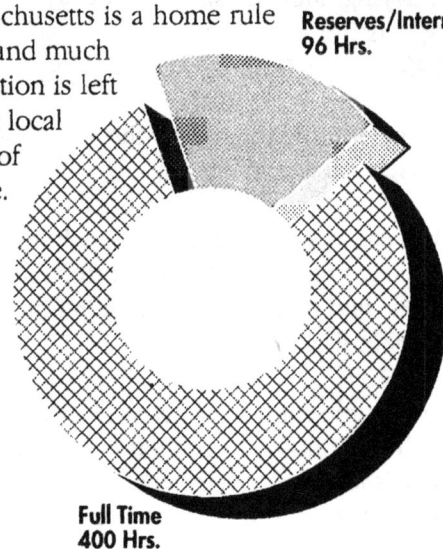

Massachusetts is unusual in that several state agencies contacted said they did not track how many full-time officers are employed in the state. The Massachusetts Criminal Justice Training Council maintains that its role is to dictate the 400 hours of basic police training required and not keep records on the number of officers currently serving. The Council only regulates the amount of training required for full and part-time paid law enforcement officers.

Erick Hoffman, president of the Massachusetts Reserve Law Enforcement Federation and a Spencer, MA, auxiliary officer, said he estimates the state has 5,000 part-time paid or volunteer officers.

Part-time paid special officers, who may also be called reserves or even auxiliaries, must complete the 96 hour Reserve/Intermittent Officer course. They also need to complete a 30-37 hour First Responder course, CPR and firearms qualification. Volunteer auxiliary officers are under state civil defense and are not required by Massachusetts to undergo any training although some towns have their auxiliary officers take the 96 hour Reserve/Intermittent training. Massachusetts is a home rule state and much discretion is left to the local chief of police.

**Reserves/Intermittent
96 Hrs.**

**Full Time
400 Hrs.**

Contact:

Erick Hoffman, President
Massachusetts Reserve Law Enforcement Federation
430 Franklin Village Drive, Suite 306
Franklin, MA 02038

Michigan

Number of Officers
25,000 Full Time
2,000 Reserves
27,000 Total Officers

Minimum Training Hours Req.
440 Full Time
Reserves trained in house

M ichigan, with 25,000 full-time officers with at least 440 hours of training, does not have a state-wide training mandate for their 2,000 reserves. Barbara Best, information manager for the Michigan Law Enforcement Officers Training Council, said the state regulates full-time officers only and that any training a reserve receives would be dictated on an in-house basis.

Many reserve programs in Michigan have come to rely on local community colleges for their structured basic and in-service training courses. Among the better known programs in Michigan is the 100 hour Police Reserve Officer Training Program held by Schoolcraft College in Livonia for southeastern Michigan area police departments. The course is typically run on Monday and Wednesday evenings from 7:00 PM to 10:00 PM for 15 weeks including seven Saturday sessions for range qualification, first aid, and CPR.

Schoolcraft also runs an extensive menu

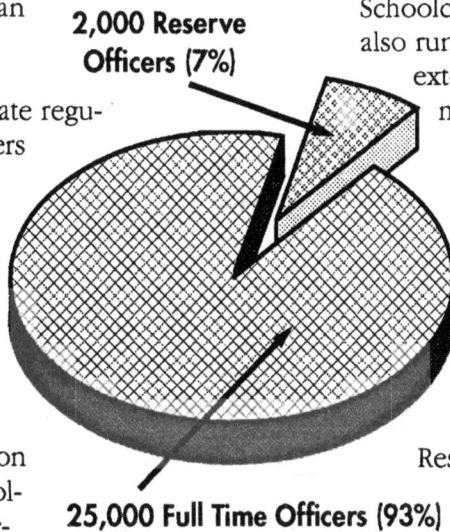

2,000 Reserve Officers (7%)

25,000 Full Time Officers (93%)

of four hour and eight hour in-service courses. Four hour courses earn .4 CEU (continuing education units) from the college and eight hour courses are pegged at .8 CEU. Among the topics taught previously: Police Shotgun Handling and Safety for Reserves, Traffic Direction and Control, Courtroom Demeanor and Testimony for Reserves, Vehicle Stops, Police Reserve Leadership, Advanced Defensive Tactics, and Introduction to Basic Narcotics for Reserves.

"Future plans include incorporating the F.A.T.S. (Firearms Training System) simulator," said Douglas M. Purcell, coordinator, continuing education services for Schoolcraft.

Contact:

Barbara Best, Information Manager
Michigan Law Enforcement Officers Training Council
7426 North Canal Road
Lansing, MI 48913

517/322-1946

Douglas M. Purcell
Schoolcraft College
18600 Haggerty Road
Livonia, MI 48152-2696

313/462-4400

Minnesota

Number of Officers
7,501 Full Time
824 Part-time
8,325 Total Officers

Minimum Training Hrs Req.
400 Full Time
No training minimum
for Part-time and
Volunteer Officers

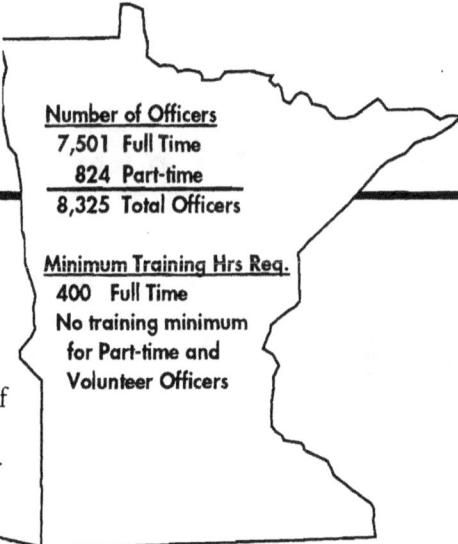

Minnesota's Board of POST (Police Officer Standards and Training) has its full-time officers pass a POST exam prior to commencing service. Connie Edwards, clerk/typist III., said, under state statute 626.84, chapter 6700, the Board mandates that full-timers hold a two year college degree.

"Clinical skills are taught by higher education facilities. The 10-12 week (400 hour) course is taught at three schools," she said adding that there were 7,501 full-time officers in the state as of January 1, 1992.

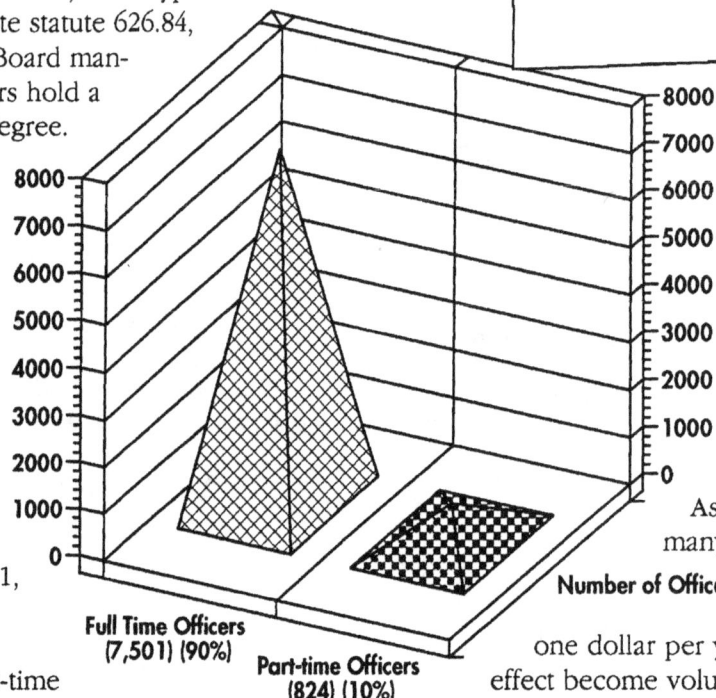

The 824 active part-time officers (working no more than 1,040 hours per year or 20 hours a week), who are also regulated by the Board of POST, carry firearms and have powers of arrest but are under no state mandate concerning training. The state does not regulate volunteer officers, therefore their number is unknown, who have no powers of arrest or carry firearms. As elsewhere, many agencies utilize armed part-timers paid one dollar per year who in effect become volunteers for their departments.

Full Time Officers
(7,501) (90%)

Part-time Officers
(824) (10%)

Number of Officers

Contact:

Connie Edwards, Clerk/Typist III.
Minnesota Board of POST
1600 University Avenue, Suite 200
St. Paul, MN 55104-3825

612/643-3060

Mississippi

Number of Officers
4,646 Full Time
2,500 Reserves
7,146 Total Officers

Min. Training Hours Req.
360 Full Time
  Volunteers and
  Part-time trained
  in house

Mississippi regulates only its full-time officers. Keith May, with operations and planning for the Mississippi Minimum Standards for Criminal Justice, said the 4,646 full-time officers undergo 360 hours (nine weeks) of basic training.

Lamar Beasley reimbursement analyst for the Board for Law Enforcement Officer Standards and Training, said training for non-full-time personnel is left up to the local agency. "A recent bill to impose training standards died in committee," he lamented. Beasley explained that the state's 2,500 (according to their 1990 figures) volunteer or paid part-time officers undergo whatever training their chief or sheriff deems appropriate.

Reserve Officers (2,500) (35%)

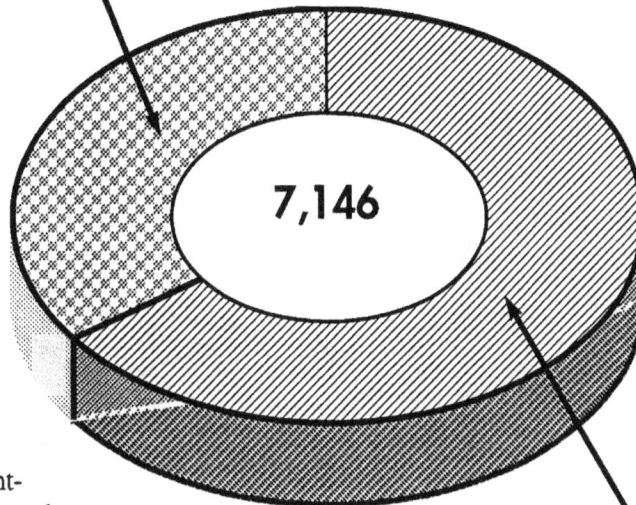

7,146

Full Time Officers (4,646) (65%)

Contact:

Keith May, Operations & Planning
Mississippi Minimum Standards for Criminal Justice
301 West Pearl Street
Jackson, MS 39203-3088

601/949-2225

Missouri

Number of Officers
14,142 Full time
  352 Certified
  400 Non-certified
14,894 Total Officers

Minimum Training Hours Req.
All certified Full Time, Part-time
    Volunteer Officers
600 Certified in larger Class 1 cities/counties
120 Certified in small Class 1,2,3,
    & 4 cities/counties
  Non-certified Volunteer Reserves
    require no minimum training

Missouri's reserve and auxiliary officers are moving toward a more professional vein via training said Missouri Reserve Peace Officers Association president David Blodgett. Blodgett, a Maryland Heights reserve officer who served as president of the Missouri Auxiliary and Reserve Police Association said that volunteer officers are used extensively in his state.

June Baker, POST program administrator with Missouri POST, said that the state regulates certified officers only. Police officer training for certification is based on county population and form of the county government. She explained that for 4th, 3rd, 2nd, and 1st class counties (without a charter form of government), the state mandate is 120 hours. Counties at 1st class rating with a charter form of government have a minimum training standard of 600 hours. A 1st class county is one with a population of 100,000 and up.

Baker said that there are 352 certified reserves

and 400 non-certified reserves in the state. It is up to the local law enforcement chief executive whether or not to utilize armed non-certified reserve officers.

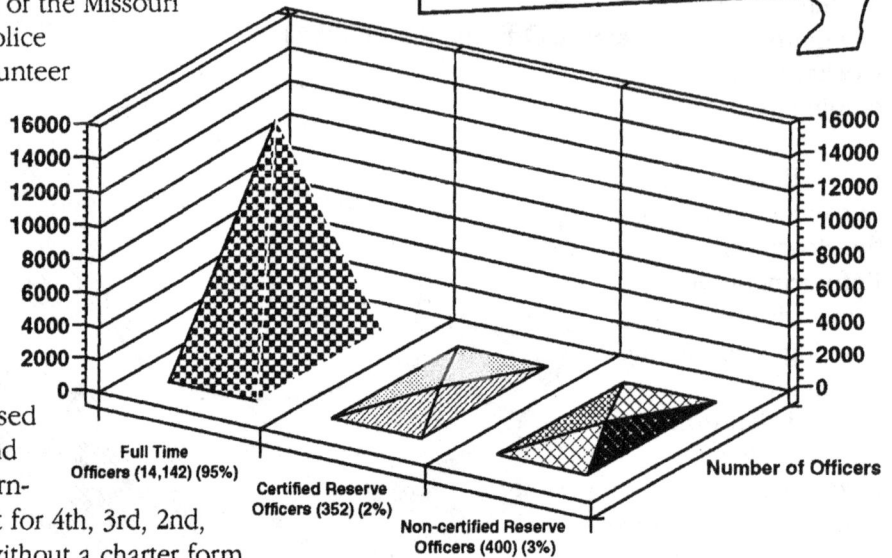

Full Time Officers (14,142) (95%)
Certified Reserve Officers (352) (2%)
Non-certified Reserve Officers (400) (3%)
Number of Officers

Contact:

June Baker, POST Program Administrator
Missouri POST
P.O. Box 749
Jefferson City, MO 65102

314/751-4905

David Blodgett, President
Missouri Reserve Peace
Officers Association
550 Blazewood Drive
Ballwin, MO 63021

Montana

Number of Officers
1,496 Full Time
71 Part-time
382 Volunteers
1,949 Total Officers

Minimum Training Hours Req.
540 Full Time
540 Part-time
180 Volunteers

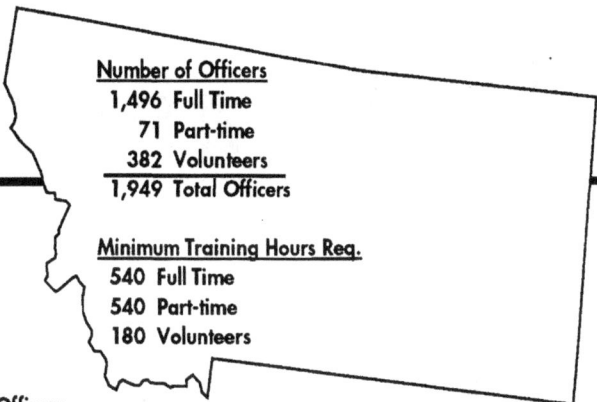

Part-ttime Reserve Officers
540 hours

Volunteer Reserve Officers
180 in-house training hours

Full Time Officers
540 hours

Minimum Training Hours

full-time officers and 71 part-time officers certified at the 540 hour or above training level. Montana's 382 volunteer officers are trained in-house, to negate traveling time as a factor for not becoming a reserve officer, to the tune of 180 hours. A certified officer must be on duty when they are serving in an official capacity.

I llustrative of states whose departments' training agendas are impacted by vast travel distances is Montana. Montanta's approach to training officers, particularly non-full-time personnel, is constrained by the expansive geography of the state.

Gene Kaiser, executive director of the Montana POST (Police Officer Standards and Training) Council which regulates all officers in the state, said certified full and part-time officers must undergo 540 hours of training. As of December 1991, there were 1,496

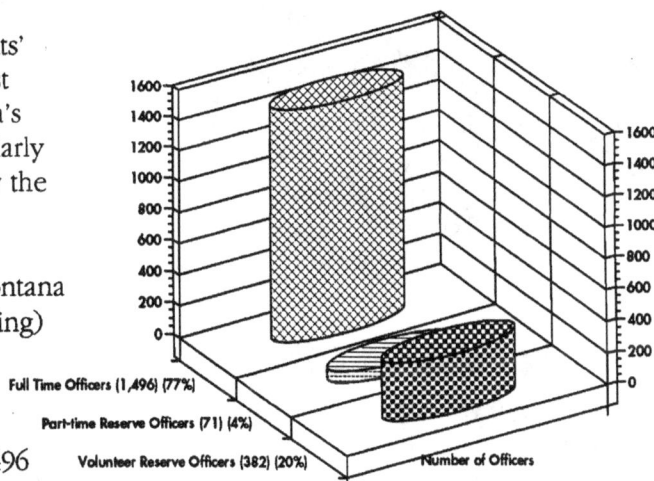

Full Time Officers (1,496) (77%)

Part-time Reserve Officers (71) (4%)

Volunteer Reserve Officers (382) (20%)

Number of Officers

Contact:

Gene Kaiser, Executive Director
Montana POST Council
303 North Roberts, Room 460
Helena, MT 59620

406/444-3604

Nebraska

Number of Officers
3,400 Full Time and Part-time
250 Volunteer Reserves
3,650 Total Officers

Minimum Training Hours Req.
500 Full Time and Part-time
134 Volunteer Reserves

Nebraska law enforcement training faces the same vast distance considerations as Montana. Bob Zipay, assistant director for the Nebraska Law Enforcement Training Center, said that the state does not differentiate between full or part-time officers. The state requires that both classifications be certified at 500 hours at a minimum and the records reflect that 3,400 officers have done so.

The state's 250 volunteer officers, who have at least 134 hours of training, can't work more than 100 hours per year and must do so under a certified officer's supervision. Zipay said the training is done over nine straight days during which the volunteer officer in training is housed in the Academy's dormitory. He explained that they come back one additional weekend for firearms.

Volunteer Reserve Officers - 250 (7%)

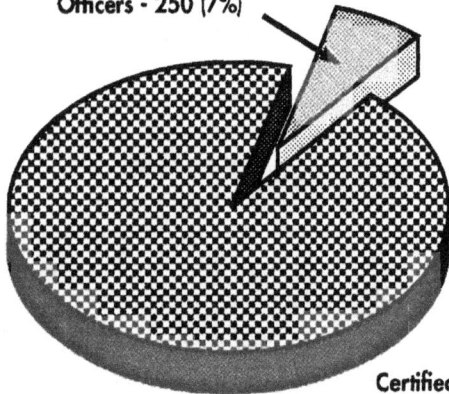

Certified Officers - 3,400 (93%)

Number of Officers

Volunteer Reserve Officers - 134 Hours

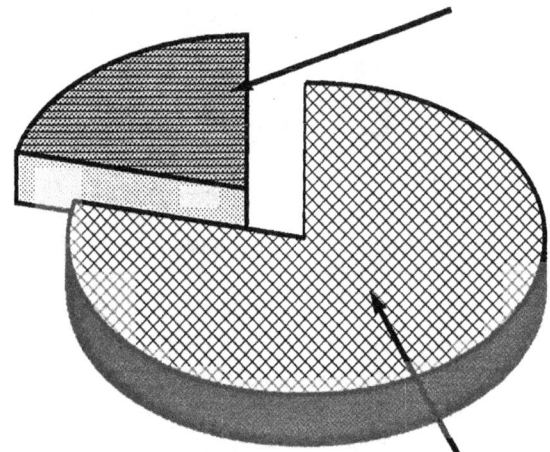

Full and Part-time Certified Officers - 500

Minimum Training Hours

Contact:

Bob Zipay, Assistant Director
Nebraska Law Enforcement Training Center
Route 3, Box 50
Grand Island, NE 68801-9403

308/381-5700

Nevada

Number of Officers
6,000 Full Time
1,000 Volunteer Reserves
7,000 Total Officers

Minimum Training Hours Req.
540 Full Time
     Volunteer Reserve
     training up to agency

Nevada's Peace Officer Standards and Training regulates full-time officers only. Wayne Taglia, training officer for POST, said that there are 6,000 full-time officers who have a minimum of 540 hours of training. The 1,000 volunteer officers' training is left up to agency discretion but most have their non-compensated officers train up to full-time officer standards.

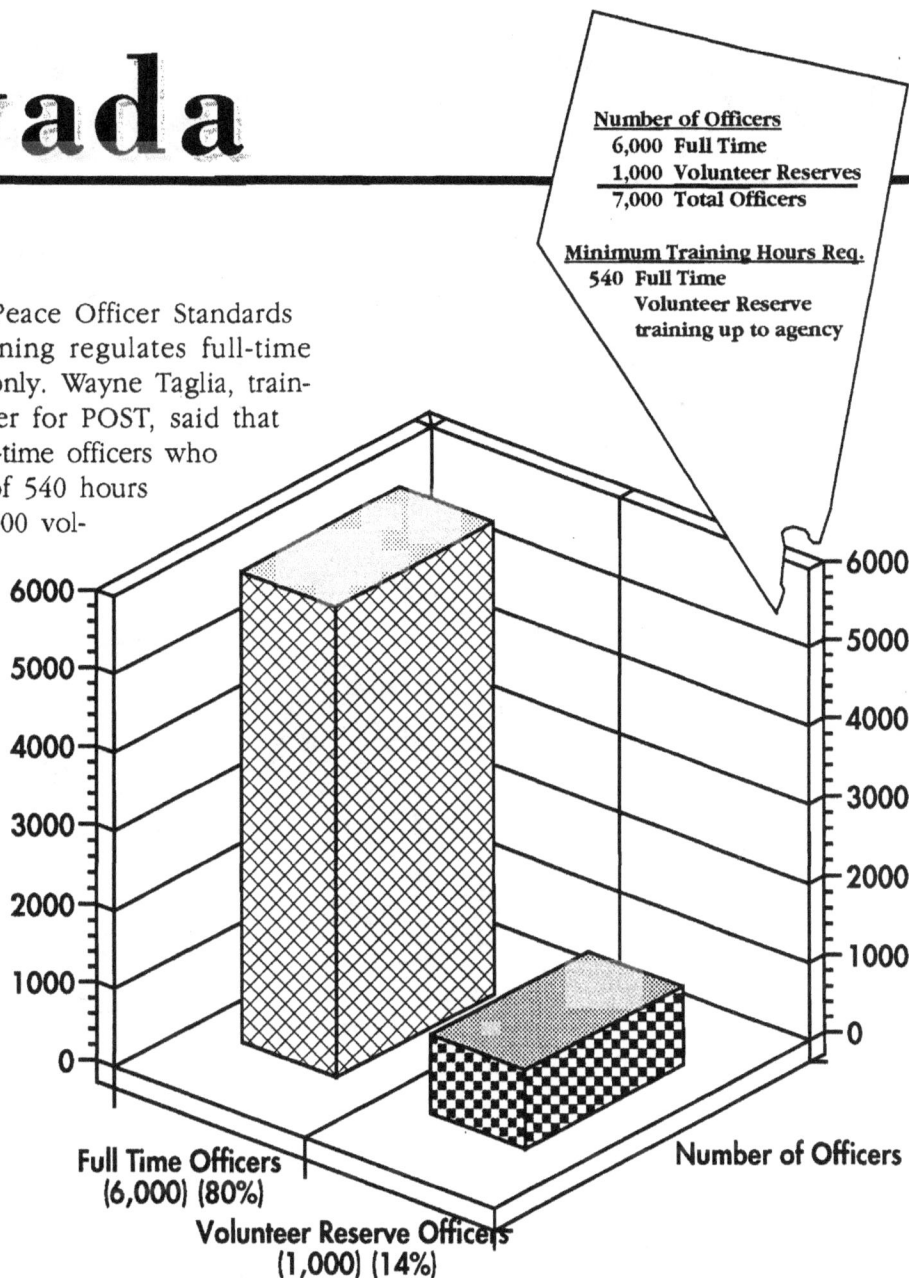

Full Time Officers
(6,000) (80%)

Volunteer Reserve Officers
(1,000) (14%)

Number of Officers

Contact:

Wayne Taglia, Training Officer
Nevada Peace Officer Standards & Training
555 Wright Way
Carson City, NV 89701

702/687-3283

New Hampshire

New Hampshire relies quite heavily on their part-time paid and volunteer personnel and even the 249-man New Hampshire State Police utilizes 31 auxiliary troopers. Under enabling legislation RSA (revised statute annotated) 188-F;22-28, the New Hampshire Police standards and Training Council requires that full-time officers, of whom there are 2,192, undergo 430 hours of training.

Part-time paid and volunteer officers complete a 100 hour training program. "Many of the part-time police officers serve with more than one department," said Nancy Otis, secretary to the Council, "1,654 part-time officers fill 1,897 positions."

involves ten weekends of training and option two involves two weeks of full-time training which takes place in the summer," said New Hampshire

Number of Officers	
2,192	Full Time
1,654	Part-time
3,846	**Total Officers**

Minimum /training Hours Req.	
430	Full Time
100	Part-time

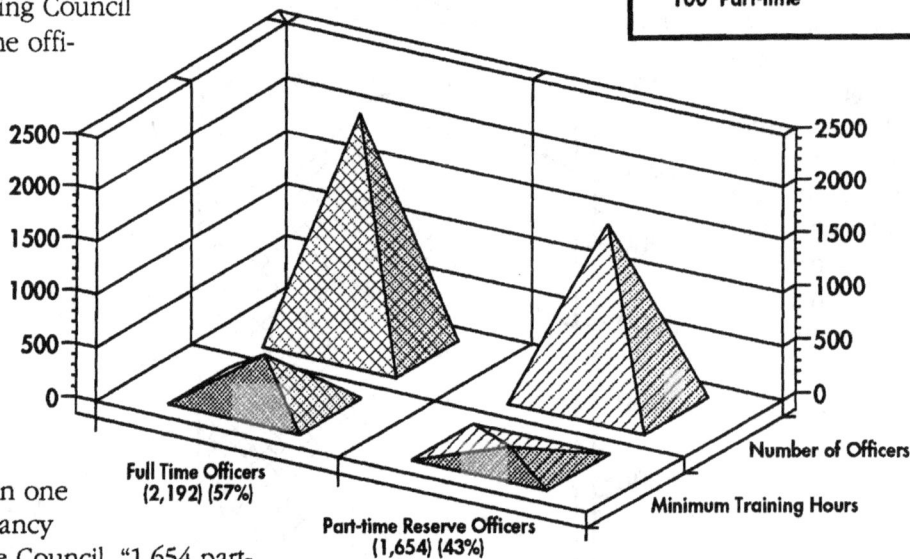

Full Time Officers (2,192) (57%)

Part-time Reserve Officers (1,654) (43%)

Number of Officers

Minimum Training Hours

Training for the part-time law enforcers at either the local or state police levels involve two training schedule options. "Option one

State Police Lt. MarkFurlone, commander of the special services unit, which oversees the auxiliary trooper program.

Contact:

Nancy Otis, Secretary
New Hampshire Police Standards
    & Training Council
17 Fan Road
Concord, NH 03301-5098

603/271-2133

Lt. Mark Furlone, Commander
Special Services Unit
New Hampshire State Police
10 Hazen Drive
Concord, NH 03305

603/271-3636

New Jersey

New Jersey's full-time law enforcer contingent is comprised of 27,337 officers. The New Jersey Police Training Commission (PTC) oversees their training standards ensuring that a certain number of performance objectives (P.O.s) are met.

Geri Schaeffer, supervisor of the standards administration unit for the PTC, said that there are no minimum training hours imposed on officers in New Jersey. Rather, performance objectives (P.O.s) are used to determine course content and length.

In hourly figures, the full-time category averages out to 669 hours.

The home state to the Center for Reserve Law Enforcement and the New Jersey Auxiliary Police Officers Association, has several different types of non-full-time personnel.

Number of Officers	
27,337	Full Time
Unknown	Part-time
	Class I. and II. Specials
96	Vol. Deputy Conservation Officers
1,000	Volunteer Aux.

Minimum Training Time Req.	
669*	Full Time
452*	Class II Specials
78*	Class I Specials
200	Vol. Deputy Conservation Officers
42	Vol. Aux. (+40 hours firearms training if armed)

*Average Hours

Contact:

Geri Schaeffer
Supervisor
Standards Administration Unit
New Jersey Police Training Commission
25 Market Street, CN 085
Trenton, NJ 08625-0085

609/984-2140

Lt. Thomas Dombroski
Auxiliary Police Coordinator
Office of Emergency Management
    New Jersey State Police
P.O. Box 7068
West Trenton, NJ 08625

609/882-2000, Ext. 6061

Lt. Mike Boyle
Training Officer
New Jersey Division of Fish and Game
RD#3, Box 386
Robbinsville, NJ 08691

609/259-3347

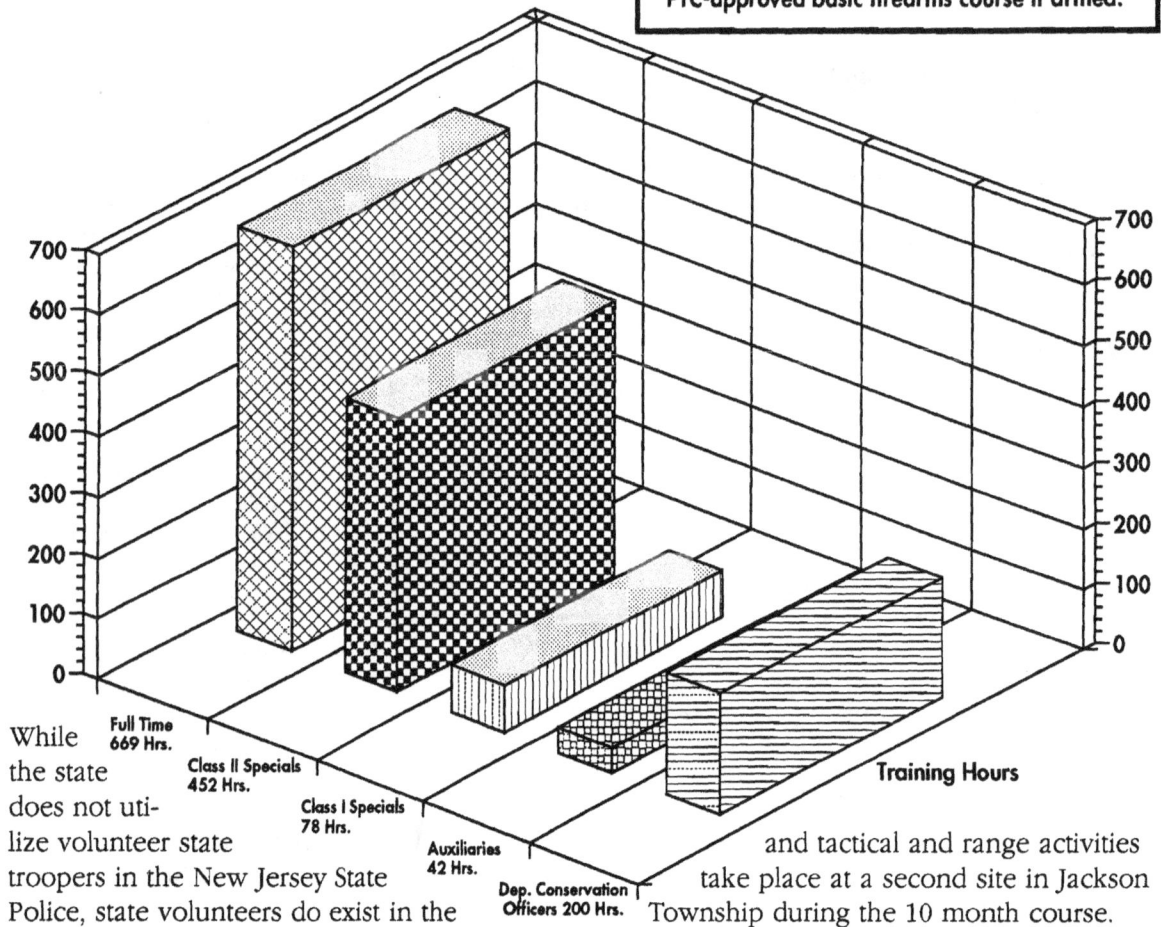

Note: Auxiliaries must take minimum 40 hour PTC-approved basic firearms course if armed.

Training Hours

- Full Time 669 Hrs.
- Class II Specials 452 Hrs.
- Class I Specials 78 Hrs.
- Auxiliaries 42 Hrs.
- Dep. Conservation Officers 200 Hrs.

While the state does not utilize volunteer state troopers in the New Jersey State Police, state volunteers do exist in the guise of "deputy conservation officers" for the New Jersey Division of Fish and Game. Lieutenant Mike Boyle, training officer, said that the division utilizes 96 trained, Glock-toting deputies throughout the Garden State, continuing a program which started in 1895.

Some 200 hours of weekend training are held for the volunteer rangers covering search and seizure, patrol, first aid, defensive tactics, wildlife laws and 48 hours of firearms. Classroom facilities are in Freehold Township, and tactical and range activities take place at a second site in Jackson Township during the 10 month course.

Boyle said they were interested in people "with a sportsman's level of knowledge." He added that a person's place of residence is compared with the area's need for deputy conservation officers. He said, for example, that the Burlington County area is in need of volunteer deputies whereas the counties of Camden and Gloucester are not. According to Boyle, interested individuals are encouraged to send a letter detailing why they would like to be appointed deputy conservation officers.

Following a review of the letter and geographically related deputy manpower needs, applications are sent out. Two interviews, a background investigation and a written exam are held, as well as a physical exam at the applicant's expense. During the initial training phase, trainees undergo psychologicals and urinalysis which are administered by the state of New Jersey.

Boyle said the uniform and firearms costs, which come to about $2,000, are borne by the deputy conservation officer. The only difference in the uniform manifests itself in a "deputy" rocker above the conservation officer shoulder patch and a "deputy" tab on the badge.

The term "reserve" has been eliminated as an official designation by the state, but many special and auxiliary officer programs have built reputations in their communities as "reserves." Numerous programs have continued to identify their officers as reserves when they may technically be specials or auxiliaries.

Special officers in New Jersey are regulated by the PTC, the same body which oversees training standards for full-time law enforcers. Special officers are part-time officers who may or may not be paid at the discretion of their local chief of police. They tend to be employed during seasonal periods at resort communities, while they are used year-round at other municipalities.

In accordance with the Special Law Enforcement Officer (SLEO) Act of 1986 (covered under New Jersey Revised Statutes Title 40A:14-146.8 through 40A:14-146.18), there are two classifications of special officers. Among many requirements, all special officers must be a resident of the state, be able to read, write and speak the English language, have a high school diploma or its equivalent, and undergo the same psychological testing as that required of the departments full-time personnel.

Class II. SLEOs are the higher trained of the two classifications. Class II.s have full police powers and can carry a firearm while on duty. Class I.s have limited powers related to crowd and traffic control and do not carry a firearm. They do not handle indictable offenses. Both must attend a PTC-certified county police academy prior to commencing official duties.

Broken down further, Class Ia. SLEOs are empowered to enforce municipal ordinances (encompassing some 40 hours of training). Class Ib. SLEOs handle the same duties with additional responsibilities for Title 39 (motor vehicle laws) involving approximately 80 hours of training.

While an unlimited number of Class I.s may be used by a department, the number of Class II.s may not exceed 25% of the number of full-timers employed by the agency. The department may also use one Class II. SLEO on a full-time basis, year-round. Local authorities may determine whether special officers must reside within the municipality or not.

The PTC's Schaeffer indicated that they do not track the number of active special officers in the state. She said many serve only for a summer and move in in some cases to a full-time slot. The PTC's records reflect that 122 Class II. SLEOs were trained in 1990-1991 at 452 average hours and that 218 Class I. SLEOs were trained during the same period at 78 average hours.

Police chiefs wishing to switch a Class II. SLEO from part-time to full-fledged, full-time officer status may apply to the PTC for a waiver covering all or part of the training. Certain academies in the state, such as the Gloucester County Police Academy with 625 hours of weeknight and weekend SLEO II. training over the course of nine and a half months, have been designated by the PTC as fully acceptable. The weekends at the Deptford Township based academy are utilized for firearms and for the three physical agility assessments. The cost is $150 for in-county attendees and $250 for those officers from outside of Gloucester County.

Other academies fall just shy of the full waiver and the officer goes back for a minimal amount of classes. One example is the Monmouth County Police Academy's Class II. training program. The 540 hour training regime runs for nine months from 6:00 PM to 11:00 PM on Tuesday, Wednesday and Thursday evenings. There are eight Saturdays for firing range and

water safety at the pool.

A more compressed version of the concept is the 365 hour Class II. SLEO program of the Passaic County Police Academy in Wayne Township, NJ. The four month program meets on Tuesday, Wednesday and Thursday nights and all day Saturdays for four months straight. The curriculum covers firearms, use of force, criminal law (2c), motor vehicle law (Title 39), criminal investigations, CPR and first responder/crash injury management (CIM) and community relations. The tuition for in-county recruits is $375, while those from other counties other than Passaic, are charged $475. Around 1,000 rounds of ammo must also be provided by the student or their department as well as $120 worth of Passaic County Police Academy physical training attire.

An even more consolidated and intense experience may be had at the 460 hour Class II. training program held in south Jersey at the Cape May County Police Academy in Cape May Courthouse, NJ. The seven week, six day-a-week, 12 plus-hour-a-day academy is held full-time under the demanding eyes of State Police Academy at Sea Girt-bred instructors. Trainees in this program held in the earliest part of the summer recall hours of physical training in 90 degree heat.

The curriculum for Class II. typically includes physical training (PT), defensive tactics, side handle baton, patrol concepts, investigations, community relations, first responder/crash injury management (CIM), CPR, criminal law (2C), motor vehicle law (Title 39) and use of force, as well as a minimum of 40 hours of firearms training.

The Class I. SLEO training programs are run out of academies in counties such as Bergen and Middlesex.

According to the "State of New Jersey Emergency Management Auxiliary Police Organization & Training Plan," auxiliary officers, who may not be paid for their services, are under the auspices of the New Jersey State Police Office of Emergency Management, and have full police powers while on duty unless administratively restricted by the local police chief (Executive Order No. 101, Directive No. 28 and Formal Opinion 1961 - No. 4).

The state police, in cooperation with the New Jersey State Association of Chiefs of Police, require that a minimum curriculum of 42 hours of training be completed prior to the auxiliary officer being certified and deployed (Directives No. 28 and 30). Most county auxiliary academies, which are held outside of normal work-hours for the convenience of the attendees who have full-time occupations, go well beyond the 42 hour minimum.

The Bergen County Auxiliary Police Academy in Mahwah, NJ, conducts 52 hours of training, while the Essex County Auxiliary Police Academy, in Cedar Grove, NJ, comes in at 77 hours. The Edison, NJ-based Middlesex County Auxiliary Police Academy, which is held in the fall, runs an 88 hour course.

Per Directive 95, they may or may not be armed at the police chief's discretion provided that they complete a minimum 40 hour PTC-approved basic firearms course. The Passaic County Police Academy runs an 80 hour course which exceeds the PTC's basic requirements.

State Police Lieutenant Thomas Dombroski, auxiliary police coordinator, said that their records indicate that some 1,000 auxiliary officers (minimum age of 18 per Informational Bulletin No. 73-2) are participating in the programs of 61 municipalities. He indicated that 600 of those volunteers officers are serving in units which have been issued a certificate of certification while 400 are not in compliance. Such certificates are issued by the New Jersey State Police attesting that the unit has completed all paperwork and responsibilities concerning in-service training and rosters for their officers.

Auxiliary officers, at a minimum, must serve eight hours per month, or 24 hours per quarter, with two hours each month dedicated to in-service training. Their service must be oriented to training objectives and they are not to replace full-time officers.

The state requires that auxiliary police officers reside in the municipality in which they are serving, exempting only those who are grandfathered in having begun their service prior to the ruling. An exception to the residency requirement involves persons residing five miles or less from a contiguous municipality in which they wish to serve.

As detailed in section VIII. of Directive 97 in the "State of New Jersey Emergency Management Auxiliary Police Organization & Training Plan," the minimum 42 hour* basic training course for auxiliary police is broken down as follows:

SUBJECT	**TIME ALLOTTED**
1. INTRODUCTION INDOCTRINATION A. School Requirements B. Note Taking C. Auxiliary Police Powers	2 hours
2. NEW JERSEY EMERGENCY MANAGEMENT CONTROL PLAN A. Definition and Purpose B. Human Relations	2 hours
3. CIVIL GOVERNMENT AND POLICE AGENCIES A. Organization of Government - Federal, State, County, Municipal B. Police Agencies Operating in the State of New Jersey	2 hours
4. TRAFFIC CONTROL A. Basic Techniques in Handling Traffic B. Title 39, R.S. (Motor Vehicle Law)	2 hours
5. PATROL FUNCTIONS A. Vehicles B. Foot C. Marine	2 hours
6. CROWDS AND ASSEMBLAGES A. The Law and Basic Procedures in Handling Disorders Resulting from Violence, Panic, Mobs, etc.	2 hours

SUBJECT	TIME ALLOTTED
7. CRIMINAL LAW	2 hours
A. General Principles of New Jersey Law	
B. Elements of Various Crimes	
8. COURTS	2 hours
A. Powers and Function of the Courts with Particular Emphasis on Magistrates' Courts	
B. Court Procedure, Testimony and Courtroom Demeanor	
9. PRESERVATION OF EVIDENCE	2 hours
A. Preserving Scene and Evidence	
B. Obtaining Witnesses	
10. ARREST AND SEIZURE	2 hours
A. Powers and Methods with Due Process of Law	
11. PROTECTION AGAINST RADIATION HAZARDS	12 hours
A. Classroom Portion of Radiological Monitor Course	
12. FIRST AID	10 hours
A. Multi Media Course - 8 hours or Standard First Aid & Personal Safety - 16 hours	
B. Emergency Childbirth - 2 hours	

* Note: Most county auxiliary police academies triple the minimum required by the New Jersey State Police and include additional defensive tactics components among others. Utilization of firearms is at the discretion of the local police chief. Officers complete a 40 hour PTC firearms course to carry a firearm while on duty.

New Mexico

Number of Officers
4,215 Full Time
Unknown number of
reserves

Min. Training Hours Req.
400 Full Time
No minimum training for
Part-time and Volunteer
Officers

The State of New Mexico does not certify or track volunteer or part-time paid officers and therefore does not have statistics on their numbers in the Land of Enchantment. New Mexico has 4,215 full-time officers with 400 hours of minimum police training.

The 300 volunteer troopers of the New Mexico Mounted Patrol, descendants of a mounted posse formed by the governor in the 1930s, have established a symbiotic relationship with the New Mexico State Police. New Mexico thus is one of eight states with a volunteer state trooper organization.

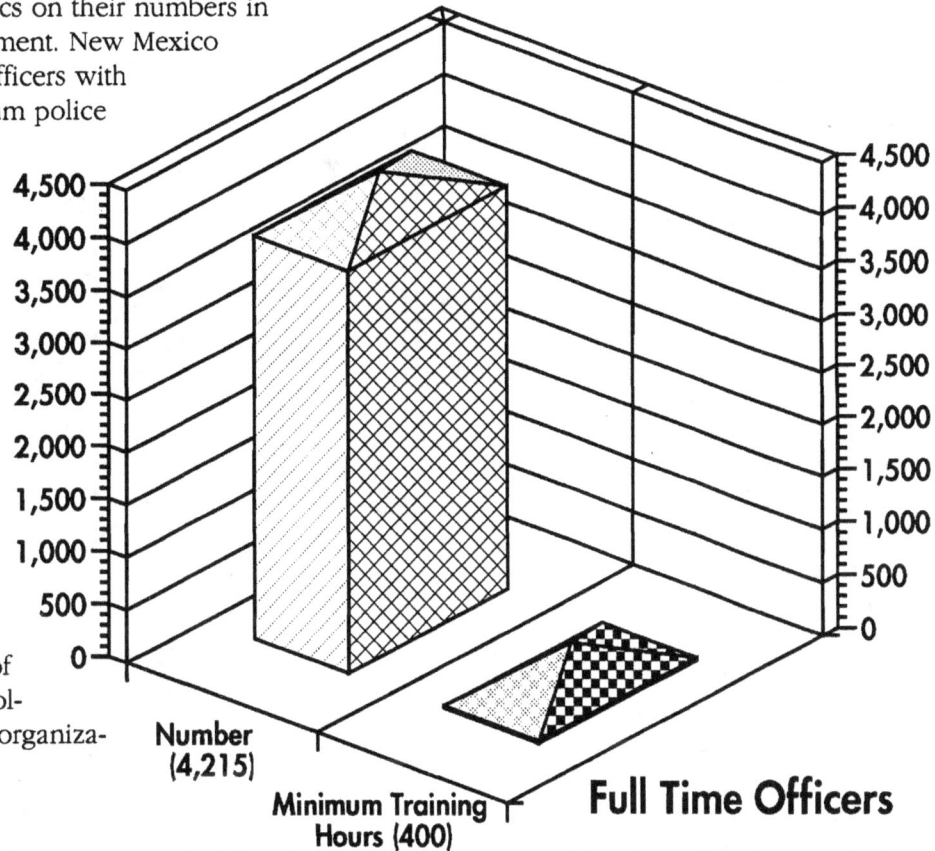

Number
(4,215)

Minimum Training
Hours (400)

Full Time Officers

Contact:

Jim Burlesome, Deputy Director
Training & Recruitment
New Mexico Department of Public Safety
4491 Cerrillos Road
Santa Fe, NM 87505

505/827-9251

New York

T he New York State Bureau of Municipal Police regulates only full- and part-time police officers. The Bureau's Richard Basile said that both classifications of officers must complete at least 445 hours of basic police training. The state has 62,953 full-timers and 2,690 part-timers.

The state's 7,240 volunteer auxiliary officers are under the New York State Emergency Management Office in Albany. That office requires only ten hours of training, although, as elsewhere, most agencies far exceed the requirement.

In an unusual twist, municipal police auxiliaries are under the policy control of the county in which the town is located. An exception is the 27,151 member New York City Police Department with its 4,402 volunteer auxiliaries trained for 54 hours over the course of 16 weeks.

Number of Officers
62,953	Full Time
2,690	Part-time
7,240	Vol. Aux.
72,803	**Total Officers**

Minimum Training Hours Req.
445 Full Time & Part-time
10 Volunteer Auxiliary

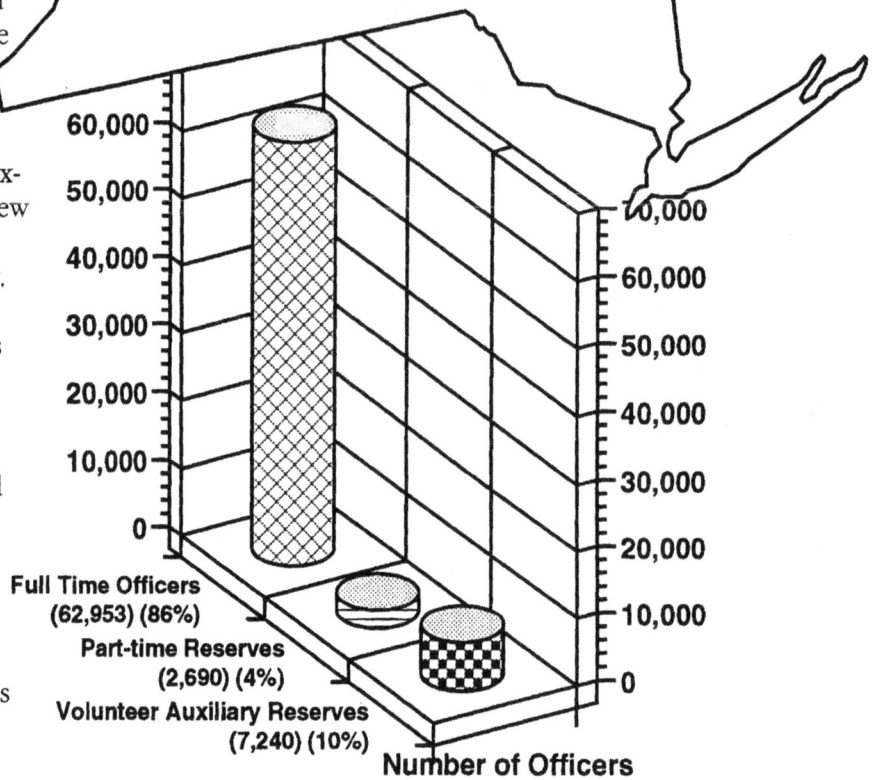

Full Time Officers
(62,953) (86%)

Part-time Reserves
(2,690) (4%)

Volunteer Auxiliary Reserves
(7,240) (10%)

Number of Officers

Contact:

Richard Basile
New York State Bureau of Municipal Police
Executive Park Tower, Stuyvesant Plaza
Albany, NY 12203

518/457-6101

North Carolina

The tar heel state of North Carolina is one of the more progressive users of reserve officers. The state has the same minimum requirements in place for them as those used for full-timers. The reserves are deployed and uniformed in a fashion which reflects their solid basic training. The state divides its sheriffs department employees from all other police officials. Combined full-time sworn police and sheriffs personnel come to 16,526 with 4,617 of that number being part-time paid or volunteer reserves.

Scott Perry, deputy director of the North Carolina Criminal Justice Standards Division in the Department of Justice, said all full-time, part-time and volunteer police officers must take 432 hours of pre-service basic training. As of the end of April 1992, the state has a total of 13,717 police personnel made up of 3,293 state law enforcers (Highway Patrol, State Bureau of Investigation, and Alcohol Law Enforcement), 271 county police, 37 other county police (park, animal), 70 local alcohol beverage control officers, and 10,046 municipal full-time and reserve police officers. Of that 10,046 number, 8,037 are full-timers and 2,009 are reserves.

Overseeing sheriff's departments is a separate agency called the North Carolina Sheriffs Education and Training Standards Commission which is also incorporated with the state's Department of Justice/Attorney General's Office umbrella. The deputy sheriffs minimum training comes in at

Number of Officers	
16,526	Full Time
4,617	Reserves
21,143	Total Officers

Minimum Training Hours Req.	
432	Police incl. Reserves
444	Sheriffs incl. Reserves

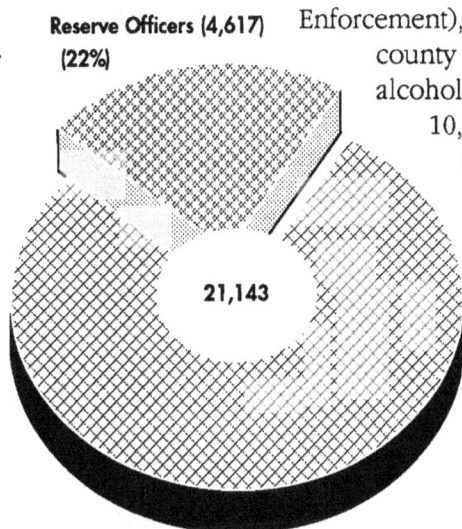

Reserve Officers (4,617) (22%)

21,143

Full Time Officers (16,526) (78%)

Contact:

Scott Perry, Deputy Director
North Carolina Criminal Justice
Standards Division
P.O. Drawer 149
Raleigh, NC 27602

919/733-2530

Joan Neuner, Director
North Carolina Sheriffs Education &
Training Standards Commission
P. O. Box 629
Raleigh, NC 27602

919/733-9236

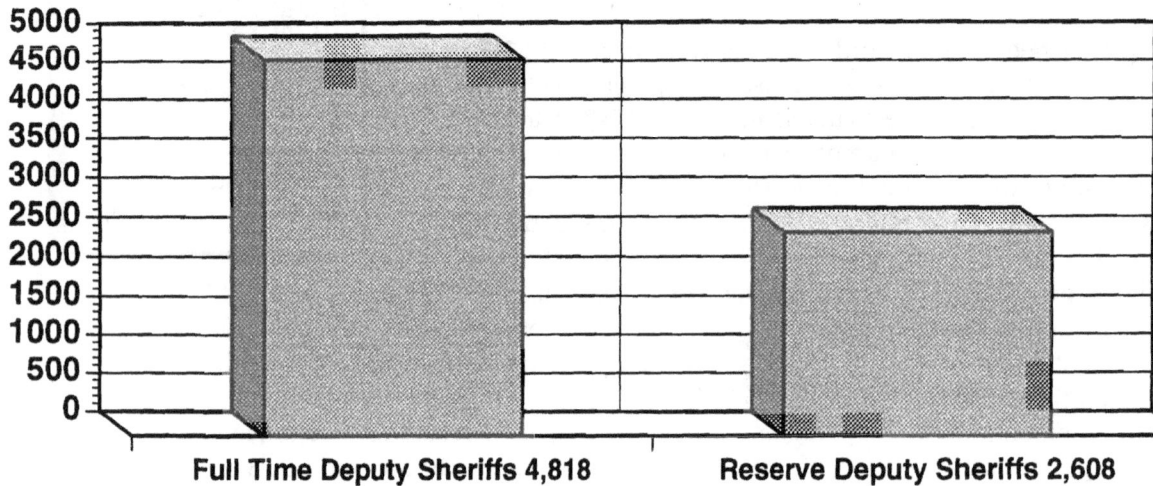

North Carolina
Number of Deputy Sheriffs

12 additional hours (444 hours) over police agencies due to the inclusion of training covering civil process and related material. Joan Neuner, director of the Commission said the state has a total of 7,601 deputy sheriffs with 4,818 working full-time and 2,608 serving as reserves.

North Dakota

Number of Officers
1,564 Full Time
200 Part-time
100 Volunteer
1,864 Total Officers
Minimum Training /Req.
360 Full Time & Part-time
Volunteer training up to agency

North Dakota is a state with the same geographical travel distance problems as Montana and the other big western states. Mark Gilbertson, director of the training division of the North Dakota Bureau of Criminal Investigations and

may take a correspondence course with classroom testing and must pass the licensing exam." The academy-training route for part-timers is the same as that for full-timers: 360 hours (nine weeks).

Some part-timers in North Dakota may in reality only be paid one dollar per year, but still receive state certification via the correspondence course/licensing exam or 360 hour academy routes. Gilbertson explained that part-timers work an average of 20 hours per week or less. North Dakota has 1,564 full-time officers and 200 part-time officers. Both classifications of officers carry firearms and have full arrest powers. There are also 100 volunteer officers whose training is up to the agency.

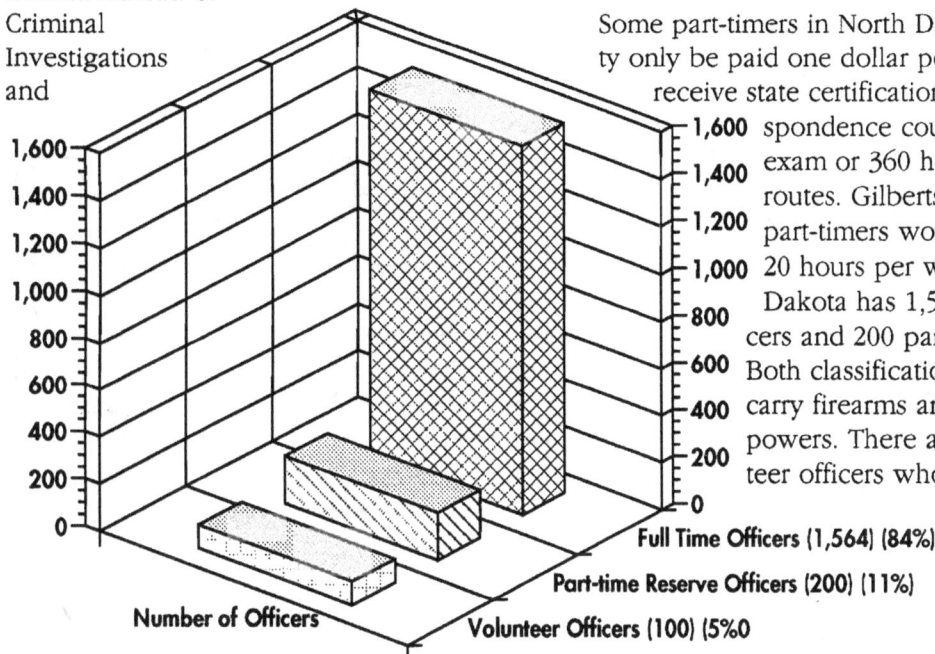

executive director of the POST Board, said the state compensates by allowing its "part-time officers assisting a small agency

Contact:

Mark Gilbertson, Director
Training Division
North Dakota Bureau of Criminal Investigations
P.O. Box 1054
Bismarck, ND 58502

701/221-6180

Ohio

Number of Officers
14,789 Full Time
18,000 Part-time, Volunteers
32,789 Total Officers

Minimum Training Hours Req.
420 All officers who are commissioned

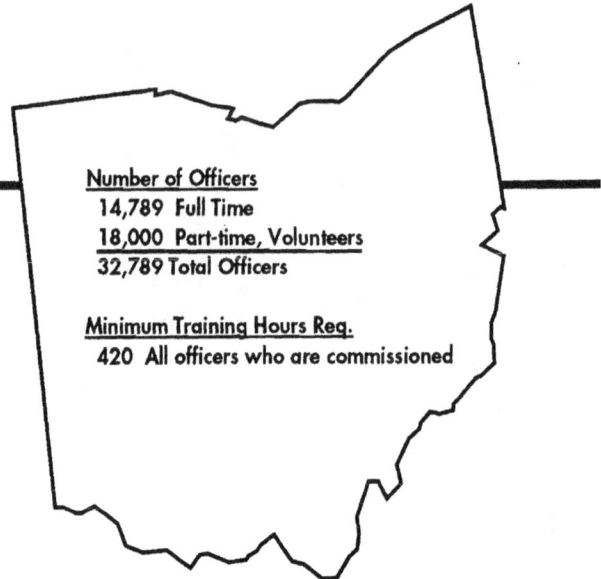

I n Ohio, the state does not differentiate between peace officers concerning their full-time, part-time or volunteer officer status.

According to the Ohio Peace Officer Training Academy's Reed Chaves, "they all have a minimum of 420 hours (of training)" and must take a POPE (Police Officer Proficiency Exam).

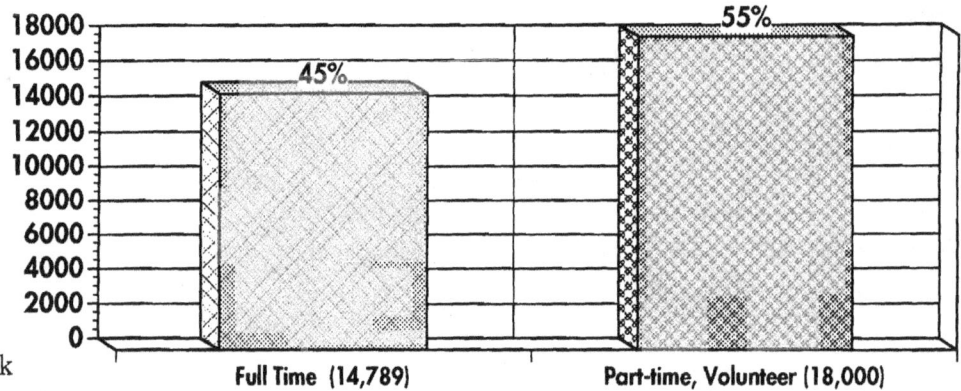

Because of the lack of differentiation, numbers of officers are hard to come by. Ohio, much like New Jersey, only issues the certificates and does not track officers over the course of their careers thus they are unable to state how many are still plying their law enforcement profession. Chaves said 1,800 peace officer certificates were issued in 1991 and he estimates that there are 25,000 in all categories.

The Ohio Police & Fire Pension Fund, which along with the Ohio Public Employee Retirement System comprises Ohio's two full-

	Full Time (14,789)	Part-time, Volunteer (18,000)
	45%	55%

Contact:

Reed Chaves
Ohio Peace Officer Training
Academy
P.O. Box 309
London, OH 43140

614/466-7771

Res. Lt. Pat Feighery
Ohio Volunteer Peace Officers
Association
P.O. Box 32481
Columbus, OH 43232-3481

614/443-7664

time officer pension systems, said they had 14,789 active police officers showing in their records as of March 1992.

The Ohio Volunteer Peace Officers

Association's Pat Feighery, himself a reserve lieutenant with the Middletown, OH, Police Department, said their research revealed that 18,000 volunteer law enforcers are in Ohio.

The Ohio Peace Officer Training Council's 420 hour Ohio Peace Officer Basic Training curriculum has a 30 hour option in physical conditioning. The unit breakdown is as follows:

UNIT	HOURS
Administration	30
Legal	49
Human Relations	49
Firearms	60
Investigation	76
Traffic Accident Investigation	15
Patrol	35
Traffic Enforcement	19
Civil Disorders	15
Unarmed Self-Defense	32
Prisoner Handling & Booking	04
First Aid	16
Physical Conditioning (optional)	30

Oklahoma

Number of Officers
7,436 Full Time
2,105 Volunteer/Paid Reserves
9,541 Total Officers

Minimum Training Hours Req.
300 Full Time
120 Volunteer/Paid Reserve

As of the end of 1991, the Sooner State of Oklahoma was home to 7,436 full-time officers and 2,105 active volunteer or paid part-time officers called reserves. Ingram said that full-timers are trained for 300 hours. Reserves, who work less than 25 hours per week, receive 120 hours of training.

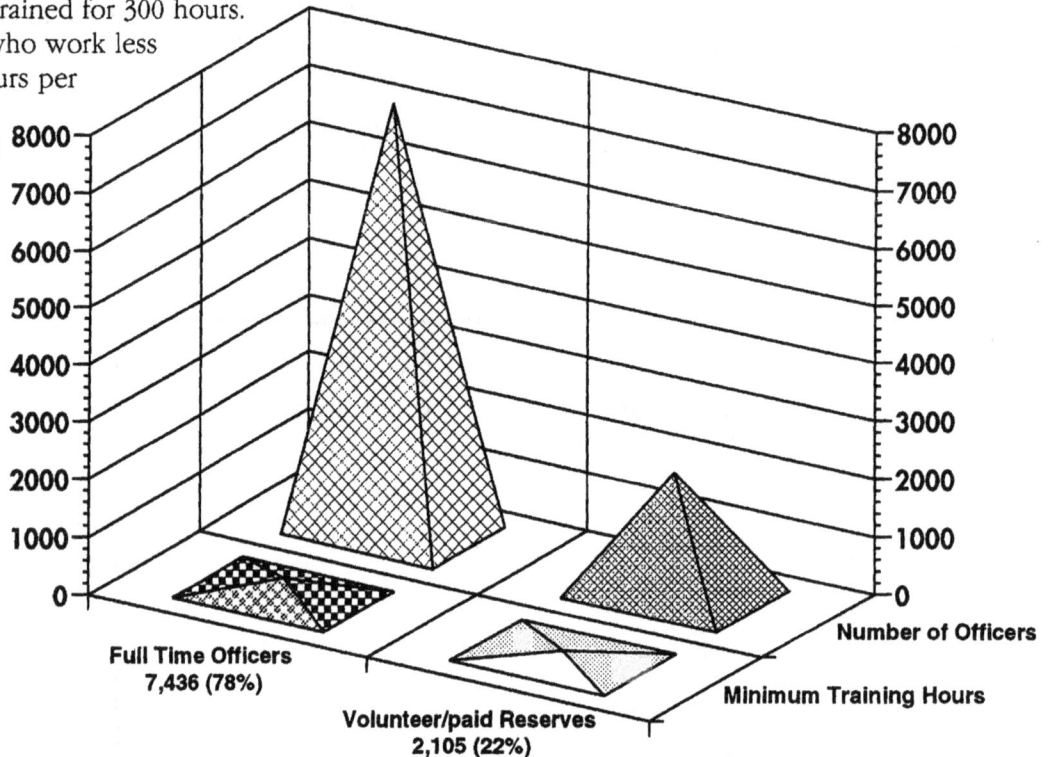

Full Time Officers
7,436 (78%)

Volunteer/paid Reserves
2,105 (22%)

Number of Officers

Minimum Training Hours

Contact:

Janet Ingram, Manager
Administrative Division
Oklahoma Council on Law Enforcement
Education & Training
P.O. Box 11476 - Cimarron Station
Oklahoma City, OK 73136

405/425-2750

Oregon

Number of Officers
4,830 Full Time
1,342 Reserves
6,172 Total Officers

Minimum Training Hours Req.
320   Full Time
No minimum training
    required for Reserves

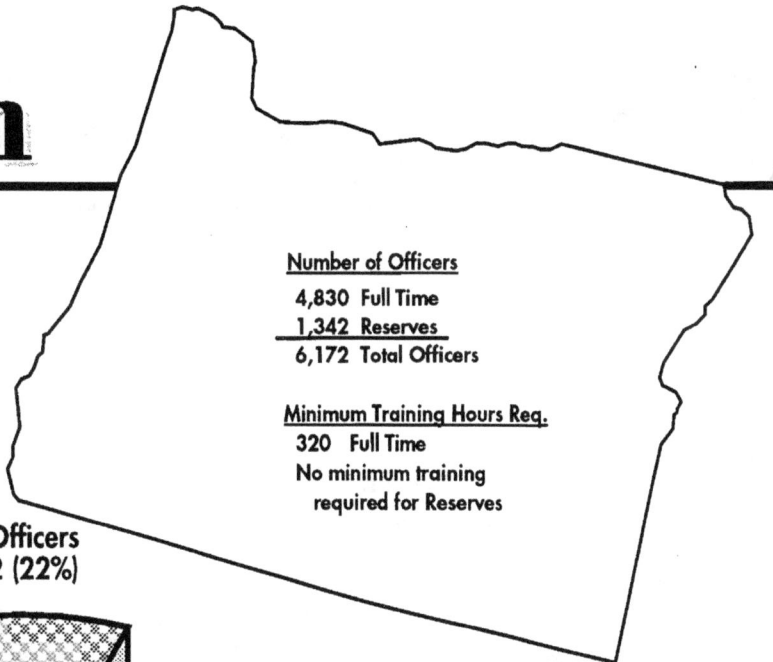

The State of Oregon has 4,830 full-time officers at the 320 hour or better training mark. According to Jeri Hemmer, research analyst for the Oregon Police Academy's training section, the state regulates full-time officers only, "although most agencies are 320 hours." The state has 1,342 reserves working for municipal police and county sheriffs agencies.

Reserve Officers
1,342 (22%)

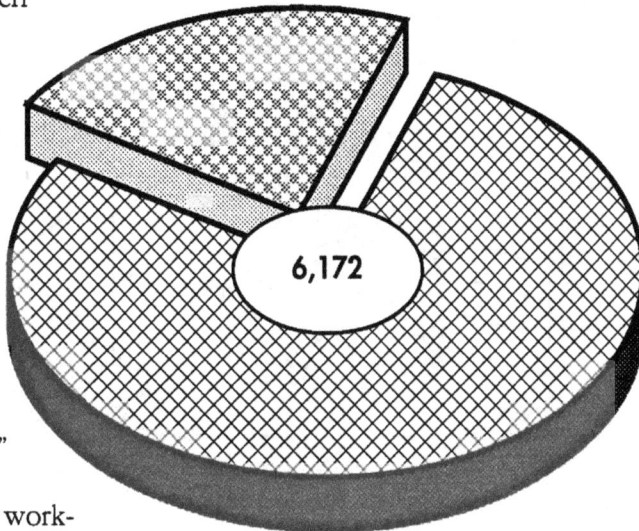

6,172

Full Time Officers
4,830 (78%)

Contact:

Jeri Hemmer, Research Analyst
Oregon Police Academy - Training Section
550 North Monmouth Avenue
Monmouth, OR 97361

503/378-2100

Pennsylvania

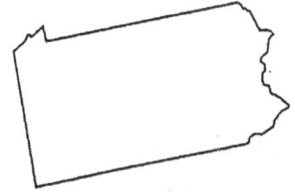

Under the mandatory Police Training Act of Pennsylvania, known as "Act 120," municipal officers for the last three years have been required to undergo 520 hours of basic police training. Robert A. Nardi, administrative officer with the Hershey-based Pennsylvania Municipal Police Officers' Education and Training Commission, said the state regulates only the 18,500 full-timers and 3,500 part-timers. They do not regulate volunteer auxiliary officers whose training is left to the local agency. Part-timers, as with other states may be paid a token $1.00 per year and function in effect as volunteer officers, however they must still meet all minimum standards and therefore have all the authority of a full-time officer.

Sheriffs in Pennsylvania are classified as peace officers (which holds less authority in Pennsylvania,

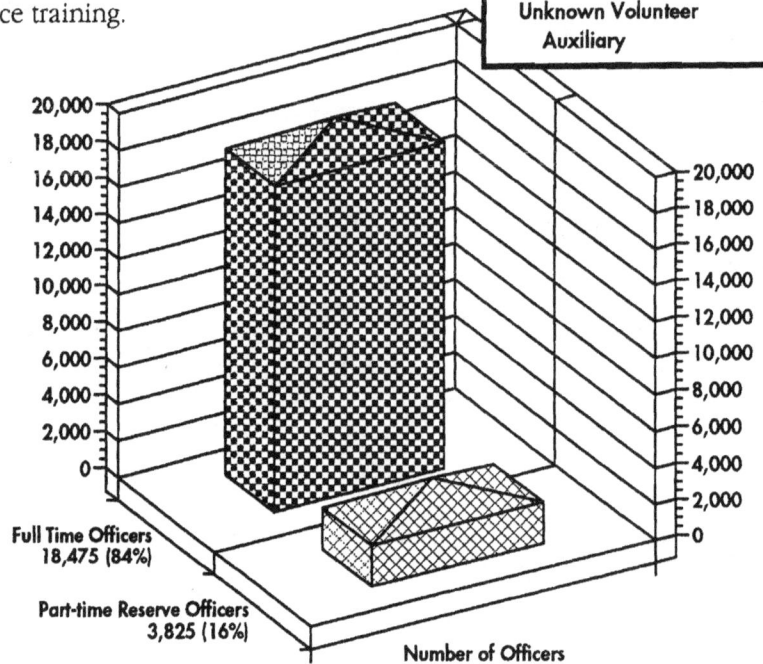

Full Time Officers
18,475 (84%)

Part-time Reserve Officers
3,825 (16%)

Number of Officers

Number of Officers

Contact:

Robert A. Nardi, Administrative Officer
Pennsylvania Municipal Police Officers' Education & Training Commission
P.O. Box 480
Hershey, PA 17033

717/533-5987

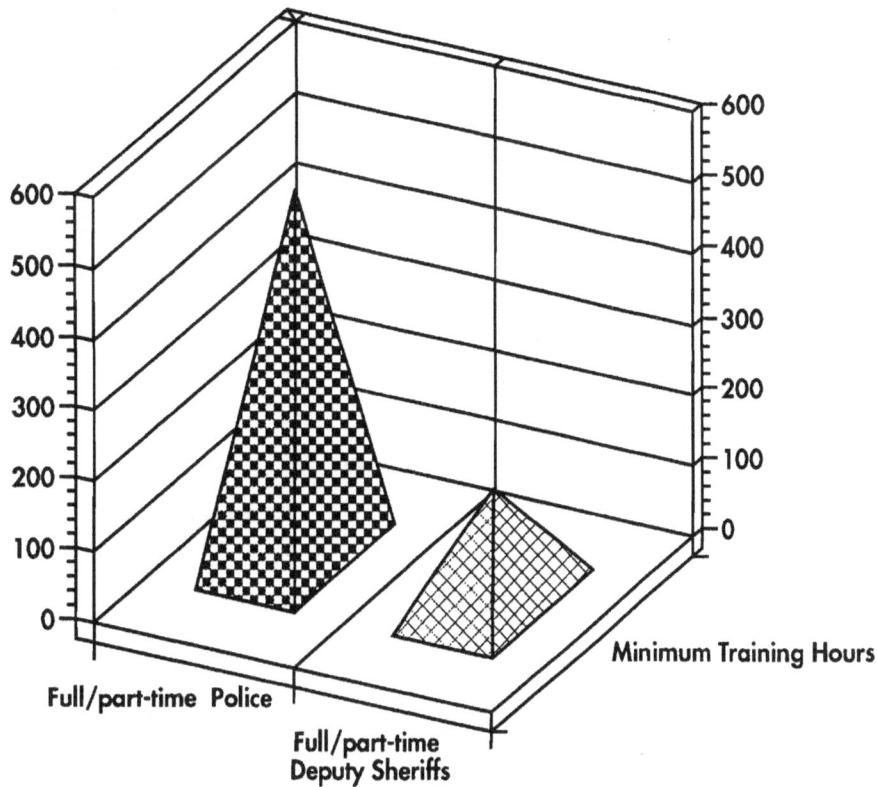

Minimum Training Hours

Full/part-time Police

Full/part-time Deputy Sheriffs

unlike in other states such as California). They serve process, transport prisoners and conduct court security. Some sheriff's offices provide major crime investigators on the county level and even an occasional patrol car.

The program manager of deputy sheriff training with the Pennsylvania Deputy Sheriffs' Training Board, Steve Spangenberg,

said the training is detailed in Act 2 of 1984. The training involves 160 hours of basic training and 20 hours of continuing education every two years. A total of 1300 deputies serve in the keystone state with 75% (975) as full-timers and 25% (325) as part-timers.

The combined totals of Pennsylvania police officers and deputy sheriffs breaks out to 19,475 full-time and 3,825 part-time.

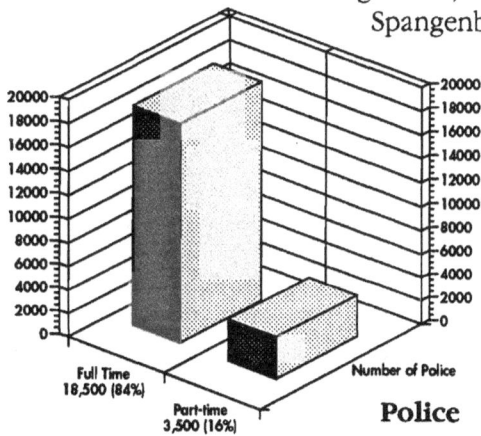

Police

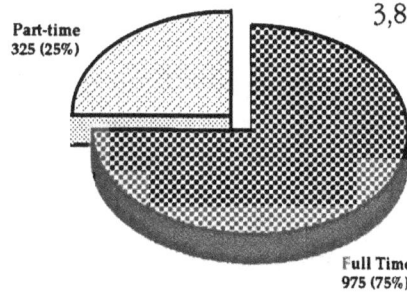

Deputy Sheriffs

Rhode Island

Rhode Island's finest, who train to the 500 hour mark, number 2,400. David Ricciarelli, coordinator of testing and instruction for the Rhode Island Municipal Police Academy, said that there is no state minimum for the 605 volunteer or part-time officers in the state. He said that the state used to have a 40 hour academy, but that it was discontinued.

Number of Officers
2,400 Full Time
  605 Part-time, Volunteer
3,005 Total Officers

Minimum Training Hours Req.
  500 average for Full, Part-time
  No minimum training for
    Volunteer and Part-time

Part-time, Volunteer Officers
605 (20%)

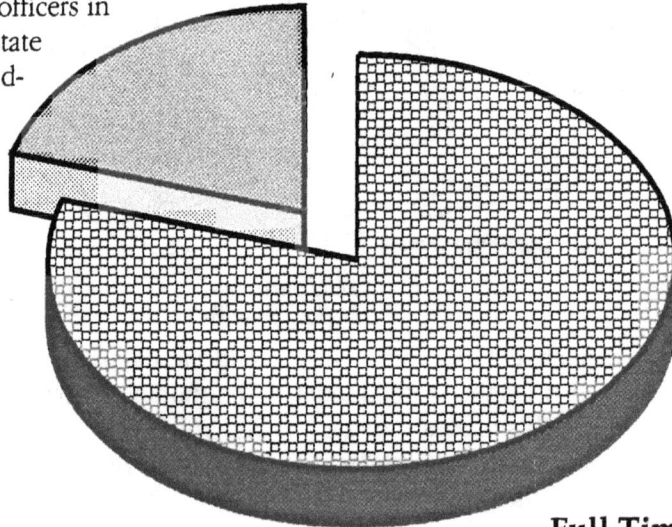

Number of Officers

Full Time Officers
2,400 (80%)

Contact:

David Ricciarelli
Coordinator, Testing and Instruction
Rhode Island Municipal Police Academy
Flanagan Campus
Community College of Rhode Island
Lincoln, RI 02865

401/277-3755

South Carolina

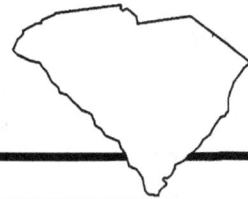

S outh Carolina requires the same 332 hours of police training for their 500 part-time officers as they do for their 7,000 full-time officers. The state, which regulates all officers, mandates that the 850 volunteer reserve officers undergo 64 hours of in-house training at their agency, as per South Carolina Code of Law 23-28-20. Henry Wengrow, general counsel for the South Carolina Criminal Justice Academy, said they must then take a test to determine police officer proficiency. Reserves in the state must work 20 hours per month including in-service training and they can't exceed their agency's combined total number of full-time and part-time paid officers.

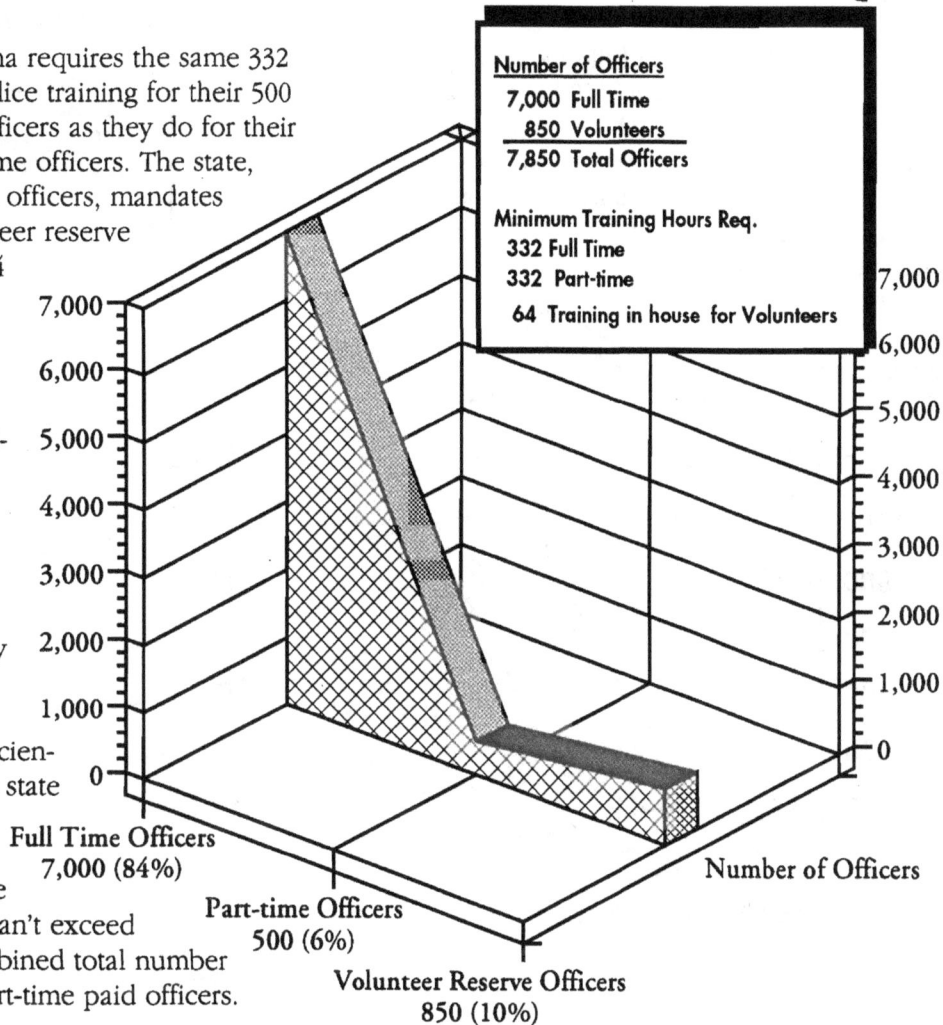

Number of Officers
7,000 Full Time
850 Volunteers
7,850 Total Officers

Minimum Training Hours Req.
332 Full Time
332 Part-time
64 Training in house for Volunteers

Full Time Officers 7,000 (84%)

Part-time Officers 500 (6%)

Volunteer Reserve Officers 850 (10%)

Number of Officers

Contact:

Henry Wengrow
General Counsel
South Carolina Criminal Justice Academy
5400 Broad River Road
Columbia, SC 29210

803/737-8400

South Dakota

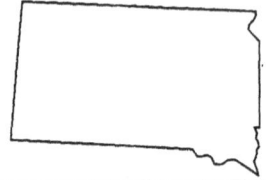

S outh Dakota's 1,023 full-time and part-time officers undergo 320 hours (eight weeks) of training. The state does not have the two categories broken apart. The 190 volunteer reserves take a 100 hour training program broken down into a 60 hour state mandated curriculum with the remaining 40 set by the local agency.

Number of Officers
1,023 Includes both Full and Part-time
190 Volunteer Reserves
1,223 Total Officers

Minimum Training Hours Req.
320 Full, part-time
100 Volunteer Reserves

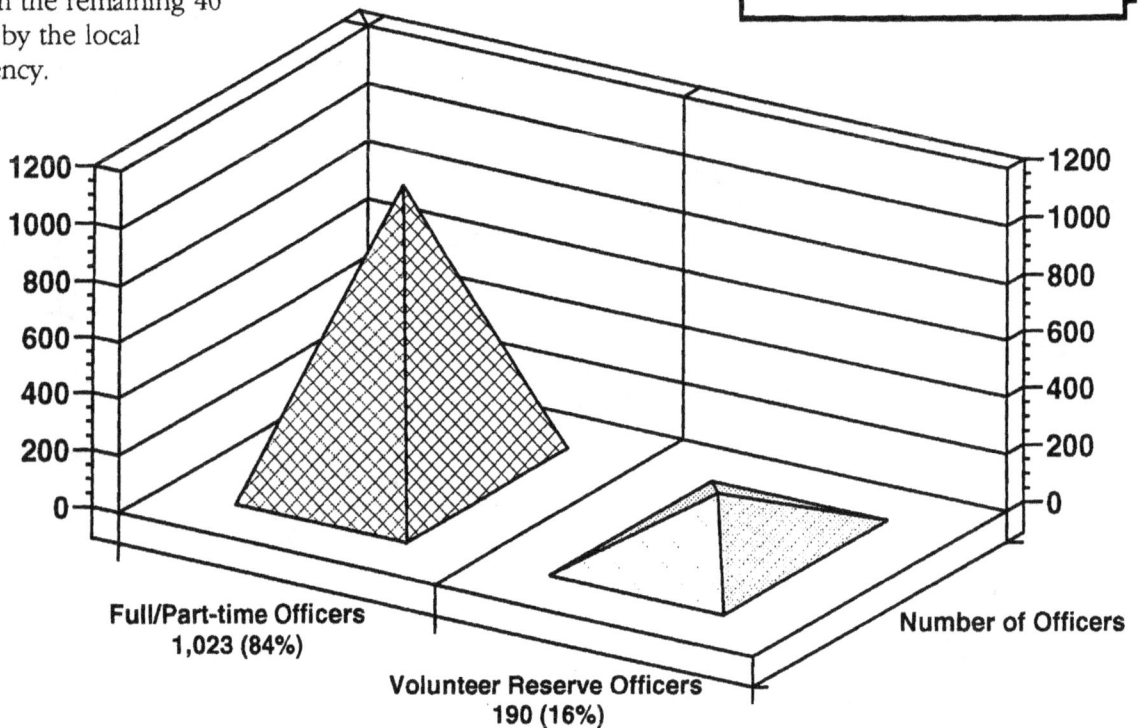

Full/Part-time Officers
1,023 (84%)

Volunteer Reserve Officers
190 (16%)

Number of Officers

Contact:

South Dakota Highway Patrol Training Academy
East Highway 34 c/o 500 East Capitol
Pierre, SD 57501

605/773-3584

Tennessee

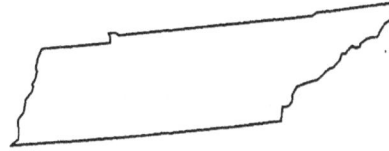

Tennessee's state Law Enforcement Training Academy administers training only and does not track the exact number of officers in the different categories. The estimated 8,000 full-time officers take 320 hours of training. Part-time officers, who work under 20 hours per week, must take a minimum of 40 hours of training during the first calendar year. The 1,000 part-timers have the same entrance standards as full-timers (minimum 18 years of age, high school graduate, no felony convictions, etc.).

The Tennessee Municipal League, which provides insurance to 214 municipalities, provided their figures concerning the numbers of officers in their files. Jim Richardson, director of loss control for the League, said their records reflect the following classifications and numbers of officers: 2,734 full-time, 84 non-certified full-time, 86 part-time certified, 100 non-certified part-time, and 414 non-certified auxiliary/reserve.

Number of Officers	
8,000	Full Time
1,000	Part-time
1,656	Non-cert. Vol. Res/Aux
10,656	Total Officers

Minimum Training Hours Req.	
320	Full Time
40	Part-time
Training up to agency for Non-cert. Vol. Res/Aux	

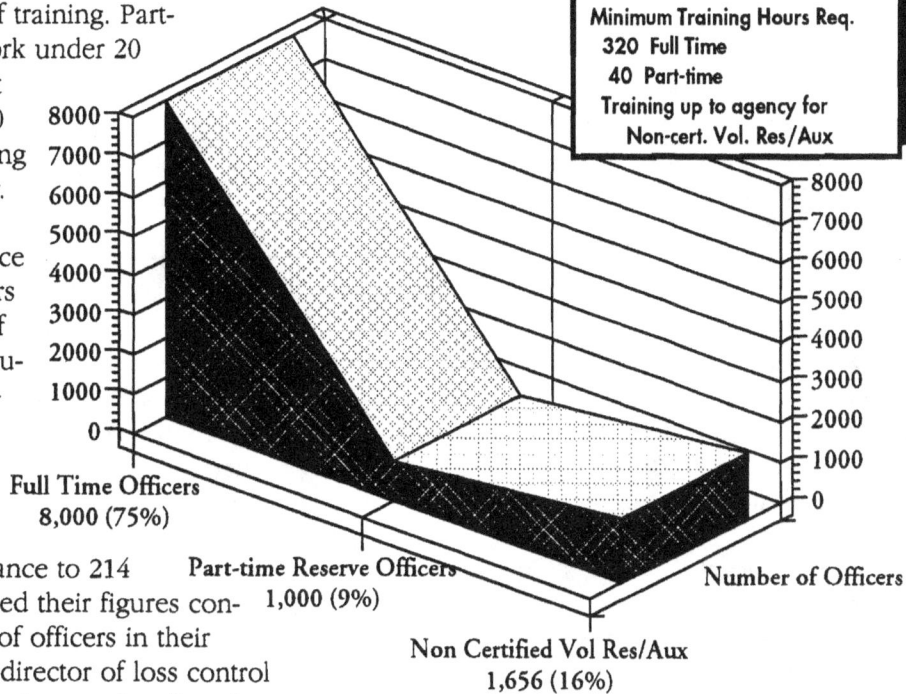

Full Time Officers
8,000 (75%)

Part-time Reserve Officers
1,000 (9%)

Non Certified Vol Res/Aux
1,656 (16%)

Number of Officers

Contact:

Tennessee State Law Enforcement
Training Academy
P.O. Box 140229
Donelson, TN 37214

615/741-4448

Jim Richardson
Director of Loss Control
Tennessee Municipal League
5100 Maryland Way
Brentwood, TN 37027

615/371-0049

Texas

Number of Officers
47,391 Full Time
5,770 Reserves
53,161 Total Officers

Minimum Training Hours Req.
400 Full Time
400 Reserves

According to the Texas Reserve Law Officers Association's Bill Martin, whose organization has 3,200 members, the numbers concerning quantity of officers and part-time/volunteer officer training standards in the state of Texas reflect the larger than life image that the Lone Star State invokes.

The manager of public information for the Texas Commission on Law Enforcement Officer Standards and Education (TCLEOSE), Peter Stone, said reserves receive their authority under three statutes in the local government code. Municipal reserves are featured under 341.012, whereas county sheriff's reserves are under section 85.004 and county constable's reserves are detailed in section 86.012.

Reserve Officers
5,770 (11%)

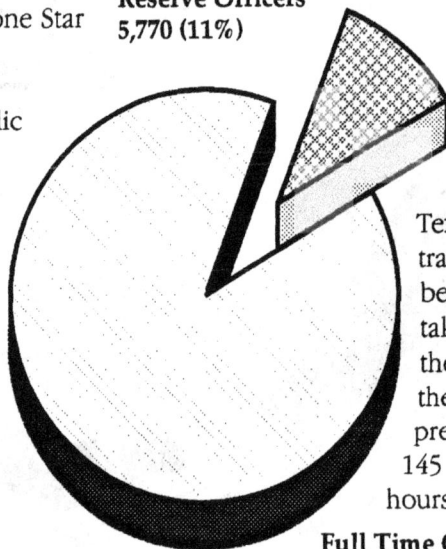

Full Time Officers
47,391 (89%)

Stone said the 47,391 full-timers in Texas take 400 hours of pre-service training. The 5,770 reserves, who must be a minimum of 21 years of age, also take the 400 hours of training, however their training is both before and during their tour of the streets of justice. The pre-service basic course is made up of 145 hours. Within two years another 131 hours must be completed and an additional 124 hours must be done within four years.

Contact:

Peter Stone
Manager of Public Information
Texas Commission on Law Enforcement
Officer Standards and Education
1033 La Podesta Street
Austin, TX 78752

512/450-0188

Bill Martin
President
Texas Reserve Law Officers
Association
P.O. Box 270407
Dallas, TX 75227

214/321-4300

Utah

Utah does not break their categories of officers down and therefore reflect a total of 5,000 full-time, part-time and volunteer officers in the state. All officers are trained for 440 hours with Category II./Special Function Reserves trained through a 160 hour reserve academy.

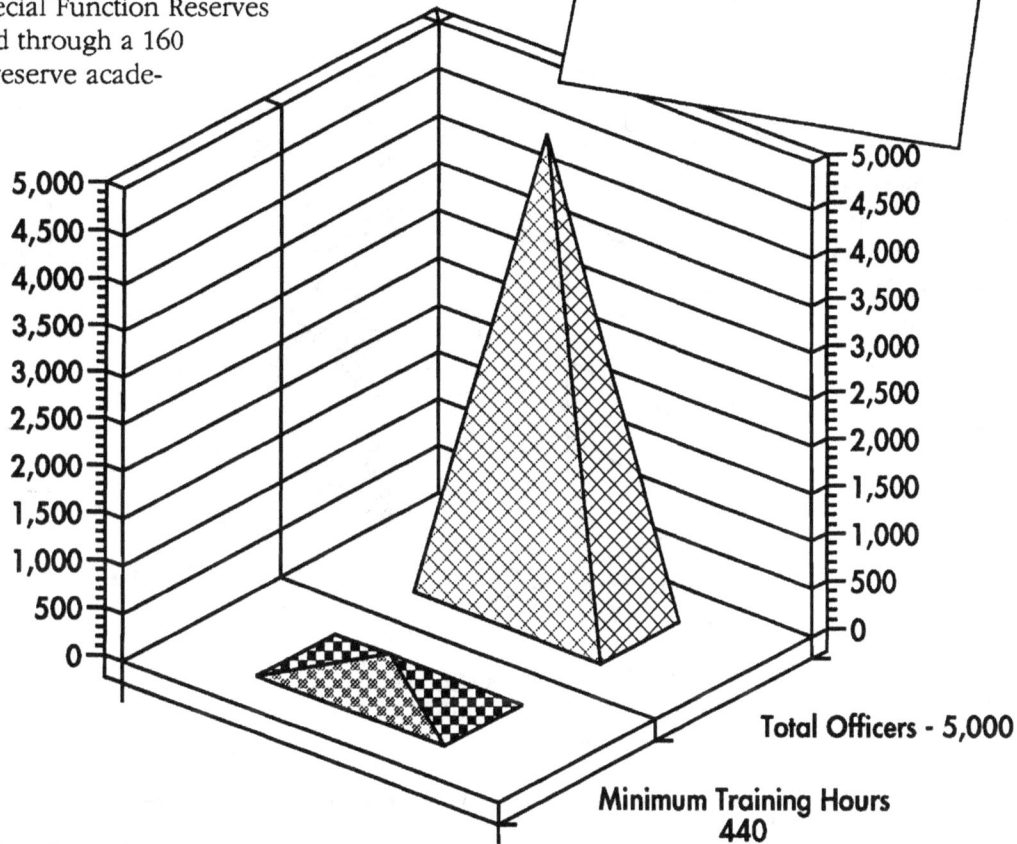

Number of Officers
5,000 Full Time, Part-time Volunteers

Minimum Training Hours Req.
440 Full Time, Part-time, Volunteer
160 Category II. Reserve/Special Function Officer

5,000	5,000
4,500	4,500
4,000	4,000
3,500	3,500
3,000	3,000
2,500	2,500
2,000	2,000
1,500	1,500
1,000	1,000
500	500
0	0

Total Officers - 5,000

Minimum Training Hours
440

Contact:

Utah Peace Officer Standards and Training
4525 South 2700 West
Salt Lake City, UT 84119

801/965-4099

Vermont

Number of Officers
600 Full Time
1,100 Special
1,700 Total Officers

Minimum Training Hours Req.
600 Full Time
168 Special

Vermont has dubbed it's version of volunteer and part-time officers as "specials" and the 1700 total law enforcement officers in the state reflect mostly specials in the ranks. Full-time officers make up 600 of the 1700 total with 1100 specials rounding out the figure.

R.J. Elrick, training coordinator for the Vermont Criminal Justice Training Council, said part-time specials must complete a three phase training program within one year. Phase I. involves a 58 hour, one week academy prior to putting a uniform on. Phase II. is an additional 50 hours which may be done in-service. A 60 hour field training officer (FTO) program completes the three step certification process. Elrick added that specials are provisional prior to full certification and must work with a certified officer.

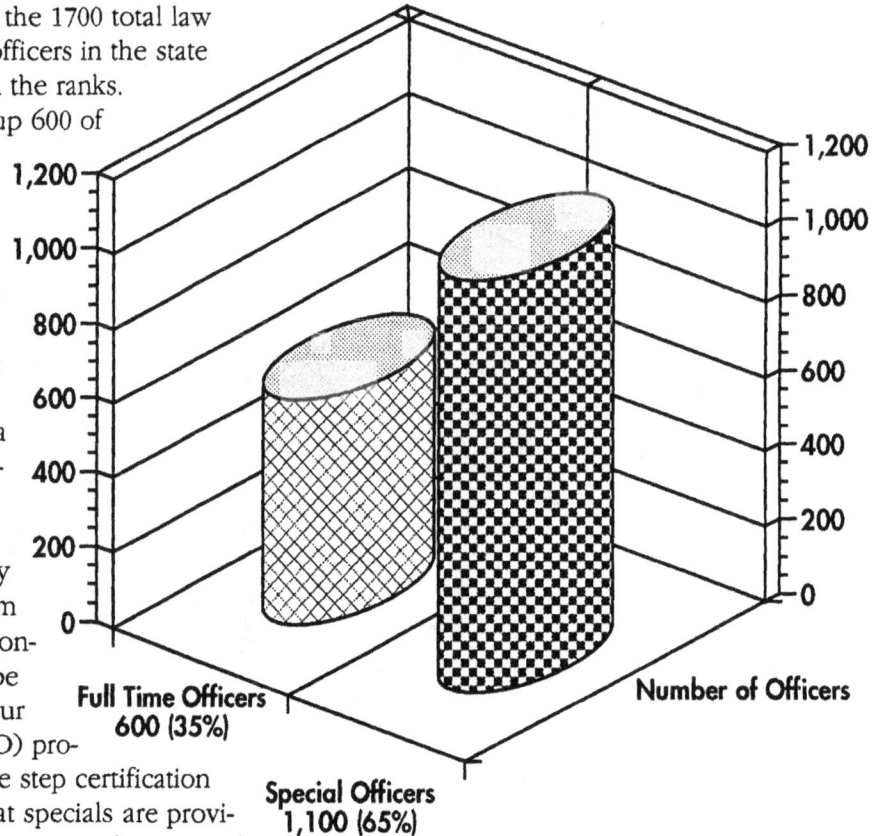

Full Time Officers
600 (35%)

Special Officers
1,100 (65%)

Number of Officers

Contact:

**R.J. Elrick
Training Coordinator
Vermont Criminal Justice Training Academy
Route 2, Box 2160
Pittsford, VT 05763-9712**

802/483-6228

Virginia

Number of Officers
24,400 Total Certified Officers
Unkown Non-certified Officers

Minimum Training Hours Req.
315 Certified Officers
Non-certified Officer training up
to local agency

Virginia's Division of Training & Standards tracks only certified officers which they tally as numbering 24,400. Bill Flink, certifications and standards program analyst for the Division, said the figure includes all full-time, part-time and volunteer officers who have completed a basic academy.

The basic academies cover 433 performance objectives (P.O.s) and come in at a minimum of 315 hours and an average of 400 hours. There are 34 academies in the Old Dominion state, although only 24 are basic training facilities.

The types of officers are covered under Title 15.1-159.2 (Auxiliary Police Forces) and Statute 9-180. Certified officers, who are nicknamed locally as "Paragraph B Officers," must requalify with their sidearm once a year. They must also complete a 60 hour Field Training Officer (FTO) program. "Paragraph A Officers" are not fully certified, but receive basic training in firearms and also requalify once a year.

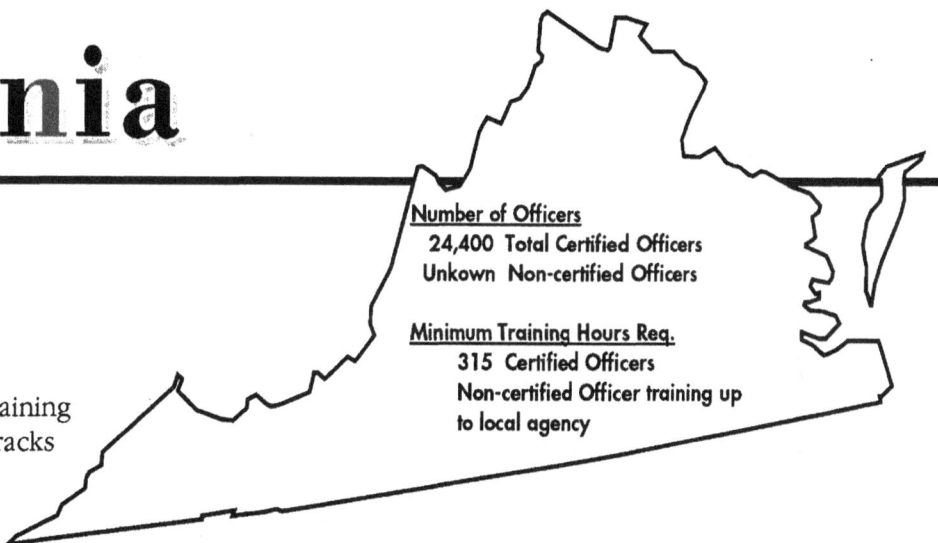

Fink added that all sheriffs who receive state funding must have all their officers up to certification standards. Conversely, those sheriffs that do not have all their officers fully certified, will operate void of state funding.

Contact:

Bill Flink
Virginia Certifications and Standards
Program Analyst
805 East Broad Street
Richmond, VA 23219

804/786-6348

Washington

Number of Officers
7,400 Full Time
2,500 Volunteer Reserves
9,900 Total Officers

Minimum Training Hours Req.
440 Full Time
No minimum requirement for
the Reserves — Optional 175
hour reserve academy

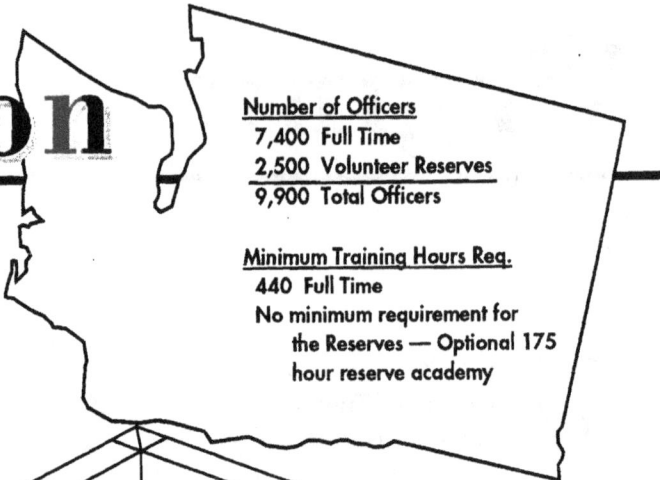

While a police chief or sheriff in Washington State can have reserves who are not trained or tested for the basic reserve certificate by the Washington Criminal Justice Training Commission, most opt for at least the optional 175 hour minimum academies offered by the state. Gary Wegner, assistant director of the Olympia-based Commission, said that reserves undergo the training at one of 29 approved academies which dot the Evergreen State.

Basic training hours are 440 for the 7,400 individuals who make their living full-time from the law enforcement profession.

The Commission does not track the total number of reserves serving. They do know that 590 people graduated last year (July 1, 1990-June 1991) from reserve academies and that 156 departments participated. The 350 member Washington State Reserve Law Enforcement Association's Terry Lattin said their group has pegged the number of reserves at 2,500. Lattin is a 23 year veteran Seattle Police Department reserve officer who serves as president of the Association.

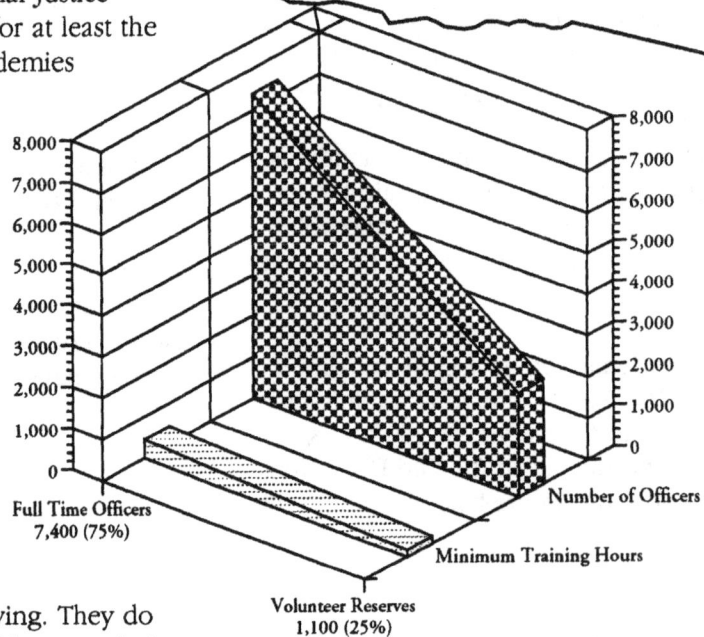

Full Time Officers
7,400 (75%)

Volunteer Reserves
1,100 (25%)

Minimum Training Hours

Number of Officers

Contact:

Gary Wegner
Assistant Director
Washington Criminal Justice
 Training Commission
Mail Stop PW-11
Olympia, WA 98504

206/459-6342

Terry Lattin
President
Washington State Reserve Law
 Enforcement Association
P.O. Box 5432
Kennewick, WA 99336-0432

West Virginia

The Mountain State of West Virginia lumps their full and part-time officers together for a total figure of 2,500 officers trained for 498 hours. The City of Charleston uses volunteer reserves while other cities use part-timers in a quasi-volunteer capacity.

Number of Officers
2,500 Both Full Time and Part-time

Minimum Training Hours Req.
498 Full Time and Part-time
No minimum training required for Volunteers

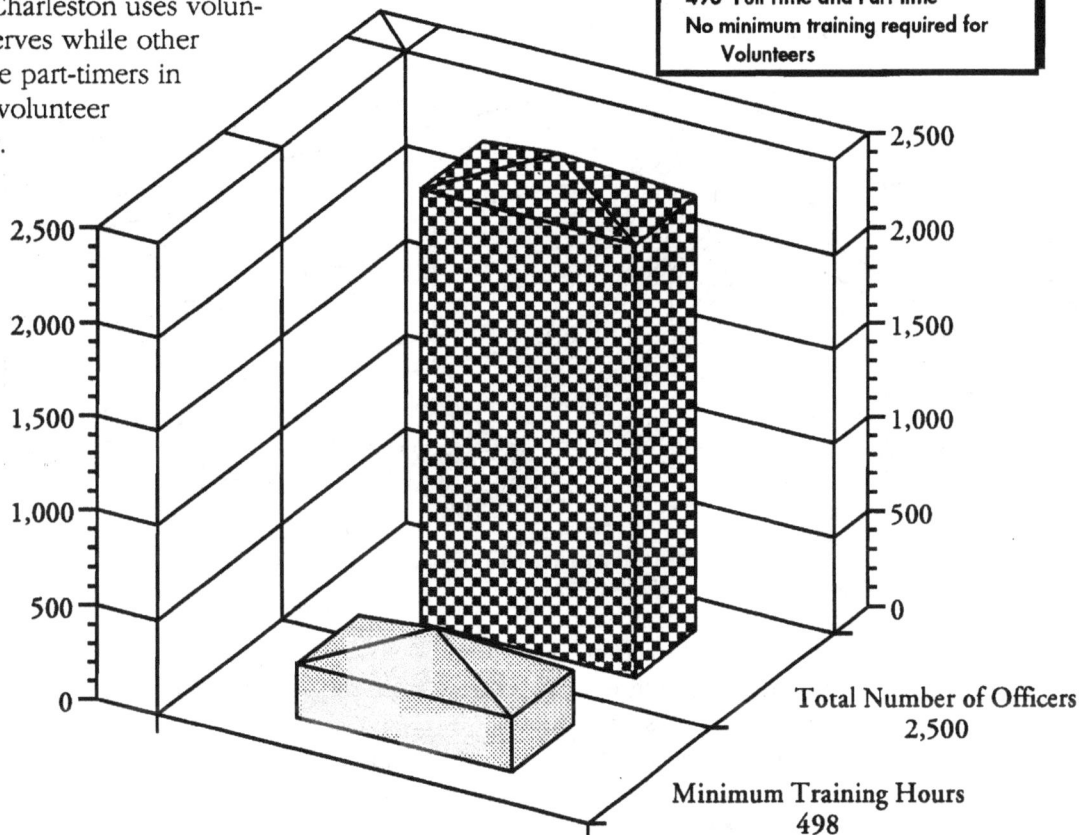

Total Number of Officers
2,500

Minimum Training Hours
498

Contact:

**Donald Davidson
Field Representative
Law Enforcement Training Sub Committee
Governor's Committee on Crime, Delinquency & Corrections**

304/558-8814

Wisconsin

Number of Officers
10,000 Full Time
2,000 Certified Part-time
1,500 Non-certified Volunteers
13,500 Total Officers

Minimum Training Hours Req.
400 All Certified Officers

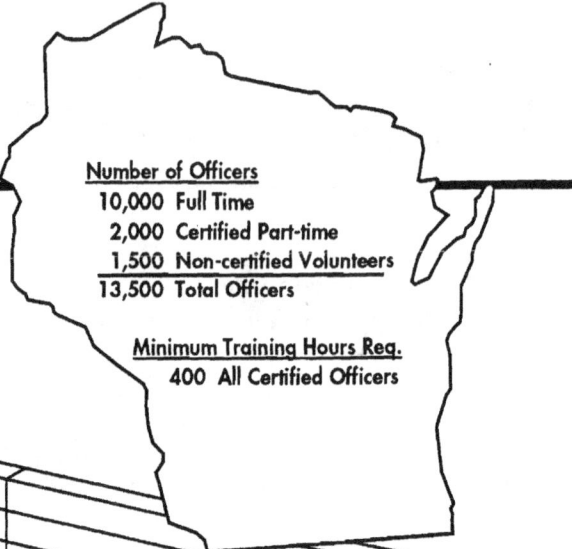

Wisconsin officers are trained on a modular system. The state regulates all certified officers. Dennis Hanson, director of the Wisconsin Training & Standards Bureau, said that all certified officers have 400 hours of training. The Badger State's 2,000 part-time officers are allowed to complete the 400 hours of training within three years. The pre or in-service training is broken into ten 40 hour modules with three formats to choose from for scheduling convenience.

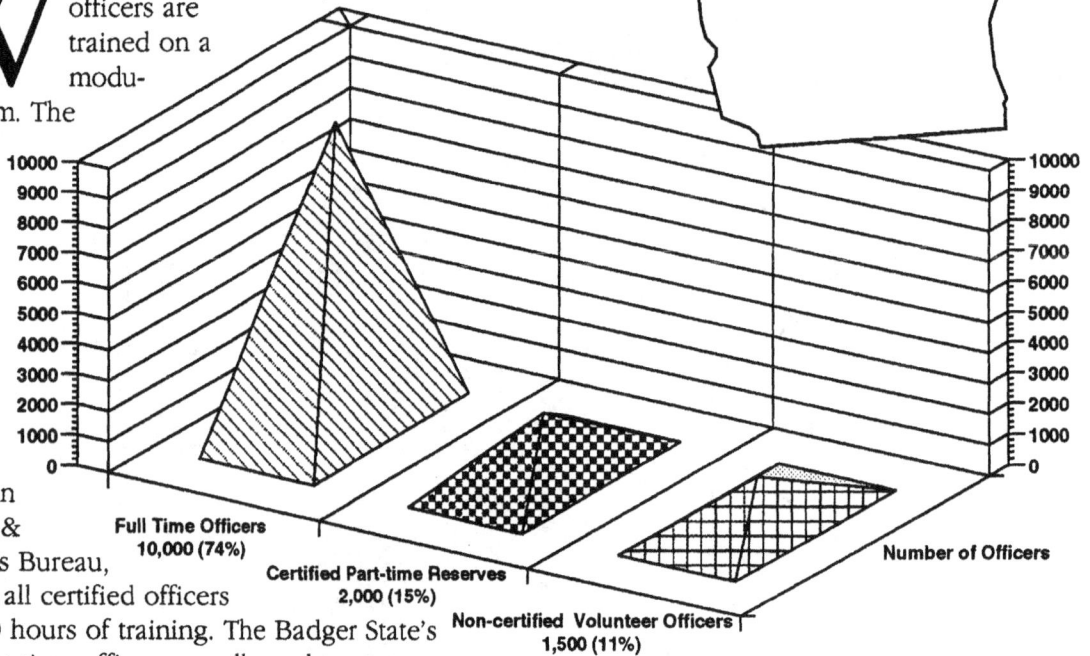

Hanson said the state also has 1,500 non-certified volunteer officers.

Full Time Officers
10,000 (74%)

Certified Part-time Reserves
2,000 (15%)

Non-certified Volunteer Officers
1,500 (11%)

Number of Officers

Contact:

Dennis Hanson
Director
Wisconsin Training & Standards Bureau
P.O. Box 7857
Madison, WI 53707-7857

608/266-8800

Wyoming

Number of Officers
1,460 Full Time
  102 Certified Reserves
1,562 Total Officers

Minimum Training Hours Req.
403 Full Time, Part-time, Volunteer
     Police and Sheriffs
205 Detention Reserves

The Equality State of Wyoming seems to live up to its name as all officers are regulated and are expected to meet the 403 hour minimum training mark. According to Donald B. Pierson, executive director of Wyoming Peace Officer Standards & Training, the 1,460 certified peace officers have one year

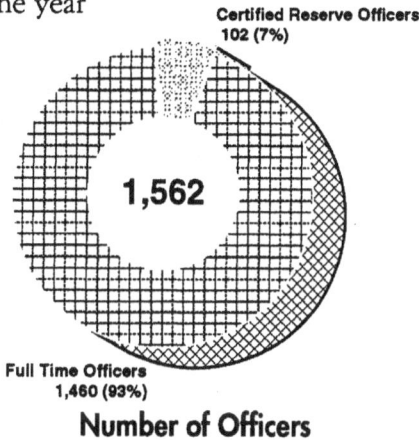

Certified Reserve Officers
102 (7%)

1,562

Full Time Officers
1,460 (93%)

Number of Officers

to acquire the training and the 102 certified reserves have two years to get it. Reserves must undergo 20 hours of job related training every two years while full-timers must do 40 hours every two years.

Pierson said that there was only one basic academy, but that three departments have an approved in-house basic academy. He added that 48 reserves are assigned to sheriffs' offices and ten are detention reserves trained for 205 hours. There are also 12 of what he dubbed as miscellaneous reserves and 32 reserve police officers.

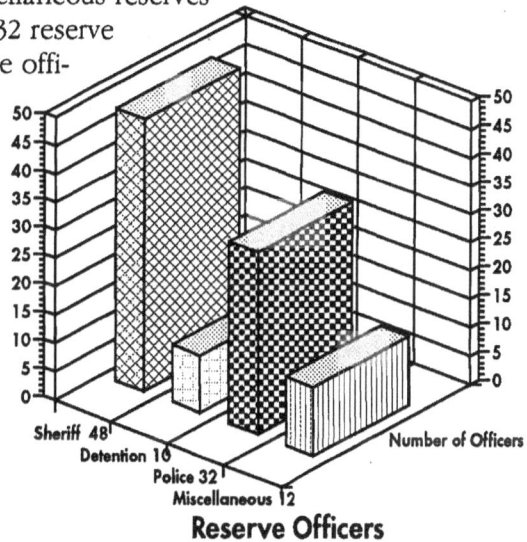

Sheriff 48
Detention 16
Police 32
Miscellaneous 12

Number of Officers

Reserve Officers

Contact:

Donald B. Pierson
Executive Director
Wyoming Peace Officer Standards & Training
1710 Pacific Avenue
Cheyenne, WY 82002

307/777-7718

SECTION
V

Section V.
Counties and Cities: Overview

	Res.	Res. Acad.	FT.	FT. Acad.	Min. Mthly. Hrs.	Min. Age	Firearm
Ada County, ID	20	160	150	390	None		yes
Akron, OH	74	420	483	420	18	21	yes
Albuquerque, NM	28	308	760	960	8	21	yes
Anchorage, AK	60	300	300	784	14	21	yes
Bloomfield, NJ	20	157	110	669	8	18	yes
Broward County, FL	25	597	900	597	16	19	yes
Burlington City, NJ	11	452/92	31	669	4	18	yes
Cass County, ND	22	360	75	360	16	18	yes
Charlotte, NC	50	432	900	640	15	21	yes
Chicago, IL	300	16	12,000	720	16	21	no
Columbus, OH	100	490	1,400	960	8	21	yes
Dade County, FL	50	700	2,800	700	20	19	yes
Dallas, TX	67	768	3,200	1,040	16	21	yes
Dearborn, MI	72	100	190	545	3.3	21	yes
Denver, CO	44	480	1,380	800	26	21	yes
Des Moines, IA	19	130	356	880	20	21	yes

	Res.	Res. Acad.	FT.	FT. Acad.	Min. Mthly. Hrs.	Min. Age	Firearm
Douglas County, NE	45	134	100	500	8	21	yes
Durham, NC	50	500	380	500	8	21	yes
Essex County, NJ	28	452-669	500	669	16	18	yes
Fort Worth, TX	75	400	1,052	682	24	21	yes
Fulton County, GA	370	280	702	280	%	25	yes
Greenwich, CT	21	498	150	498	15	21	yes
Harris County, TX	316	400	3,300	400	20	21	yes
High Point, NC	20	432	180	432	16	21	yes
Honolulu, HI	83	720	1,913	1,088	20	25	yes
Indianapolis, IN	46	500	953	500	20	21	yes
Jackson, MS	45	360	445	480	8	21	yes
Jacksonville, FL	200	750	1,800	720	16	21	yes
Jefferson County, LA	1,376	400/16	242	400	20	21	yes
Jefferson Parish, KY	200	580	800	860	28	21	yes
Laramie County, WY	20	410	30	410	20	21	yes
Las Vegas, NV	52	680/200	1,105	680	16	21	yes
Los Angeles County, CA	963	391/249	8,000	840	20	21	yes
Los Angeles, CA	650	720/267	7,700	720	16	21/18	yes
Maplewood, NJ	27	117	56	669	14	18	yes

	Res.	Res. Acad.	FT.	FT. Acad.	Min. Mthly. Hrs.	Min. Age	Firearm
Maricopa County, AZ	80	440	460	680	16	21	yes
Middletown, OH	20	450	72	450	21	21	yes
Mobile, AL	20	280	472	680	12	21	yes
Multnomah County, OR	63	328	56	328	21.66	21	yes
Newark, NJ	170	77	825	669	8	18	no
New Orleans, LA	175	500	1,300	500	24	21	yes
New York City, NY	4,402	54	27,157	640	16	17	no
Norfolk, VA	14	560	687	840	24	21	yes
Oklahoma County, OK	300	190/160	80	300	24/8	21	yes
Olympia, WA	25	175	68	480	16	21	yes
Orange County, CA	252	180/160/64	1,300	888	18	18	yes
Orange County, FL	144	600/160	909	600	24/14	21	yes
Palm Beach County, FL	35	740/200	850	740	21	21	yes
Phoenix, AZ	26	480	2,100	620	33.3	21	yes
Portland, OR	52	280	858	850	16	21	yes
Pulaski County, AR	75	102	136	320	16	21	yes
Ramsey County, MN	70	400/36	280	400	10	21	yes
Reno, NV	70	600/480	285	600	10	21	yes
Rockland County, NY	50	550	250	550	None	21	yes

	Res.	Res. Acad.	FT.	FT. Acad.	Min. Mthly. Hrs.	Min. Age	Firearm
St. Louis, MO	56	240	1,550	680	20	21	yes
Sacramento, CA	93	214/146/64	597	720	16	21	yes
San Bernardino County, CA	1,091	254/156/66	980	1,200	20/8		yes
San Diego County, CA	325	565	1,528	712	16	21	yes
San Diego, CA	100	468	1,990	944	24	21	yes
San Francisco, CA	37	146/64	1,400	900	None	21	yes
Salt Lake City, UT	16	200	330	400	24	21	yes
Seattle, WA	50	260	1,250	440	20	21	yes
Shelby County, AL	27	280	58	280	19	21	yes
Shelby County, TN	280	430	800	430	32	21	yes
Tampa, FL	80	570/132	800	570	12	21	yes
Trenton, NJ	29	87	390	669	8	18	no
Tucson, AZ	52	500/365	776	440	24	21	yes
Vineland, NJ	30	452/78	113	669	None	18	yes
Virginia Beach, VA	60	520	640	520	20	21	yes
Washington, DC	180	160	4,400	480		21	no
Winston-Salem, NC	16	432	450	432	22	21	yes
Worcester, MA	25	96	375	720	9	18	yes
Yellowstone County, MT	35	180	40	400	8	21	yes

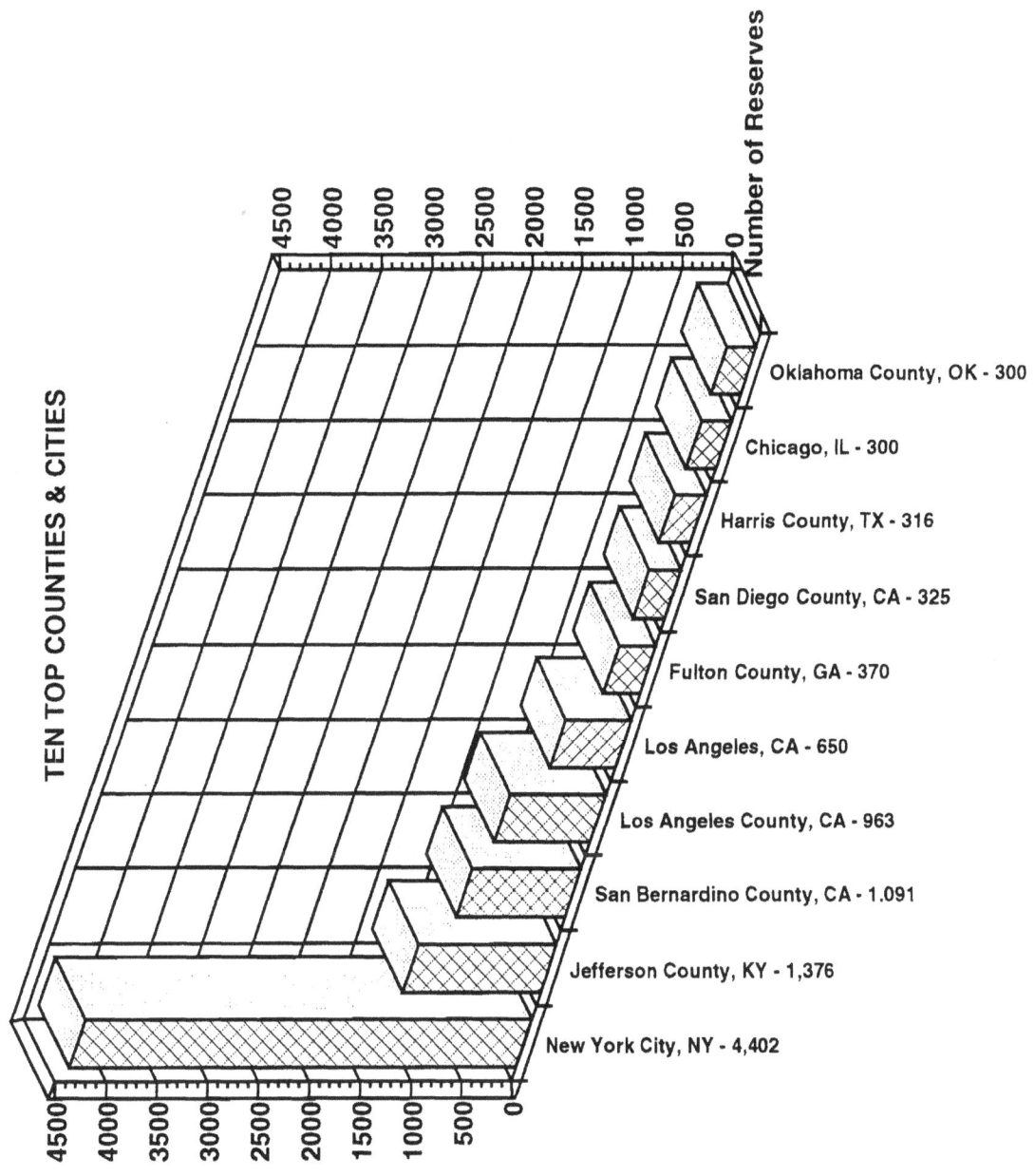

TEN TOP COUNTIES & CITIES

Number of Reserves

Oklahoma County, OK - 300

Chicago, IL - 300

Harris County, TX - 316

San Diego County, CA - 325

Fulton County, GA - 370

Los Angeles, CA - 650

Los Angeles County, CA - 963

San Bernardino County, CA - 1.091

Jefferson County, KY - 1,376

New York City, NY - 4,402

SECTION
VI

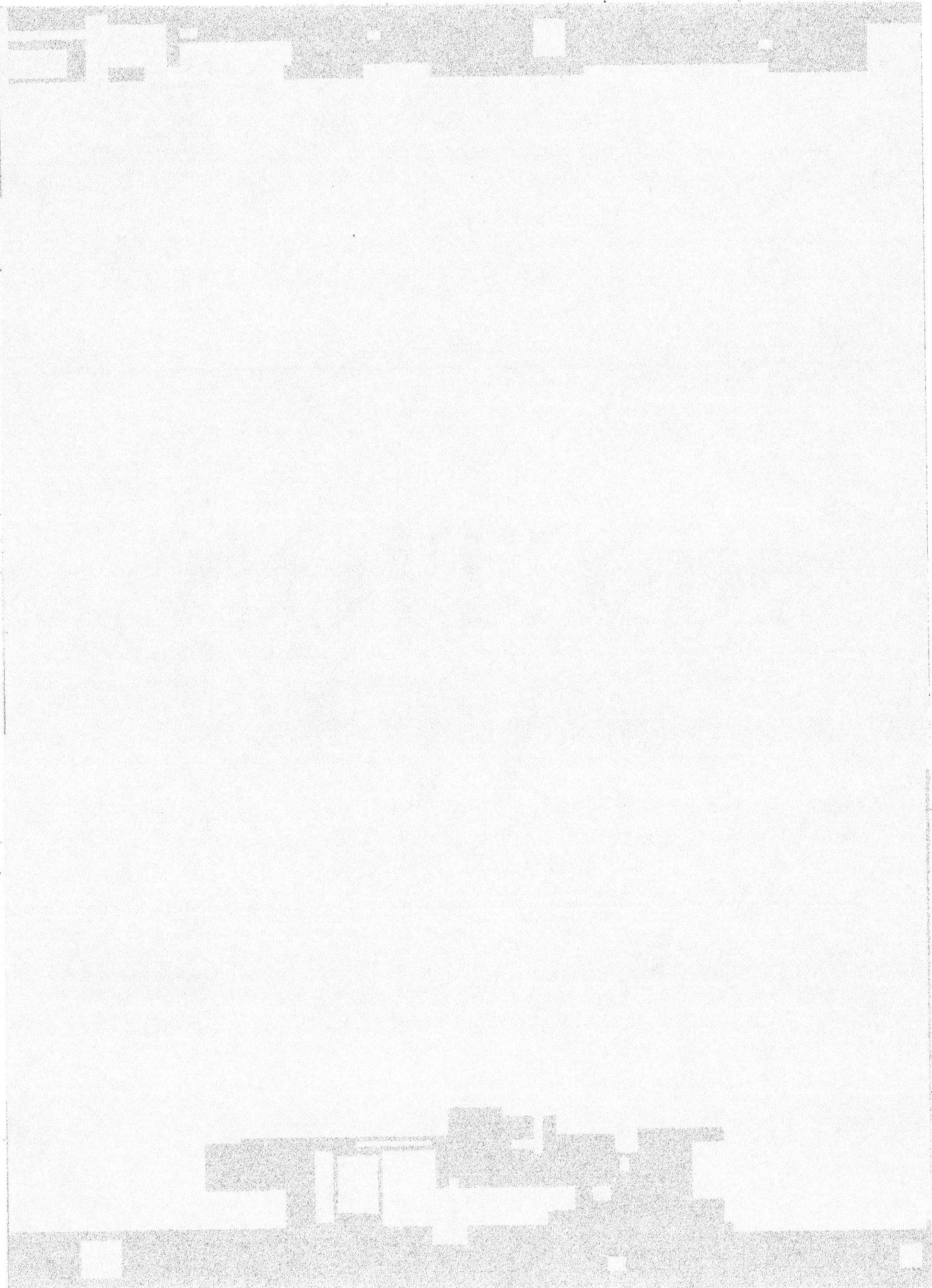

Section VI.
Cities & Counties

As previously noted in this book, local jurisdictions in most cases far exceed the minimum hourly basic training requirements set by their states. States with training and standards entities where rules concerning reserve officers were carefully laid out appeared to have city and county agencies who took an even more detailed approach with their part-time paid or volunteer law enforcers.

Additionally, it seems that by and large the states have underestimated the numbers of non-full-time personnel working for law enforcement agencies.

Surprisingly, the following major city police departments do not utilize volunteer or part-time paid personnel in a reserve capacity: Atlanta, Boston, Houston, Louisville, Nashville, Philadelphia, and Providence.

Ada County
Sheriff's Office

City of Boise, Idaho

Number of Officers
150 Full Time
20 Reserves
170 Total Officers

Minimum Training Hours Req.
390 Full Time
160 Reserve

Ada County, one of the nation's fastest growing regions, has so many people "knocking on the door," according to Jim Fox, the deputy sheriff who oversees their program, that no minimum hourly requirements need to be set for the 20 reserve deputies. He estimated that well over 2,000 hours were donated last year, not counting the eight hours spent on in-service training each month.

The department's 150 commissioned deputy sheriffs have 390 hours of police academy training and a 560 hour field training officer (FTO) program. Ada County's reserve deputies have all been trained in-house for 160 hours for two evenings a week and some Saturdays for six months during the winter. At the conclusion of the training, reserves must pass a proficiency exam, similar to that given to full-time patrolmen, for Idaho Peace Officer Training and Standards (POST) Level I. Reserve certification.

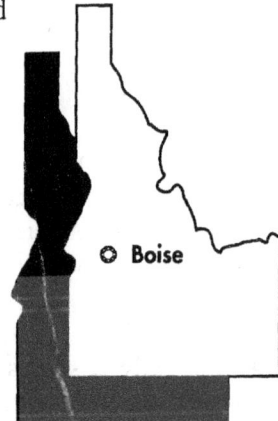

Fox pointed out that a new alternate route is available to reserves and involves a correspondence course conducted by Idaho State University in Pocatello, ID. Following the correspondence portion of the course, which has a tuition of $360, reservists attend the POST Academy in Boise for one week of practical training (shooting, driving, etc.). The proficiency exam is taken during that on-site week.

Reserve deputies are used as the second officer in a patrol car with a salaried deputy sheriff, but also do occasional solo patrol. Reserves also work foothills patrol in pairs in Ford Broncos, as well as boat patrol in the area reservoirs and in the detention center.

The Ada County Sheriff's Office furnishes all uniforms, which bear identical badges and shoulder patches and look the same as the full-timers' attire, but the reserves buy their own sidearm. The firearm may be a 4" or 6"

Contact:

Deputy Sheriff Jim Fox
Reserve Liaison
Ada County Sheriff's Office
7200 Barrister Drive
Boise, ID 83704

208/377-6500

double action Smith and Wesson or Ruger revolver. Semi-automatics may be carried provided the volunteer deputy completes an eight hour transition course. Accepted double action semi-autos are Smith and Wesson, Ruger, Glock or Sig Saur in 9mm, .40 caliber or .45 caliber.

The honing of firearms skills is taken seriously. All personnel qualify twice a year on the range. A class is held once a year on legal issues of deadly force and shoot don't shoot scenarios are annually played out realistically on a Firearms Training Systems simulator (F.A.T.S.).

The screening process imitates the full-time entry hurdles. It includes a written test, oral interview, polygraph, physical assessment and final interview with the undersheriff or administrative official of similar stature. Fox said one of their biggest problems is that reserve deputy sheriffs are routinely leaving to go full-time for their department or another law enforcement agency.

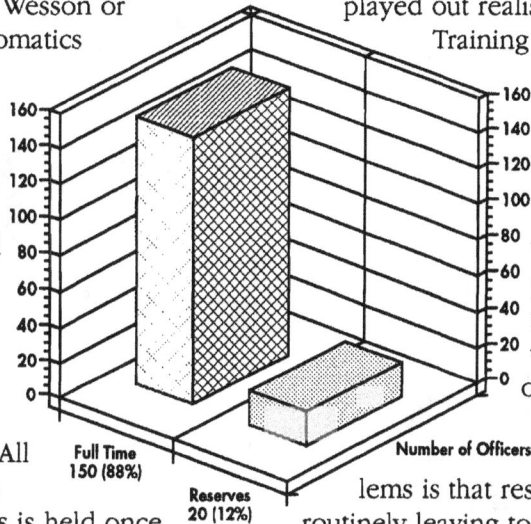

Full Time 150 (88%)

Reserves 20 (12%)

Number of Officers

Akron
Police Department

City of Akron, Ohio

The City of Akron used to invite members of the community to apply to become reserve police officers, but nowadays the 483 officer strong department limits new inductees in the program to retired full-time officers. The agency has 74 active reserves. They also have one honorary reserve officer on the roster who was shot and paralyzed in the line of duty as a reservist some years ago.

Because the reserves are former salaried officers, Sergeant Earl Wykoff, the administrative supervisor for the reserves, said the 420 hour state certification and the 1,920 hour field training officer (FTO) program have been completed already at the time of entry into the program. Finished prior to commencing full-time employment, with a minimum age of 21, is the background investigation, medical, psychological and oral interview. All that is needed to switch status from full-time to reserve is the chief's approval.

Akron ⊙

The reserve officers must work at least 16 hours a month and last year donated 15,315 hours. They must also attend two hours of monthly in-service training plus any training scheduled for the full-timers.

The uniform is paid for by the agency and is identical to that worn by the regular officers. The one difference is that the badge does say "reserve." The reserve officer must purchase the Smith and Wesson or Colt .38 revolver or Smith and Wesson 5906 9mm semi-automatic and qualify at least once a year on the chosen weapon.

The reserve police officers do everything full-time officers do except work one man patrol and traffic cars. They work on special events a great deal of the time. Other assignments include court officer, report officer and detective.

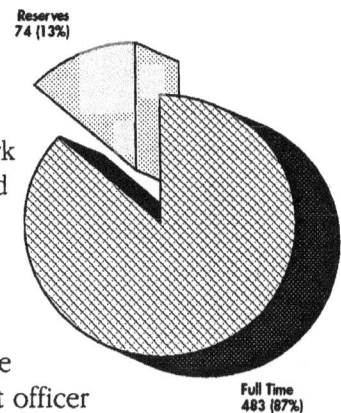

Reserves
74 (13%)

Full Time
483 (87%)

Contact:

Sergeant Earl Wykoff
Administrative Supervisor, Reserves
Traffic Bureau
Akron Police Department
217 South High Street
Akron, OH 44308

216/375-2506

Albuquerque Police Department

City of Albuquerque, New Mexico

Number of Officers	
760	Full Time
28	Reserve
788	Total Officers

Min. Training Hours Req.	
960	Full Time
308	Reserve

Officer Vic Webb, the Albuquerque Police Department's reserve coordinator, said his 28 reserve officers undergo 308 hours of pre-service academy training. The academy schedule is Tuesday and Thursday nights and all day Saturday. A subsequent 48 hour field training officer (FTO) program must be completed over six consecutive weeks. The 760 full-time officers are trained for 960 hours with a 480 hour FTO component following.

The state of New Mexico does not have a mandated training program for reserves, but Webb said his agency was working on securing state certification for their academy trained reserves.

Reserves must serve in uniform field services patrol at least eight hours a month, though Webb said

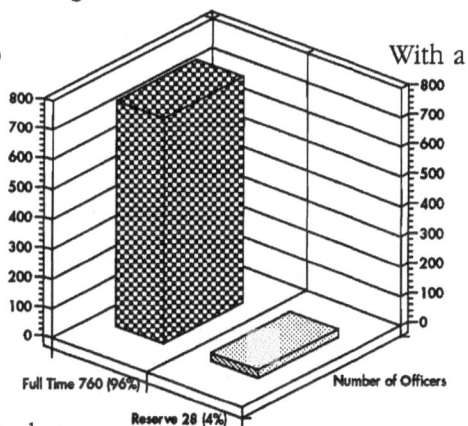

Full Time 760 (96%)
Reserve 28 (4%)
Number of Officers

most average 24 hours a month. In addition to patrol with a regular officer, they may serve their extra hours in such specialized assignments as vice, narcotics and SWAT.

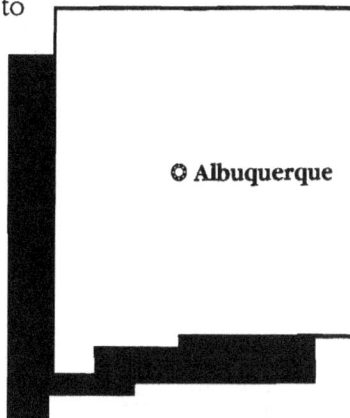

○ Albuquerque

With a minimum age of 21, reserves pass a gauntlet of obstacles including physical, psychological, written test, background investigation and oral selection committee.

Reservists in the city with a population of 500,000 pay for their uniforms (about $60 a set). Qualifying at the rate of twice annually, the reserve police officers may use a department issued .38 special revolver or they may purchase their own 9mm.

Contact:

Officer Vic Webb
Reserve Coordinator
Albuquerque Police Dept.
400 Roma, N.W.
Albuquerque, NM 87102

505/768-2200

Anchorage
Police Department

City of Anchorage, Alaska

Anchorage's reserve program, whose 60 reserve officers make up the lion's share of the Alaska Police Standards Council's (APSC) estimated 110 reserves in the state, is under the stewardship of reserve captain Mel Kalkowski. Utilizing snow machines sometimes to accomplish their mission, the reserve officers, minimum age of 21, are trained for 300 hours over the course of four months. A 240 hour field training officer (FTO) program follows. The 300 full-time officers attend the police academy for 784 hours and complete a 640 hour FTO program.

"Our reserves in calendar year 1992 donated 6,830 hours," beamed a proud Kalkowski who works as a full-time university relations director. He explained

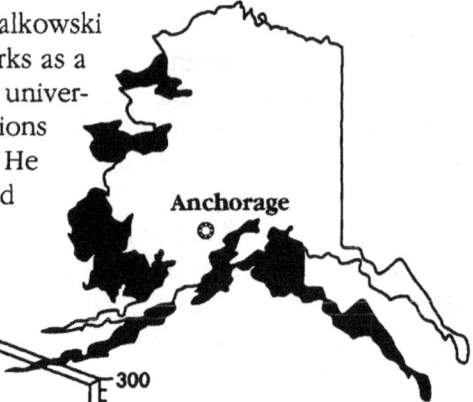

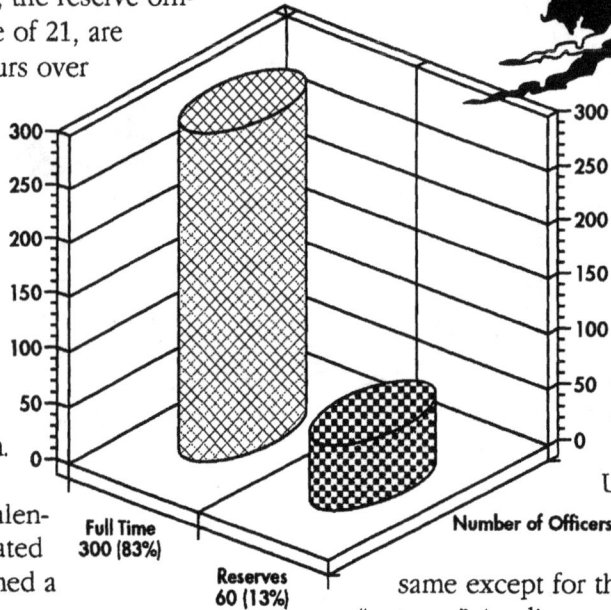

Anchorage

Full Time
300 (83%)

Reserves
60 (13%)

Number of Officers

that the reserve officers patrol with a regular officer and must work a minimum of 14 hours per month (ten hours on patrol plus four hours of in-service training).

Uniforms and firearms are provided by the city. The uniforms are the same except for the badge which says "reserve." Applicants are subjected to a polygraph, physical agility test, written exam, oral interview and background investigation.

Contact:

Res. Capt. Mel Kalkowski
Anchorage Police Department
4501 South Bragaw Street
Anchorage, AK 99507-1599

907/786-8500

Bloomfield Police Department

City of Bloomfield, New Jersey

Number of Officers	
110	Full Time
20	Reserves
130	Total Officers

Minimum Training Hours Req.	
669	Full Time
157	Reserve

Supervisory auxiliary officers in the 20 auxiliary officer strong Bloomfield program have recently switched from Smith and Wesson Model 10 .38 revolvers to Glock 9mm Model 19 semi-automatics. Auxiliary Sergeant William Vloyanetes, a Doppler radar operator who is also a certified instructor for firearms and Monadnock PR-24 sidehandle police baton, said the remaining patrolmen will be making the transition as funds become available for the agency to purchase additional Glocks.

Both Vloyanetes and Auxiliary Lieutenant Albert G. Lurker, the auxiliary officer in charge, said that their auxiliaries receive a total of 157 hours of pre-service training. The training is broken up into two components: the 77 hour Essex County Auxiliary Police Academy and an 80 hour firearms course held in a neighboring county police academy.

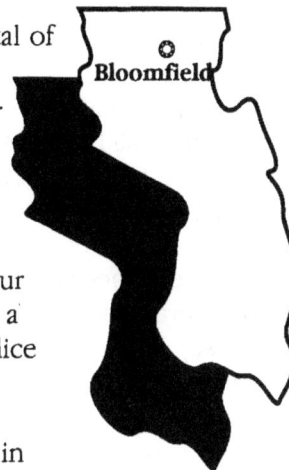

While full-time officers in New Jersey get 669 average hours of training, Bloomfield's auxiliary officers attend the Essex County Auxiliary Police Academy held at the Essex County Police Academy in Cedar Grove. The 77 hour course is held on Tuesday and Thursday nights for three months. It exceeds the 42 hour minimum guidelines set by the New Jersey State Police/Office of Emergency Management, the

Contact:

Auxiliary Lieutenant Albert G. Lurker, OIC
or
Auxiliary Sergeant William Vloyanetes
Bloomfield Police Department
Law Enforcement Building
1 Municipal Plaza
Bloomfield, NJ 07003

201 580-4118

governmental body which oversees auxiliary officer standards in the Garden State.

Following academy graduation, the officers are sent to an 80 hour basic firearms course at the Passaic County Police Academy in Wayne Township. The 80 hours exceeds the 40 hour basic firearms curriculum set by the New Jersey Police Training Commission (PTC). The firearms course is held Monday and Tuesday evenings and all day Saturday for five weeks.

The auxiliary police officer field training officer (FTO) program consists of at least two nights a week (four hours a night) for three months with a supervisor. The total for the FTO program is 96 hours. The normal duty minimum matches the eight hours set by the state, however most officers surpass it. Lurker said the auxiliary officers donated 3,000 basic duty hours last year, not counting special events and emergency call-ins.

In-service training is scheduled for four hours a month and the volunteer officers qualify on their sidearm and shotgun two times a year on day and night fire. Vloyanetes, the firearms instructor, said the auxiliaries train monthly on the firearms range.

The department supplies the weapons, equip-ment and uniforms. Badges and shoulder patches say "auxiliary." Auxiliary patrolmen wear light blue shirts and auxiliary superiors wear gray shirts. Full-time patrolmen are garbed in navy blue shirts and regular supervisors are in white shirts.

Auxiliaries patrol either with another auxiliary or a regular officer. They also conduct foot patrols in the downtown business district and at special events for traffic and crowd control. Auxiliaries additionally work fires and other emergency call-in situations.

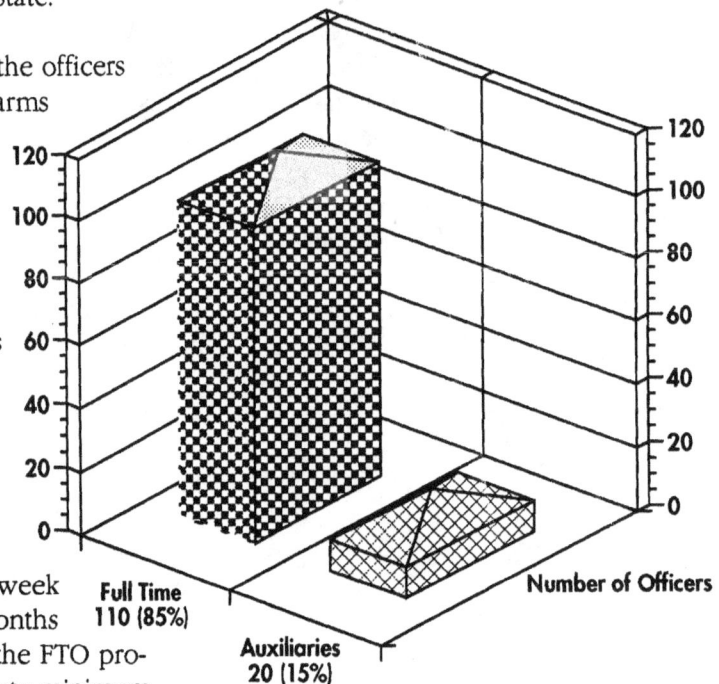

Full Time
110 (85%)

Auxiliaries
20 (15%)

Number of Officers

Broward County Sheriff's Office

City of Fort Lauderdale, Florida

Number of Officers
900 Full Time
25 Reserve
925 Total Officers

Minimum Training Hours Req.
597 Full Time
597 Reserves

Under the leadership of outgoing Sheriff Nick Navarro, known for his TV appearances on such shows as "COPS," and incoming Sheriff Ron Cochran, the Broward County Sheriff's reserve deputy program has become a sophisticated component of South Florida's crime fighting and police service team. Reserve Captain Jeff Nelson heads a committed group of 25 reserves who donated 14,000 hours in 1992. The minimum monthly service requirement is sixteen hours with the reserve deputy sheriffs averaging 45 hours each.

Trained to the tune of 597 hours over the course of six months (Monday through Friday evenings and some Saturdays), thereby exceeding the state's 520 hour minimum for certified officers, the reserves also undergo an intensive 360 hour field training officer (FTO) program (within one year). The FTO system is comprised of 15 FTO stints on each of the three shifts. The reserves' requirement to complete a 240 hour FTO program was raised to 360 hours when the regular deputies had their standards elevated.

Fort Lauderdale ⊙

Annual in-service training comes in at 48 hours. The reserves must also qualify a minimum of four times a year with their sidearm and once a year with their shotgun.

Nelson's reserves must buy all leather and weapons with Broward supplying the uniform, badge and ID card. The five point star badge, ID card and patch are identical to those utilized by the full-time deputies with no mention of the volunteers reserve status.

Getting into this crack team of reservists is tough. The selection and training requirements for reserves are indistinguishable from those applied to the regular deputy sheriffs. Nelson, a 17 year veteran of the Broward County

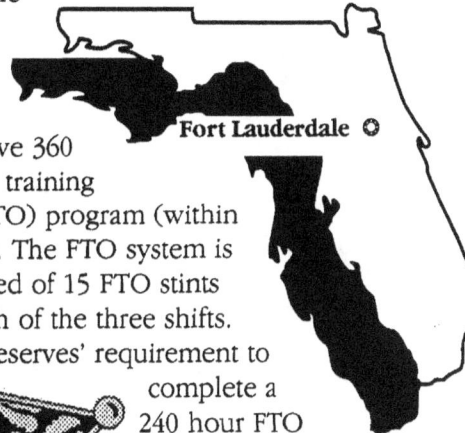

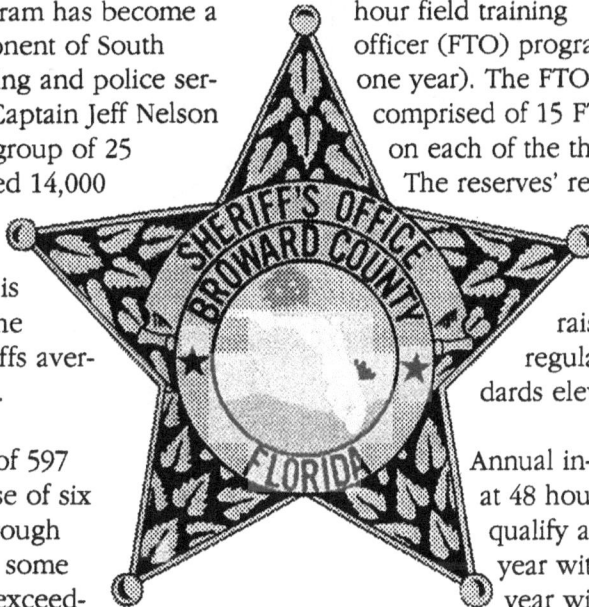

Contact:

Reserve Captain Jeff Nelson
Broward County Sheriff's Office
P.O. Box 9507
Fort Lauderdale, Fl 33310

305/797-0994

hopefuls were chosen to go to the academy during the last selection period. The minimum age is 19 and the candidate must pass a polygraph, written test, physical agility test, urinalysis and eight hour psychological.

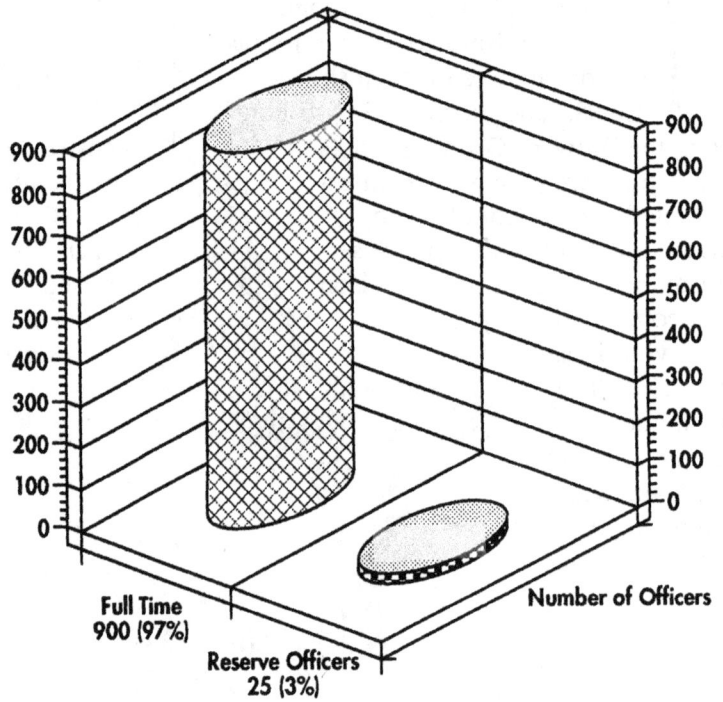

900
800
700
600
500
400
300
200
100
0

900
800
700
600
500
400
300
200
100
0

Full Time
900 (97%)

Reserve Officers
25 (3%)

Number of Officers

Burlington Police Department

City of Burlington, New Jersey

Number of Officers
31 Full Time
11 Reserves
42 Total Officers

Minimum Training Hours Req.
669 Full Time
452 special Class II.
92 special Class I.

The 11 reserves in the City of Burlington, who are technically special law enforcement officers (SLEOs), are utilized extensively by the 31 full-time officer-strong police department. Lieutenant Bryon K. Marshall, the administrative lieutenant who oversees the reserve officer program, which worked in excess of 3,000 hours last year far surpassing the four hour monthly minimum, said they patrol in a police unit with either another reserve or a regular officer. Other duties involve patrolling the city's promenade park and crowd and traffic control at special events.

Four of the 11 reserve officers are Class II. specials trained at 452 average hours. They carry Smith and Wesson .38 revolvers, although Marshall indicated that a transition to Smith and Wesson 6906 9mm semi-automatics will happen soon.

The remaining seven officers are Class I. SLEOs who have 78 average hours of training. The Burlington County Police Academy, where most of the reserves get state certified as Class I. special officers, tallies in at 92 hours of training.

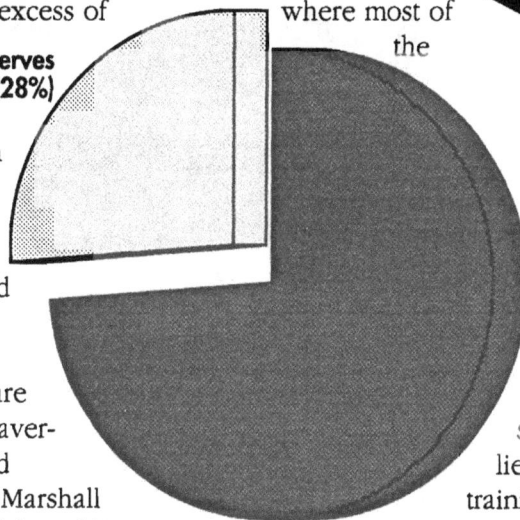

Reserves 11 (28%)

Full Time 31 (74%)

Burlington ○

The reserve field training officer (FTO) program comes in at 40 hours with a regular and an additional 40 hours with a senior reservist. Qualification with the agency provided firearm is two times a year with both day and night fire. The department also pays for the identical uniform which has a badge and shoulder patch that says "reserve."

Marshall said he has quite a few applicants waiting for the opportunity to become City of Burlington reserve

Contact:

Lieutenant Bryon K. Marshall
Administrative Lieutenant
City of Burlington Police Department
437 High Street
Burlington, NJ 08016

609/386-0262

police officers. The entry process, for persons 18 and over, mirrors that utilized for the full-timers and includes background investigation, psychological, physical and drug screening.

Cass County Sheriff's Office

City of Fargo, North Dakota

Number of Officers
75 Full Time
22 Reserve
97 Total Officers

Minimum Training Hours Req.
360 Full Time
360 Reserve

According to Cass County's Kim D. Murphy, the deputy sheriff who oversees the reserve deputy program, their sworn volunteers receive North Dakota state certification via their training and label as part-time officers. All of the 75 full-time and 22 volunteer reserves get 360 hours of basic police training and a 100 hour field training officer (FTO) program. The reserves attend evening classes at night for six months.

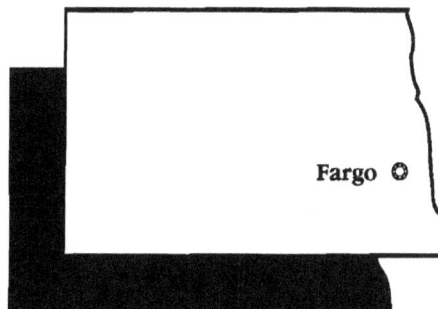

Fargo ⊙

The department provides the identical uniform and badge, although the reserve has a choice of accepting the issued Smith and Wesson .357 Model 66 firearm or purchasing his own. Qualification of the firearm takes place four times a year and the deputies undergo four hours of monthly in-service training.

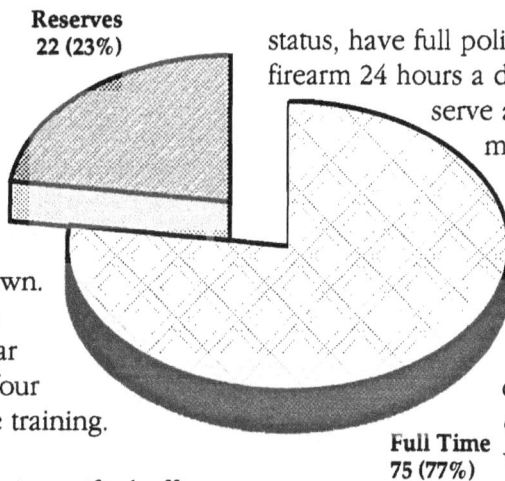

Reserves
22 (23%)

Full Time
75 (77%)

The reserves, because of their certified officer status, have full police powers and carry their firearm 24 hours a day on and off duty. They serve at least 16 hours per month in an unlimited capacity. Their assignments include solo patrol, patrol as a second deputy, special events (such as dances), warrants, court security and detectives. The reserve deputy sheriffs also work water patrol on the Red River.

Applicants may be 18, although Murphy said they prefer 21 and older. The two step selection process begins with a group orientation and 15 minute private interview, along with a psychological and physical. Step two involves a much more indepth, hour long interview before a board of six people.

Contact:

Deputy Sheriff Kim D. Murphy
Cass County Sheriff's Office
P.O. Box 488
Fargo, ND 58107

701/241-5800, Extension 3544

Charlotte
Police Department

City of Charlotte, North Carolina

Number of Officers	
900	Full Time
50	Reserves
950	Total Officers

Minimum Training Hours Req.	
640	Full Time
432	Reserve

The 50 police reserves in Charlotte are responsible for getting their own basic academy training through local community colleges such as Mitchell Community College. All programs are full law enforcement certification courses and are at least 432 hours in length.

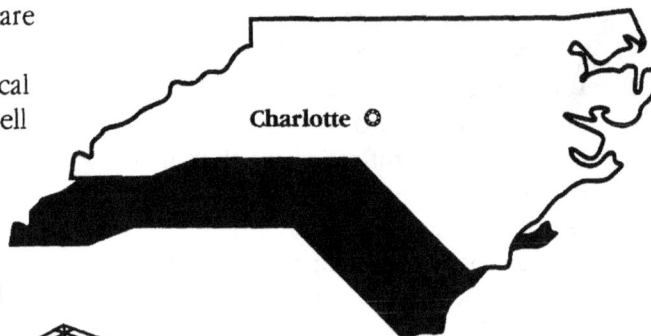

Charlotte ○

The 900 full-time police officers have a 640 hour academy and both classifications of officers go through a 960 hour field training officer (FTO) program. Reserves go to all in-service training that the regulars attend. Captain H.G. Dozier said that he is reviewing the policy to see if the reserve officers can be excused from some sessions due to their time constraints.

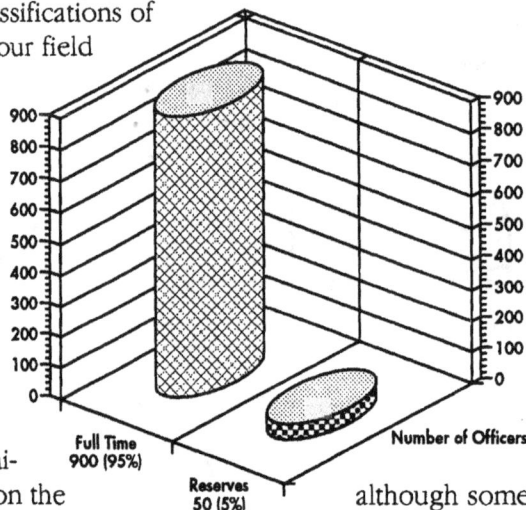

Full Time 900 (95%)

Reserves 50 (5%)

Number of Officers

Model 4046 .40 caliber semi-automatic firearm. Day and night fire qualification takes place once a year.

Reserves must serve at least 15 hours a month and donated 14,400 hours last year. They work mostly in patrol, although some work in vice and other specialized areas. They must be 21 or older and pass a background investigation, polygraph, drug screening and oral review board in order to be sworn in as a reserve police officer.

The agency supplies the uniform which says "reserve" on the badge and shoulder patch. The department also furnishes the Smith and Wesson

Contact:

Captain H.G. Dozier
Charlotte Police Department
825 East 4th Street
Charlotte, NC 28202

704/336-2404

Chicago Police Department

City of Chicago, Illinois

Number of Officers	
12,000	Full Time
300	Auxiliary
12,300 Total Officers	

Minimum Training Hours Req.	
720	Full Time
16	Auxiliary

Chicago, with over 12,000 full-time officers trained for 720 hours, follows the old, civil defense version of volunteers in uniform. Called "auxiliary aides," the Windy City's 300 dedicated men and women, with sixteen hours of training over two consecutive Saturdays, do not have police powers, do not carry firearms, and assist at parades and the like. For many years the auxiliary aides did not wear a uniform and were confined to duties inside the stationhouses to duties not requiring contact with the general public. The auxiliaries must be 21 years of age or older and serve at least 16 hours per month.

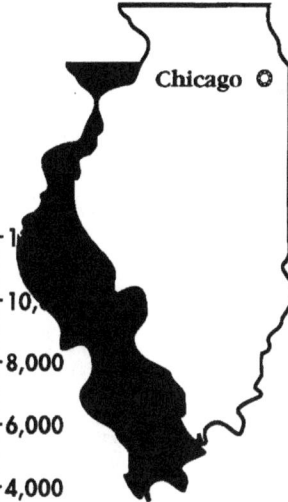

Chicago ○

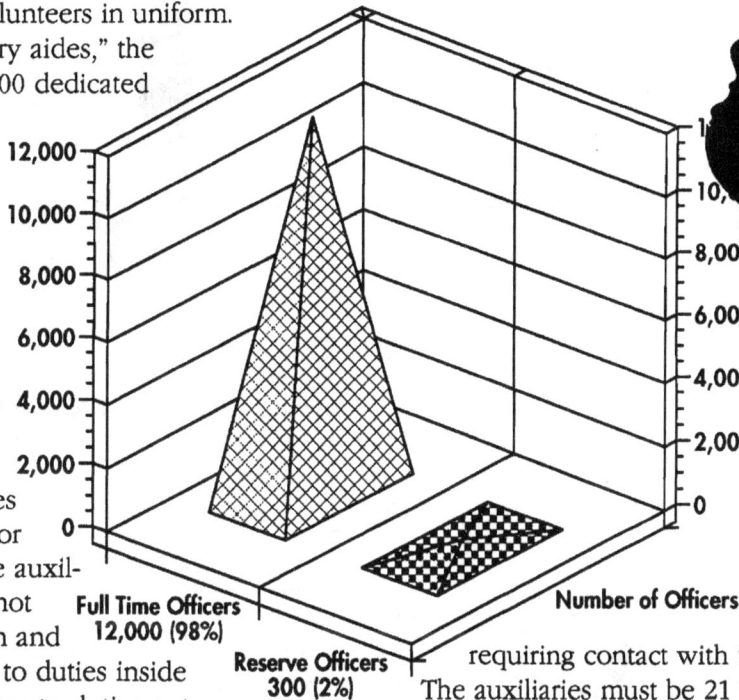

Full Time Officers
12,000 (98%)

Reserve Officers
300 (2%)

Number of Officers

Contact:

Coordinator
Special Events Section
Chicago Police Department
1121 South State Street
Chicago, IL 60605

312/747-6609

Columbus
Police Department

City of Columbus, Ohio

Founded in 1951, the Columbus Police reserve officer program has 100 officers who are fully certified with 490 hours of basic police training and a 40 hour field training officer (FTO) program. The 1,400 regular officers have 960 hours of training and a 320 hour FTO program.

Officer Gary P. Barth, who oversees the reserves from his office at the Columbus Police Training Academy, said the training exceeds state minimums and attracts other agencies from the suburbs of the city. The driver training, for example, exceeds the 20 hour state minimum by 40 hours for a total of 60 hours. The training academy runs for four hours on Monday through Thursday nights and several eight hour Saturdays for nine months.

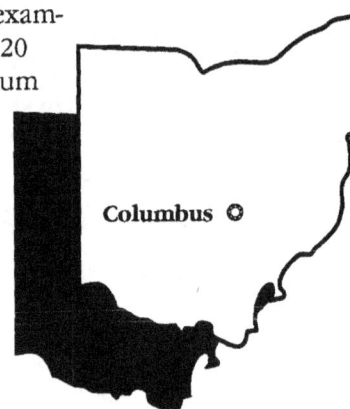

Columbus ○

The program, which saw a reserve officer killed in 1969 while assisting at an armed robbery, has a demanding screening process which mirrors the full-timers with the exception that the civil service test is waived for reserves slots. Barth said he goes through 250 people to come up with a 50 person class. Hopeful applicants, minimum age of 21, go through a background investigation, health investigation, oral board and polygraph.

The uniform and body armor is supplied by the police department. The only difference manifests itself on the badge which says "reserve." They used to have a different patch, but the department eliminated it for officer safety reasons. The firearms, also agency furnished, are being switched from revolver to semi-automatic and qualification takes place four times a year, with general in-service training happening four hours a month.

Contact:

Officer Gary P. Barth
Training Academy
Columbus Police Department
2609 McKinley Avenue
Columbus, OH 43204

614/645-4800

Reservists find themselves serving as a second officer on patrol and at special civic functions such as parades. Reserve police officers must donate a minimum of 8 hours a month and not more than 32 hours per week. Barth explained that this was done to prevent the reserve from getting exhausted and causing his full-time occupation to suffer. Last year, Columbus reserves donated 200,000 hours. Retirement badges are awarded to reserves who leave after ten years of service or more.

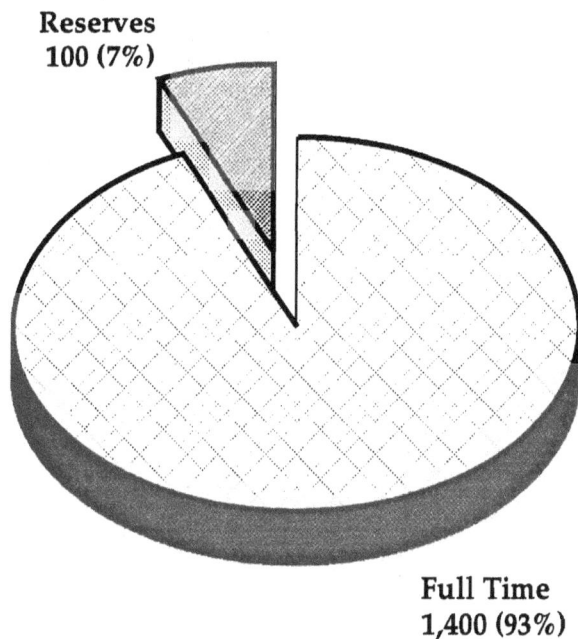

Reserves
100 (7%)

Full Time
1,400 (93%)

Dade County Police Department

City of Miami, Florida

Number of Officers
2,800 Full Time
  50 Reserves
2,850 Total Officers

Minimum Training Hours Req.
700 Full Time
700 Reserve

The Metropolitan Dade County Police Department's reserve program was modeled after Los Angeles' successful approach. Eschewing the use of ranks, Metro Dade expects its 50 reserve officers and 2,800 full-time officers to exceed the state 520 hour certified officer requirement and reach the 700 hours required by all officers attending the Dade County Police Academy.

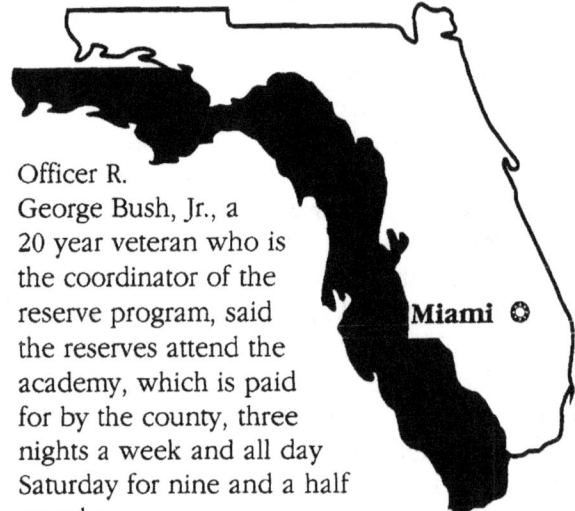

Officer R. George Bush, Jr., a 20 year veteran who is the coordinator of the reserve program, said the reserves attend the academy, which is paid for by the county, three nights a week and all day Saturday for nine and a half months.

**Reserve Officers
50 (2%)**

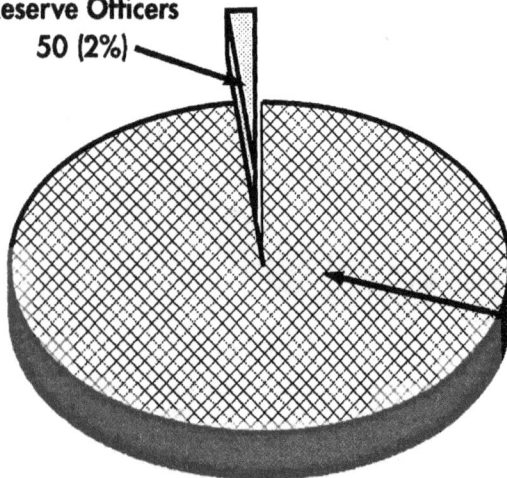

2,800 (98%) Full Time Officers

Miami ⊙

The reservists have a minimum commitment of 16 hours a month. With a rigorous in-service training regime, the obligation averages out at 20 hours per month. The reserve officers, who have full police powers and may carry a firearm, provided by the department, 24 hours a day, re-qualify once a year. Other mandatory annual in-service training topics include CPR, first responder, and PR-24 side handle baton.

Dade County is aiming for a total strength of 125 reserve officers and requires successful applicants to be 19 years of age or older, and pass the same entrance hurdles as full-timers - polygraph, urinalysis, etc.

Contact:

Officer R. George Bush, Jr.
Reserve Program Coordinator
Metro Dade County Police Department
9105 N.W. 25th Street, Suite 3102
Miami, FL 33172

305/471-1887

Residents of the 27 municipalities within Dade County barely notice the presence of the reserves as they are uniformed the same as the full-time officers. The volunteer law enforcers work patrol before being eligible to transfer to special branches such as the crime lab, special investigations division, the training bureau, community relations, marine patrol, or aviation.

Dallas
Police Department

City of Dallas, Texas

Number of Officers
3,200 Full Time
67 Reserves
3,267 Total Officers

Minimum Training Hours Req.
1,040 Full Time
768 Reserve

In existence since 1953, the Dallas Police Reserve Battalion currently has 67 armed reserve officers. According to Lieutenant Terry Hauch, the reserve coordinator, the volunteers ride primarily in uniform patrol with a regular officer during their 16 hours per month of minimum service. The reservists donated 25,000 hours in 1992.

Instructed to the tune of 768 hours of pre-service academy training and 120 hours of field training, each of the reserves receive a Texas basic peace officers certification. The academy is held for 16 hours a week on Tuesday and Thursday nights and all day Saturday for ten months. The department's 3,200 full-timers are trained for 26 weeks (1,040 hours) and undergo a three month (480 hour) FTO program.

Reserves must be at least 21 years of age and pass a physical with urinalysis (minus physical agility test), poly-

◎ Dallas

Training Required

Number
Full Time 3,200 (98%)
Reserve 67 (2%)

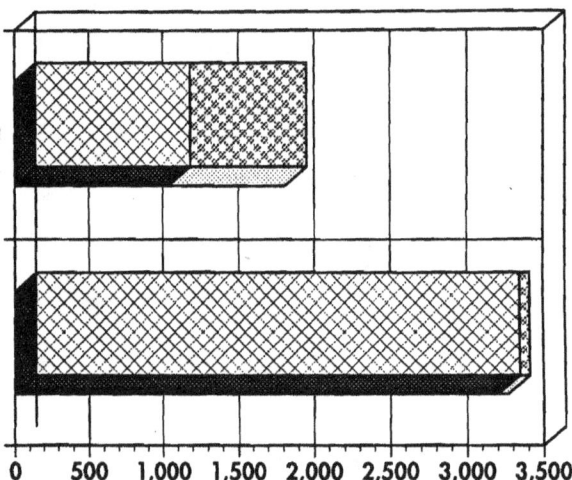

0   500   1,000 1,500 2,000 2,500 3,000 3,500

☒ Full Time Officers
☒ Reserve Officers

Contact:

Lieutenant Terry Hauch
Reserve Coordinator
Dallas Police Department
3112 Canton Street, Room 1A
Dallas, TX 75226-1687

214/670-4548

graph, psychological, background and oral interview board.

The uniform and Sig 226 firearm (which the reserves must requalify on twice a year) is provided by the department. The reserve officers' badge differs slightly from the full-time officers' with the placement of the word "reserve" on them. The patch used to indicate reserve also but was changed some time back to match the regular shoulder patch.

Dearborn Police Department

City of Dearborn, Michigan

Dearborn's program, authorized by City Ordinance No. 68-1600 on June 27, 1968, finds their 72 volunteer reserve officers, minimum age of 21, utilized in a variety of different activities. Six different volunteer details are available to reserve officers. They are: uniform patrol with a regular officer, Freeway patrol with two reserves, uniform patrol with two reserves, inclement weather patrol in marked unit, plainclothes surveillance with two reserves and house checks with two uniformed reserves.

The reserve officers in Dearborn have been heavily involved in dignitary security details for the President and Nelson Mandella. Reserves are expected to serve at least 40 hours per year, not counting classroom and range training activities. They must complete a 20 hour FTO program with different senior reservists.

Corporal Douglas R. Laurain, the reserve and training officer for the 190 full-time officer department, said his reserves, who are uniformed like the full-timers, save for the badge which states "reserve," undergo training at Schoolcraft College's 100 hour Police Reserve Officer Training Program in Livonia, MI. Full-timers are trained for 545 hours.

The $170 tuition for the school is paid for by reserve officer candidate with reimbursement by the city conditional on successful completion of the school and subsequent probationary period. Also paid for is the officer's uniform and initial leather gear, although cleaning and maintenance is the responsibility of the individual officer. Many of the reserves purchase their own $400 Motorola radios.

Reserves purchase their own handguns, participate in monthly range training, and must qualify twice a year. The department is in transition from the Smith & Wesson .357 Model 66 to the Sig Saur 9mm which some reserves are carrying already.

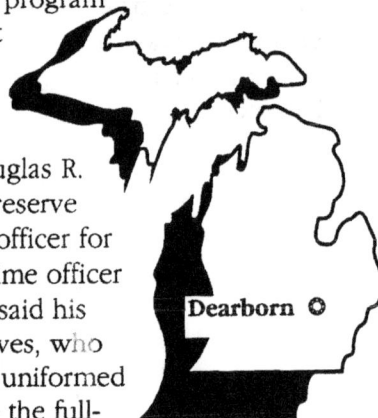

Contact:

Corporal Douglas R. Laurain
Reserve Coordinator
Dearborn Police Department
16099 Michigan Avenue
Dearborn, MI 48126

313/943-2117

The unit, which includes a lawyer and quite a few Ford Motor Company engineers and managers, will be celebrating it's 25th anniversary of protecting the 90,000 population, 25 square mile town on May 22, 1993.

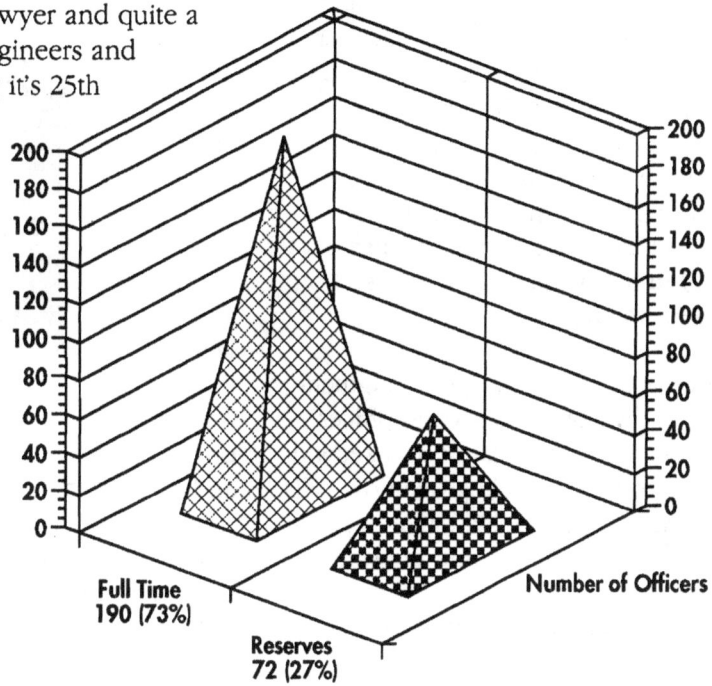

Full Time
190 (73%)

Reserves
72 (27%)

Number of Officers

Denver Police Department

City of Denver, Colorado

Number of Officers	
1,380	Full Time
44	Reserves
1,424	Total Officers

Minimum Training Hours Req.	
800	Full Time
480	Reserve

Not counting in-service training time, reserve officers with the Denver Police Department are required to donate at least 26 hours each month. "At least one eight hour shift a month is spent on special events such as Bronco games and Nuggets games," said Stephen Palka, the technician (uniformed equivalent to a detective) in the special operations section who oversees the reserves.

The rest of the time may be spent "augmenting the patrol division" as a second officer with a regular in a district car or as a second reserve in a scout car handling overflow calls for the city with a metropolitan area population of 1,000,000 people. During the summer, May through September, reserves work enforcement units in the city parks. He said that the total service for "1991 was 16,240 manpower hours."

All reserve police officers in Denver are trained past the top tier Classification I. 358 hour level set by Colorado Peace Officer Standards and Training. Reservists, who must be 21 or older, undergo 480 hours of training at the Denver Police Academy

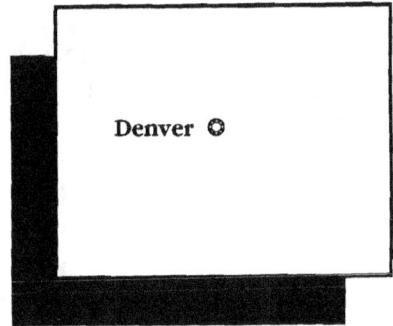

on Tuesday, Wednesday and Thursday nights and every other Saturday for seven months. In-service training runs at least four hours per quarter. The field training officer (FTO) program lasts 40 hours. Full-timers get 800 hours of training and a 480 hour FTO program.

"We provide about 50% of the uniform," said Palka who pointed out that the department attempts to give them all the clothing items out of uniform supply. Reserves buy their leather, shoes, body armor and the like. They pick from the approved .45 or 9 mm semi-automatic

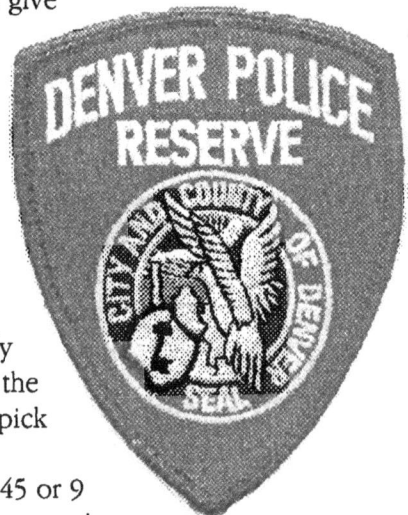

Contact:

Technician Stephen Palka
Special Operations Section
Denver Police Department
1390 Decatur Street
Denver, CO 80204

303/640-2881

firearm list and must purchase the weapon themselves. The Denver Police Department did away with revolvers four years ago and it was the reserve officers who first toted the semi-automatics.

Screening for the reserves mirrors the regular department. Following an initial phone interview, the interested party is invited to take a written test, oral board, physical fitness test, polygraph, background investigation, psychological evaluation and medical examination.

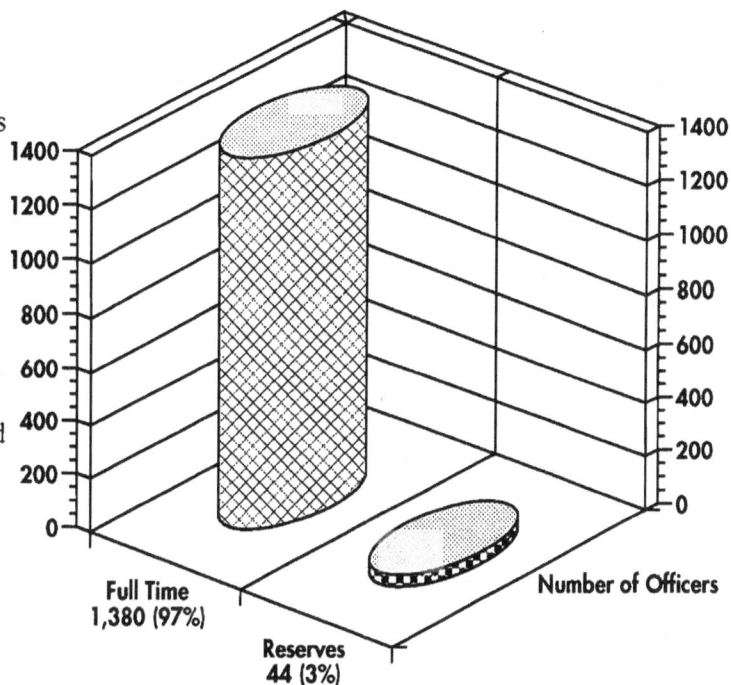

Full Time
1,380 (97%)

Reserves
44 (3%)

Number of Officers

Des Moines Police Department

City of Des Moines, Iowa

Number of Officers	
356	Full Time
19	Reserves
375	Total Officers

Minimum Training Hours Req.	
880	Full Time
130	Reserve

While Iowa state law requires 30 hours of pre-service training with an additional 150 within four years, the Des Moines Police Department mandates that their reserves have 130 hours before they even hit the streets. Speaking from his office at the police academy, Lieutenant Neil Leighter said the training takes place over the course of six months for one night a week from 6:00 PM to 10:00 PM and Saturdays from 8:00 AM to 4:00 PM. Saturday training covers firearms, PR-24 and a twelve hour defensive driving course which includes a skid pad.

In-service training takes place during a twelve hour period once a year. All officers qualify on one of four different 9mm model of firearms (Beretta, Glock, Sig Saur or Smith & Wesson) twice a year and reserves purchase their own weapon. Uniforms are provided by the agency with the exception of the shoes. The uniform is the same color with "reserve" appearing over the shoulder patch and on the badge.

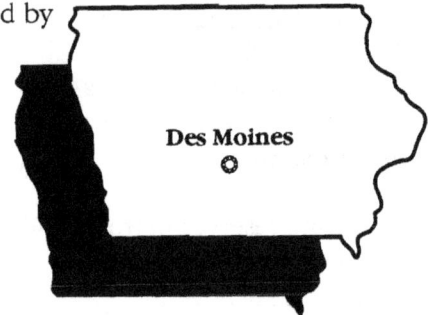

The 19 reserve officers, who must serve a minimum of 20 hours per month, supplement the full-time force of 356 by riding as a second man in the uniform division. The regulars undergo 880 hours of training at the academy and a 240 hour field training officer (FTO) program.

Reserves must be at least 21 years old and are processed in the same manner, except for a physical agility test, as full-time officers. The process includes background investigation, polygraph, MPI, physical, drug screening, psychological and written test.

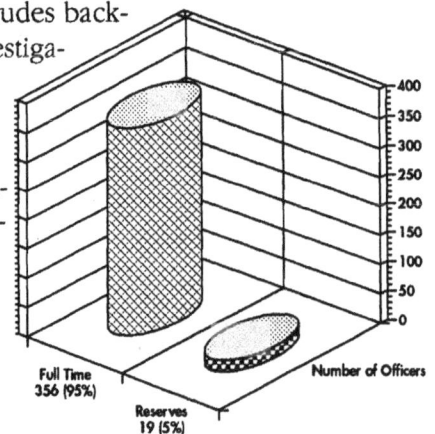

Des Moines

Contact:

Lt. Neil Leighter
Police Academy
Des Moines Police Dept.
433 S.E. Army Post Road
Des Moines, IA 50315

515/242-2964

Full Time 356 (95%)
Reserves 19 (5%)
Number of Officers

Douglas County Sheriff's Office

City of Omaha, Nebraska

Number of Officers
100 Full Time
45 Reserve
145 Total Officers

Minimum Training Hours Req.
500 Full Time
134 Reserve

To get on the department, newly accepted volunteer deputies with the Douglas County Sheriff's Office have to travel from Omaha and stay nine consecutive days at the Nebraska Law Enforcement Training Center in Grand Island. They also are required to come back one additional weekend for their firearms training in order to earn their Nebraska certification as a 134 hour trained reserve officer.

Douglas County's 100 full-time deputy sheriffs have 500 hours of academy training at Grand Island and complete a 320 hour field training officer (FTO) program. The 45 reserves are not restricted and are used in patrol, court security, traffic and criminal investigations.

The badge number for reserves differs slightly on the identical uniform which is purchased by the reserve deputy. The Smith and Wesson 9mm firearm is also bought by the reserve and qualification is held three times a year. Outfitting the reserve deputy sheriff costs around $1,000.

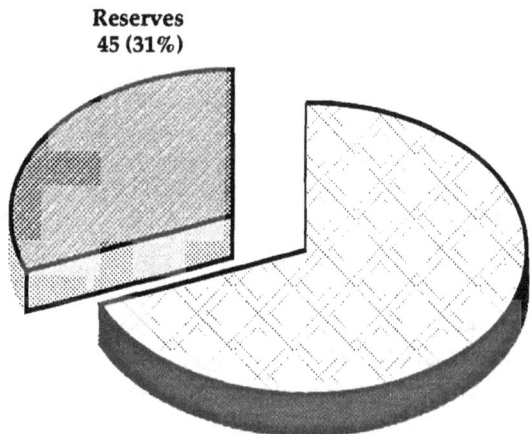

Three monthly hours of in-service training is held for the reserves who must serve at least eight hours a month. A criminal records and background check, drug analysis, polygraph, psychological and interview are conducted on all deputy sheriff candidates.

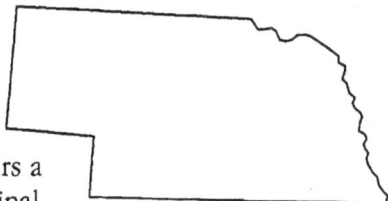

Reserves
45 (31%)

Full Time
100 (69%)

Contact:

Captain Robert R.J. Tramp
Administrative Services Bureau
Douglas County Sheriff's Office
225 North 115th Street
Omaha, NE 68154

402/444-6026

Durham Police Department

City of Durham, North Carolina

Number of Officers
380 Full Time
50 Reserves
430 Total Officers

Minimum Training Hours Req.
500 Full Time
500 Reserve

Both the 380 full-time officers and 50 reserve officers in Durham are trained past the 432 hour North Carolina state imposed minimum for 500 hours. The regular officers complete a 480 hour field training officer (FTO) program, while the reserves serve a minimum of 16 hours a month for six months (96 hours total) with a full-time officer FTO. Reserves normally have an eight hour monthly service minimum.

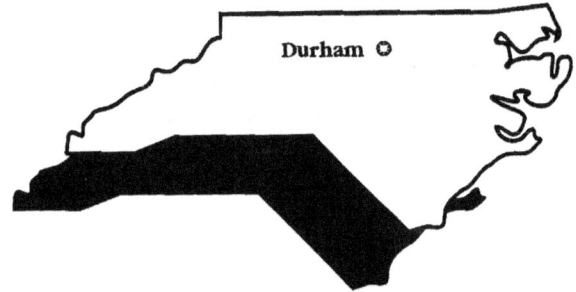

Durham ○

Sergeant N.S. Beck, the coordinator of the reserves, said the academy is held three nights a week and some Saturdays for seven months. Reserves must qualify day and night fire on the agency provided Smith and Wesson .45 sidearm and a shotgun two times a year.

Beck said the reserves donated 8,000 hours last year and saved the city a quarter of a million dollars. Among the tasks taken on by the volunteer officers are special events, multi-county drug raids, warrant service and patrolling as a second officer. Experienced reserves patrol solo.

The uniform is paid for by the Durham Police Department. A rocker underneath the shoulder patch says "reserve," as does the badge.

Contact:

Sergeant N.S. Beck
Coordinator, Reserves
Durham Police Department
505 West Chapel Hill Street
Durham, NC 27701

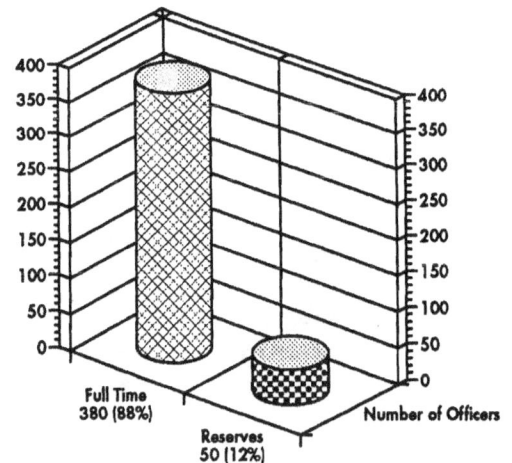

919/560-4314

Full Time 380 (88%)
Reserves 50 (12%)
Number of Officers

Essex County Sheriff's Office

City of Newark, New Jersey

The 28 volunteers of the Essex County Sheriff's Office, with their gold five pointed deputy sheriff badges, occupy a unique place in the Garden State's law enforcement landscape. Based in New Jersey's largest city, the deputies patrol a 127.44 square mile county populated by 778,206 people. In addition to a 6,000 acre county parks patrol, their county beat encompassing 23 municipalities includes upscale suburban enclaves such as Millburn/Short Hills and Livingston, as well as the urban environments of Newark, East Orange and Irvington.

Essex County Sheriff Armando B. Fontoura, who runs the state's largest sheriff's office with 500 full-timers, said his deputy sheriffs volunteer their time and are certified by New Jersey's Police Training Commission (PTC). They have police powers and carry Smith and Wesson 9mm 6906 semi-automatic firearms. "They patrol the county roads and highways and handle crowd control at concerts and other events," said Fontoura, a former City of Newark Police captain and an FBI National Academy graduate. He added that the non-compensated deputies pay approximately $1,000 for their uniforms and equipment.

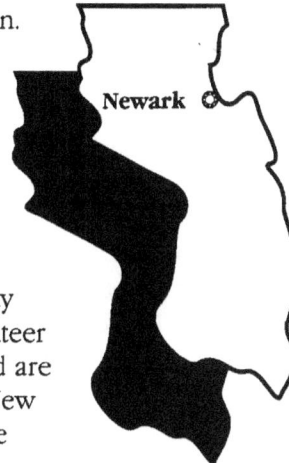

Director Eric A. Mayer, the head of the deputy sheriffs division, explained that the officers have handled a variety of high profile assignments including presidential protection details for President George Bush and President Ronald Reagan. They also participated in an illegal dumping task force, as well as being paired up with investigators from the Essex County Prosecutor's Office for a successful carjacking task force. The deputies each serve around 16 to 20

Contact:

Director Eric A. Mayer
or
Captain Peter J. Corbo
Essex County Sheriff's Office
Essex County Courts Building
Newark, NJ 07102

201/621-4105

hours per month, though most far exceed that number. Last year, the volunteer officers donated 8,000 hours.

The training and field officer, Captain Peter J. Corbo, a 14 year veteran who is a state certified instructor, said the deputy sheriffs, minimum age of 18, must graduate from a certified police academy. The PTC approved average hours range from 452 to 669 hours. Mayer indicated that a new class of approximately 50 people is about to start. The screening includes oral interview, background investigation, medical exam, urinalysis and psychological.

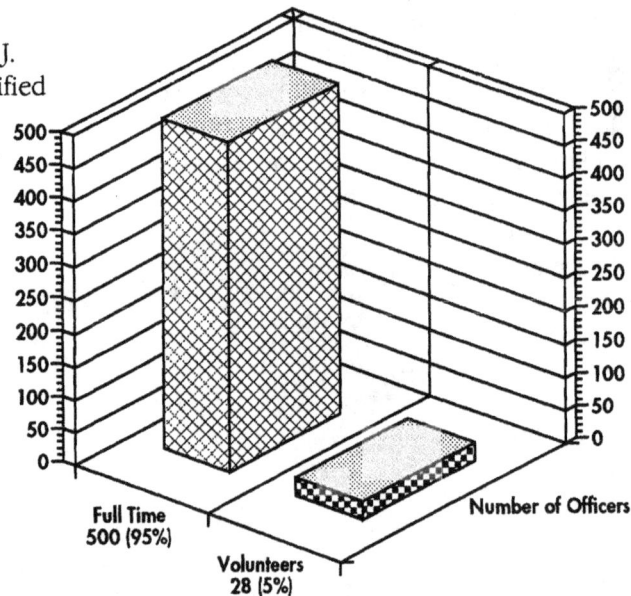

Full Time
500 (95%)

Volunteers
28 (5%)

Number of Officers

Armando B. Fontoura
Essex County, N.J. Sheriff

Essex County, NJ deputy sheriff Jeff Brophy, one of Sheriff Armando B. Fontoura's volunteer officers, stands next to a four wheel drive patrol vehicle while sporting his commando sweater and Smith and Wesson 6906 9mm firearm.

Fort Worth Police Department

City of Fort Worth, Texas

Number of Officers	
1,052	Full Time
75	Reserves
1,127	Total Officers

Minimum Training Hours Req.	
682	Full Time
400	Reserve

In accordance with Texas Commission on Law Enforcement Officer Standards and Education (TCLEOSE) regulations, the 75 reserve officers with the Fort Worth Police Department have their training broken up into three components. The department has dubbed them Grade I., II. and III. The reserve officers' call letters on the radio reflect their level of training.

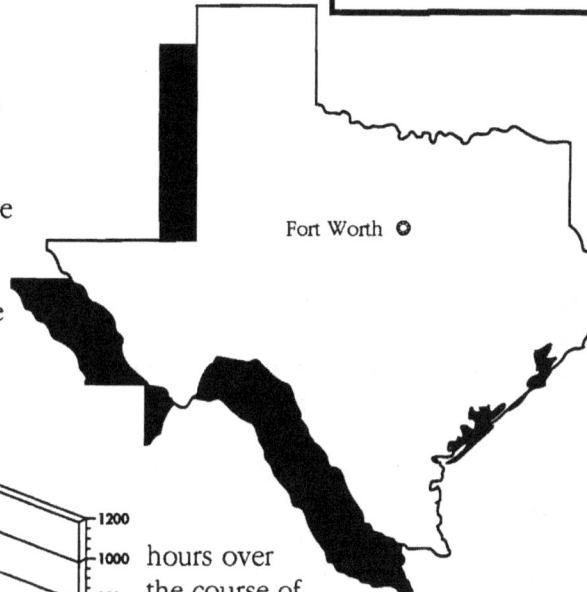

Fort Worth ⊙

Following their completion of the 145 hour, 12 week reserve basic course, they are dubbed a Grade III. reserve and patrol only as a second officer. Within two years, the intermediate course, which lasts 131 hours over the course of 11 weeks, must be completed and the designation Grade II. reserve is earned and they are allowed to patrol solo. The ten week last portion, the Grade I. reserve advanced course of 124 hours, must be done within four years.

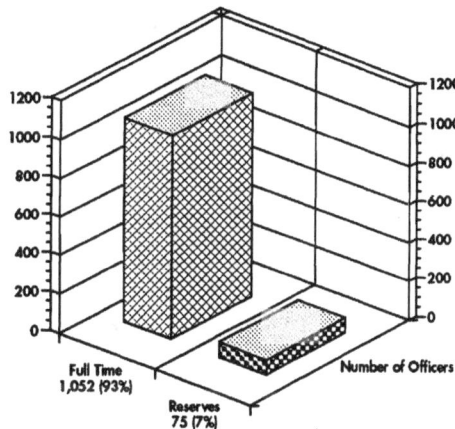

Number of Officers

Full Time
1,052 (93%)

Reserves
75 (7%)

Following completion of the 400 total hours, reserves take their TCLEOSE exam for a basic law enforcement officer's certificate. Reserves may carry their firearm off-duty within the City of Fort Worth once they've attained their Grade I. status.

The full-time police officers, of which there are 1,052, go through a 682 hour pre-service academy and a 560 hour field training officer (FTO) program.

Last year, the reserves spent 20,712 hours on patrol and an additional 3,639 hours on spe-

Contact:

Lieutenant R.H. Autry
Fort Worth Police Department
1100 Nashville Avenue
Fort Worth, TX 76105

817/871-7139

cial details for a total of 24,351 hours. Hours spent in training were not available. The monthly minimum is 24 hours of service.

The police department provides all uniforms, equipment and .357 revolver, on which they must qualify two times annually. The uniform is the same as the regulars, but the badge says "reserve." Officers may purchase their own semi-automatic if they prefer.

With a minimum age of 21, applicants go through an identical weeding out process as for full-time slots including background investigation, polygraph, drug screening and psychological.

Fulton County Sheriff's Office

City of Atlanta, Georgia

Number of Officers
702 Full Time
370 Reserves
1,072 Total Officers

Minimum Training Hours Req.
280 All Officers

Under the visionary leadership of Major Richard H. Davis, this 370 reserve deputy strong unit, including reserves who double as full-time officers with 40 other agencies, has made its mark in the reserve law enforcement world. It's reach extends far beyond it's local boundaries and effects the 2.8 million people in the metro Atlanta region, the ninth largest metropolitan area in the U.S.

Five main divisions comprise this program. They are: Four wheel drive, motorcycle, horse, foot patrol, and correction. The volunteers wishing to serve in one of the first three divisions must provide the four wheel drive, motorcycle, or horse (with horse trailer) as appropriate. There is also an elite 20 member Special Emergency Response Team (SERT), as well as a 26 member search and rescue all-terrain-vehicle (ATV) team. All reserve deputies must pay for their own uniform including firearm.

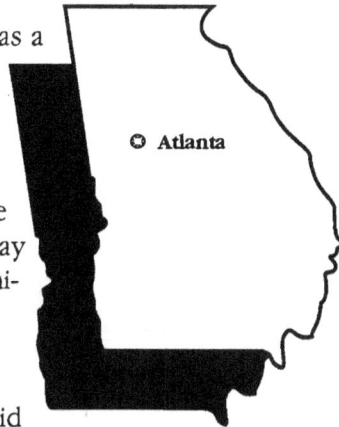

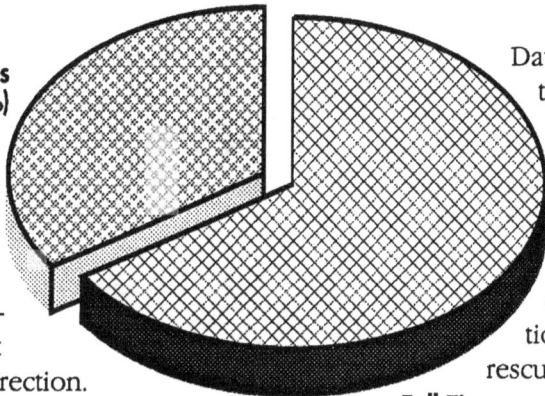

Davis said the Fulton County reserve unit has donated $13,220,900 to the community last year in manpower and equipment. The figure includes 70 four-wheel drives, 50 motorcycles, 20 horses, six vehicles, two mobile command centers, one communication van with its own repeater, one rescue bronco, one drug awareness bus, and 53 ATVs which were donated by Honda.

Reserves 370 (35%)

Full Time 702 (65%)

○ Atlanta

Contact:

**Major Richard H. Davis
Fulton County Sheriff's Office
137 Peachtree Street, S.W.
Atlanta, GA 30303**

404/730-5100

Reserve deputies serving with this tightly run outfit are required to attend eight out of 12 monthly meetings which take place at 7:30 PM the second Tuesday of each month. They must also attend 12 regularly scheduled activities a year. To keep their certification within the organization, officers must work 24 hours per quarter, with corrections personnel obligated to work two monthly shifts of eight hours each. The penalty for missing an assignment without proper notification is $50 the first time, $100 the second time and dismissal the third time. A $150 initiation fee is paid by all reserve deputy sheriffs when they join.

Entry requirements include minimum age of 25 and an ability to withstand the same scrutiny in a background investigation as that applied to a full-time deputy sheriff candidate.

Because of the vast amount of services that the county sheriff's reserve have been providing at the request of the City of Atlanta Police Department, it is

Reserve Law Enforcement in the United States

only recently that the 1,600 full-time officer agency is exploring the possibility of implementing its own reserve force, particularly in light of the upcoming Olympics set to take place there in 1996.

Davis said the Fulton County Sheriff's Reserve's certified officers and the 702 full-time deputies are trained to Georgia state standards of 280 hours and have a nondescript "command division" rocker under their shoulder patch so as to avoid public confusion. The 280 hours of training takes place three nights a week and alternate Saturdays for fifteen weeks.

Greenwich Police Department

City of Greenwich, Connecticut

Number of Officers	
150	Full Time
21	Specials
171	Total Officers

Minimum Training Hours Req.	
498	Full Time
498	Special

Greenwich
o

As with the 150 full-time officers, Greenwich's 21 special officers, serving the affluent suburban community in the shadow of New York City, complete 498 hours of basic police training. They are fully certified by the Connecticut Municipal Police Training Council (CMPTC) and carry their firearm off duty.

Special Sergeant Eric Omdahl, who oversees the Special Police Division, said the volunteer officers attend the training at night and on the weekends. "Most of time, we've run the program out of Greenwich, but a few of our guys got the training regionally at Fairfield, Norwalk or Trumbull," said Omdahl who added that budget constraints have lead the course to be offered on a sporadic basis. Firearms and driver training topics are taught only in Meriden at the state academy. He said that the training was broken up into five 100 hour blocks and that Greenwich picks up the cost of around $500.

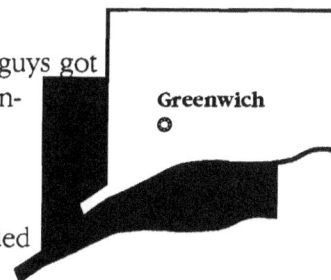

After the first block, the non-certified officer is provisionally certified and armed and may patrol in a light blue shirt under the supervision of a certified officer. Fully certified officers, who have completed all of the mandated training and hang a CMPTC certificate identical to the regular officers' certificates on their wall, wear the same dark blue shirt as full-time Greenwich police officers and have full police authority. All specials have their status indicated on their badge and shoulder patch.

The field training officer (FTO) program for both full-time and special officers lasts 80 hours. In order to maintain state certification, all officers have to also take 40 hours of refresher training every three years. Sergeants and above must take 60 hours during the same time frame. The extra 20 hours of supervisory training is only offered in

Contact:

Special Sergeant Eric Omdahl
Special Police Division
Greenwich Police Department
Havemyer Place
Greenwich, CT 06830

205/434-7791

Meriden.

The specials, minimum age of 21, carry agency furnished Smith and Wesson 9mm semi-automatics and must qualify four times a year. Uniforms are also provided by the municipality, though budget constraints have forced many specials to shell out the money themselves.

Special police officers, who work at least 15 hours per month, patrol with a regular or with another special. Solo patrols happen in the parks. The specials are also used heavily in the marine section and the department often pairs a full-time officer with a special on a police boat. The marine uniform consists of Khaki police shirt and shorts.

Omdahl said the screening process was just like that used for the full-time officers. Among the hurdles to be passed are a physical, drug screening and psychological.

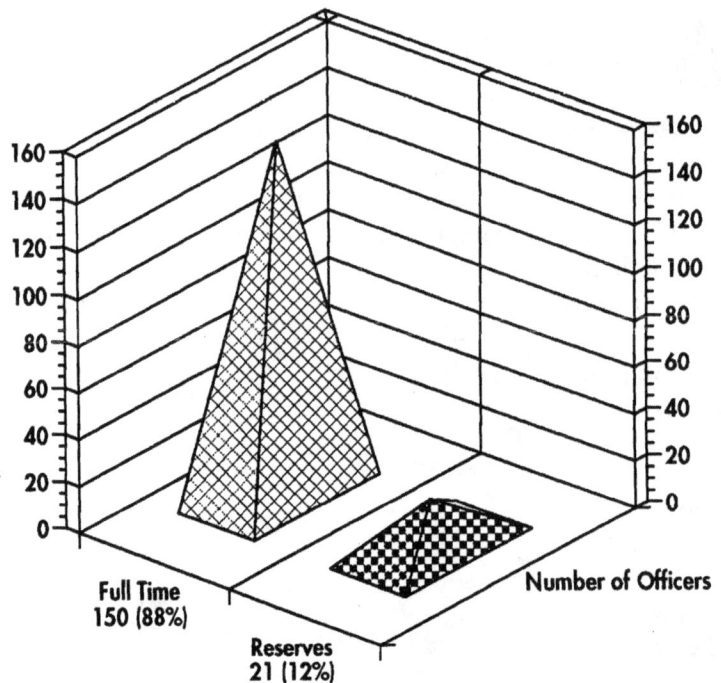

Full Time
150 (88%)

Reserves
21 (12%)

Number of Officers

Harris County Sheriff's Office

City of Houston, Texas

Number of Officers
3,300 Full Time
  316 Reserves
3,613 Total Officers

Minimum Training Hours Req.
400 Full Time
400 Reserves

The chief of the 316 reserve deputies working for the Harris County Sheriff's Office, L. Ray Vickers, said their 14 groups assist the 3,300 full-time deputy department in numerous ways. The groups include four devoted to patrol, as well as detention, community relations, mounted, detectives and personnel and training. With a minimum of 20 monthly hours of service, Vickers' people average 43 hours each month per reserve.

eight years and sits on the Sheriff Johnnie Klevenhagen's command staff, said only 20% of the applicants, minimum age of 21, make it successfully through the process. The hurdles, which

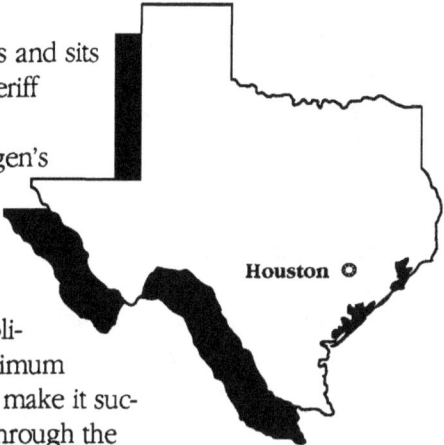

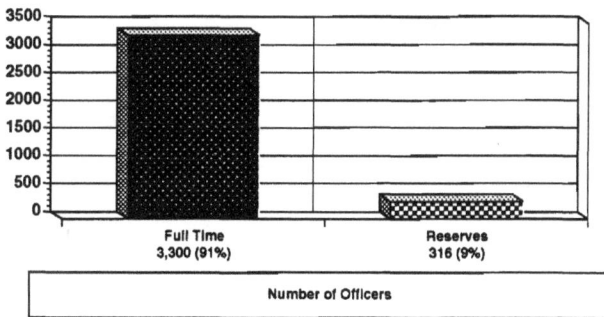

Houston

Full Time 3,300 (91%)	**Reserves** 316 (9%)

Number of Officers

Screening to get into the volunteer outfit is rigorous. Vickers, who has been reserve chief for

are identical to those striving for regular deputy sheriff status, include a reading comprehension test, psychological, drug testing and personal interview.

While the regulars receive their 400 hours of state certified training pre-service, the reserve deputies have two years to acquire it. After 145 initial hours, the reserve receives a badge, uniform and ID from the department (firearms are paid for by the reserve) for limited duty with the marine division or detention area.

Contact:

L. Ray Vickers
Chief of Reserves
Harris County Sheriff's Office
1301 Franklin
Houston, TX 77002

713/755-7286

After the next 131 hours they can go on street patrol with senior officer. The advanced training consists of 124 hours for a total of 400 hours within two years. Also mandated is a 40 hour jail school.

The program based in Houston, the nation's fourth largest metropolitan area, is insured by the department and has an extensive field training officer (FTO) program. The reserve allows certain qualified reserves to operate as one man patrol units and holds random drug testing which all volunteers from the top down are subject to. Vickers said that 20% of their reserve deputies are former full-time officers.

High Point Police Department

City of High Point, North Carolina

Number of Officers	
180	Full Time
20	Reserves
200	Total Officers

Minimum Training Hours Req.	
432	Full Time
432	Reserve

According to R.J. "Jerry" Culler, the executive officer of the reserve program, High Point's reserve officers, who must serve at least 16 hours monthly and worked 5,150 hours last year, are used in a variety of different places in addition to patrol. He said the officers work with the Tac Team, as well as with the detectives, the warrant section and traffic enforcement.

Training is the key to High Point's success. Like the regulars, the reserves get 432 hours of training. Culler said the volunteer officers go for six months to Guilford County Technical College in Jamestown, NC, four nights a week and every other Saturday.

The reserve field training officer (FTO) program is 192 hours long while the 180 full-timers must complete 560 hours. In-service training is extensive. Culler pointed out that two reserves are slated to attend a hostage negotiation school in Baltimore.

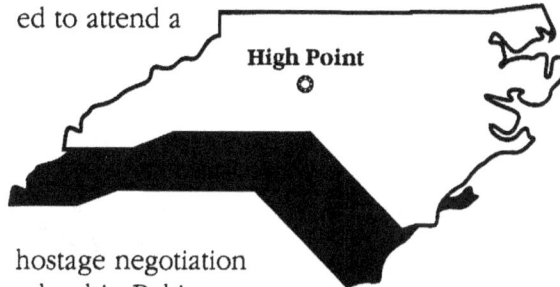

High Point has 18 sworn reserve officers and two non-sworn reservists. One serves as the department's chaplain and the other works as a crime lab technician.

Reserve hopefuls must be at least 21 and go through personnel in the same fashion as a full-time officer. Components of the screening process includes polygraph, psychological and review board.

The department furnishes everything for the reserve officers including the Smith & Wesson 9mm 6906 firearm. The badge states "reserve" on it in small letters and the ID card has "reserve officer" stamped on it.

Contact:

R. J. Culler
Executive Officer of Reserves
High Point Police Dept.
1009 Leonard Street
High Point, NC 27260

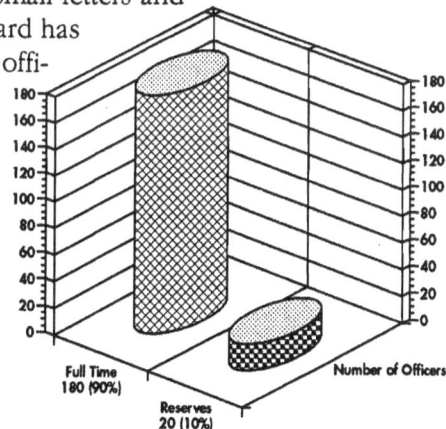

919/431-1756

Honolulu Police Department

City of Honolulu, Hawaii

According to Lieutenant Daryl Sakai, the reserve coordinator, the 1,913 member Honolulu Police Department has 83 reserve officers. The last class of reserves, in February 1992, received 720 hours of pre-service academy training. Full-timers get 1,088 hours of academy training. The state of Hawaii has not established minimum training hours for their full-time or reserve officers. Standards are set by the local agency.

Honolulu's volunteer officers' uniforms are the same and they work routine patrol duties. Some of the reserve officers are assigned to the criminal investigation division (CID). The first three sets of uniforms are provided with the department picking up 75% of the cost for additional uniforms. The agency issues a .38 Smith & Wesson revolver, however they will be soon converting to a Smith & Wesson 9mm.

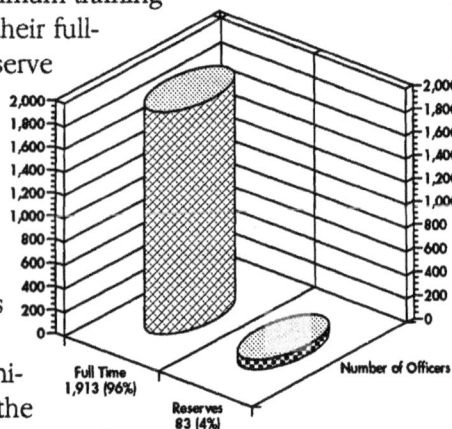

Full Time 1,913 (96%)
Reserves 83 (4%)
Number of Officers

The reserves, who worked 40,000 hours last year, must serve a minimum of ten hours per week during their first year's field training probationary period. They have to work at least five hours per week after the first year, though Sakai indicated that each reserve officer averages 40 hours a month.

Honolulu Police reserve officers must be at least 25 and no older than 45. The screening process for entry includes a physical, psychological, background investigation and oral interview.

Contact:

Lieutenant Daryl Sakai
Reserve Coordinator
Honolulu Police Department
801 Beretania Street
Honolulu, HI 96813

808/529-3385

Indianapolis
Police Department

City of Indianapolis, Indiana

Number of Officers
953 Full Time
46 Reserves
999 Total Officers

Minimum Training Hours Req.
500 Full Time
500 Reserve

Indianapolis Police Sergeant Thomas DuBois, the reserve unit supervisor, said his 46 reserves serve the 953-member full-time force currently and last year, when their manpower stood at 36, the reserves donated 15,000 hours. "One guy had 1,200 hours by himself," said DuBois who added that the minimum monthly hours required is 20.

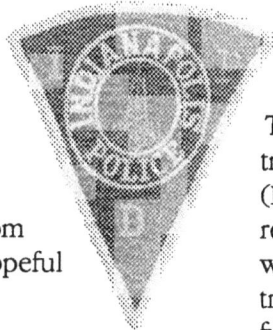

The 25 people currently in the academy to become reserve officers with the Indianapolis Police Department were culled from an applicant pool of 160 hopeful individuals.

Aspiring reserves, minimum age of 21, must successfully get by the scrutiny of the department's personnel branch. The process includes preliminary application, polygraph, written exam, oral interview, psychological screening, background investigation and physical exam.

Indianapolis reserves go through the same 500 hour academy as the regular officers. The seven month course takes place on Tuesday and Thursday nights for four hours each and on Saturdays for eight hours. The full-time field training officer (FTO) program is 800 hours long while the reserves is 270 hours. The reserves qualify with their firearm twice a year and in-service training is scheduled as it comes up for the full-timers.

The department issues the uniform, which is identical, along with the Beretta 92G 9mm firearm. DuBois said the badge is identical "except for a real small 'R' in front of the badge number."

Contact:

Sergeant Thomas DuBois
Reserve Unit Supervisor
Indianapolis Police Department
901 North Post Road
Indianapolis, IN 46219

317/898-6519

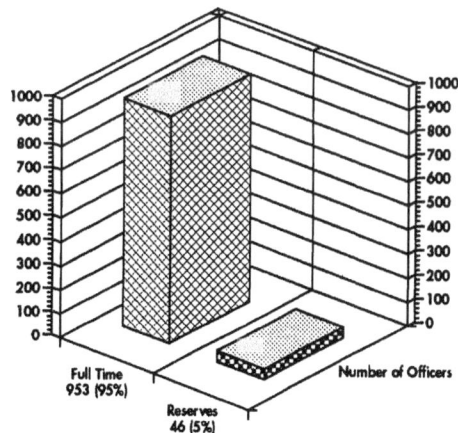

DuBois explained that the reserves serve the 750,000 population city in a number of different areas. Three squads are stationed out of different districts and an additional squad runs the prisoner wagons. He also said he has one reserve each running the Explorer Post, in tactical air patrol and in the firearms training unit.

Jackson
Police Department

City of Jackson, Mississippi

Number of Officers	
445	Full Time
45	Reserves
490	Total Officers

Minimum Training Hours Req.	
480	Full Time
360	Reserve

Officer Joe L. Austin, Jackson's reserve coordinator said the 45 currently serving reserve officers will be boosted shortly by the 30 reservists in the 360 hour police reserve academy. The academy is held on Tuesday and Thursday nights and every other Saturday for seven months. The 445 regular officers attend the academy for 480 hours with a 960 hour field training officer (FTO) program.

In-service training used to come in at a set 40 hours a month, but nowadays the reserves are required to attend any courses mandated for the full-timers. The monthly minimum, which is about to be upgraded, is eight hours, but Austin indicated that some reserve officers serve 160 hours.

The agency provides the identical uniform and badge, which says "reserve" on it, as well as the Glock Model 17 9mm firearm. Reserves do have the option of purchasing their own Glock. Qualification on the weapon is scheduled every three months.

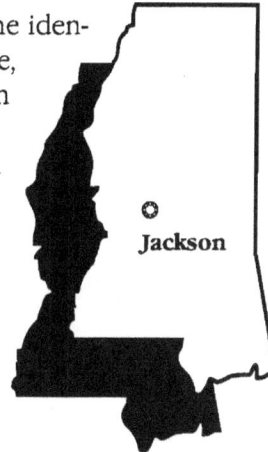

Jackson

Reserve officers, who ride as a second officer with a full-timer, are certified, have full police powers and carry their Glock 24 hours a day. They must be at least 21 years old and pass the same screening process as salaried personnel. The process includes a knowledge test, drug test, physical, MMPI psychological, background investigation and oral board.

Contact:

Officer Joe L. Austin
Reserve Coordinator
Jackson Police Department
3000 St. Charles Street
Jackson, MS 39209

601/960-1378

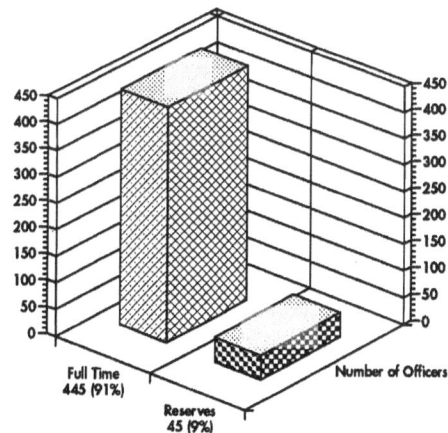

Full Time
445 (91%)

Reserves
45 (9%)

Number of Officers

Jacksonville/Duval County Sheriff's Office

City of Jacksonville, Florida

In an unusual setup, the 1,800 officer Jacksonville Sheriff's Office is headed by a sheriff and is the combined Jacksonville Police Department and Duval County Sheriff's Office. The departments reserves used to receive 124 hours of training two evenings a week and on seven consecutive Saturdays. The old reserves, who technically were auxiliaries under Florida state statute, have been grandfathered into a newly revamped program which calls for new members to undergo 750 hours of training reflective of the certified reserve level.

The reserves, minimum age of 21, must also complete 12 field training officer (FTO) rides for a total of 96 hours, while the full-time Jacksonville Sheriff's officers are academy trained for 720 hours with a 120 hour FTO program. Officers must demonstrate proficiency with the agency provided Glock Model 17 firearm at qualifications held two times annually. In-service training is slated for at least eight hours per quarter.

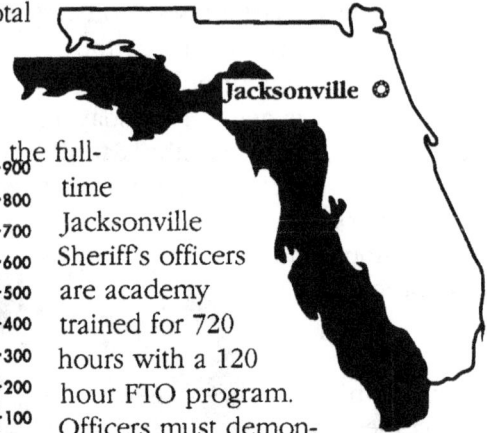

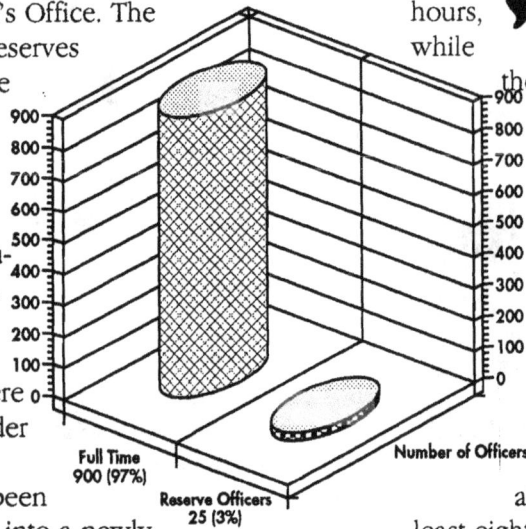

Officer Harley Johnson, the reserve liaison, said the reserves

Full Time
900 (97%)

Reserve Officers
25 (3%)

Number of Officers

Jacksonville ◉

Contact:

Officer Harley Johnson
Reserve Liaison
Jacksonville Sheriff's Office
501 East Bay Street, Room 216
Jacksonville, FL 32202

904/630-2742

must serve a minimum of 16 hours monthly. They worked 35,760 hours last year in the uniformed division as a second officer in a car and at major events. The aviation unit has 12 reservists who get extra insurance protection through Jacksonville Risk Management.

Uniforms (except for the shoes and underwear) are purchased by the agency. They look the same except for the 1/2" by 2" patch on left shoulder which says "reserve," as does the badge.

Screening for entry into the reserves is the same as the regulars and includes physical, background investigation, physical agility Cooper Test, drug screening and polygraph.

Jefferson County Sheriff's Office

City of Louisville, Kentucky

Based in Louisville, KY, the Jefferson County's Sheriff's Office has two distinct classifications of non-full-time deputy sheriffs. The 116 sworn volunteer deputies refered to as the uniformed division of support services, formerly called the working 100 group, have full police powers 24 hours a day, seven days a week. The department's 1,260 special deputy sheriffs have no police powers and do not carry firearms.

Major Gene Koch, who oversees the sworn volunteer and special deputy sheriffs from his support services office, said the special deputies, who are issued a badge, do not have a uniform and don a traffic vest if they are called out for traffic direction duties. Their other function involves delivering some of the 5,000 to 9,000 tax notices that need to be hand delivered each year throughout Jefferson County. They get sixteen hours of training.

Koch's support service's uniformed division people, who are broken up into four squads, purchase their own 9mm or .357 firearm and buy identical uniforms ($790 to $900 for the uniform, firearm and radio) to those worn by the 242 regular deputies. They undergo 400 hours of training, the same as the full-timers, and

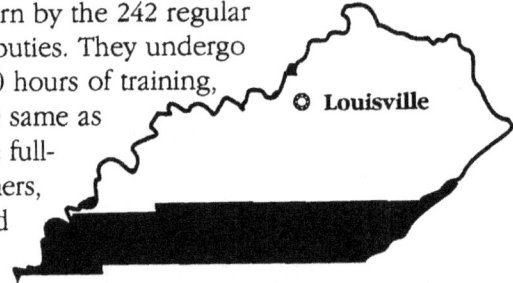

○ Louisville

undergo a 120 hour field training officer (FTO) program. Salaried deputy sheriffs have a 640 hour FTO program.

Sworn personnel, who must be 21 or older, go through an entry process which includes drug screening, background investigation and review board.

Both the volunteer and full-time deputy sheriffs get at least 40 hours of in-service training annually with firearms qualification taking place twice a year.

Contact:

Major Gene Koch
Support Services
Jefferson County Sheriff's Office
701 Fiscal Court Building
Louisville, KY 40202

502/625-5199

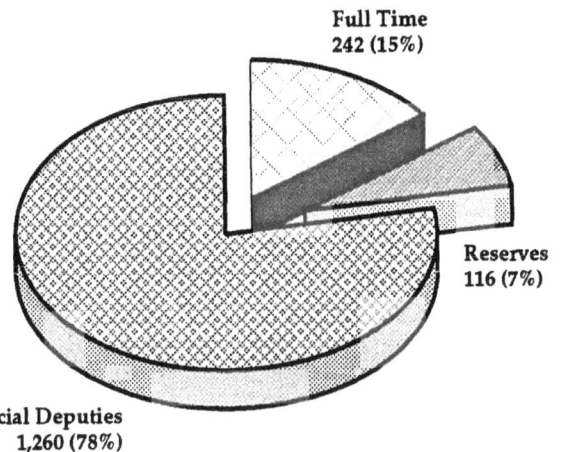

Full Time
242 (15%)

Reserves
116 (7%)

Special Deputies
1,260 (78%)

The sworn, non-compensated deputies are required to work 25 details a year with each detail running from four to ten hours apiece. Koch said the minimum service is 20 hours a month.

The most famous of the activities that the deputies patrol is the Kentucky Derby. Koch said they are celebrating the two year anniversary of the emergency vehicle assist program which has 54 hours of donated patrol work along highways I65, I64, I71 and A41. "We have 10,500 volunteer hours for this program," said Koch who said his deputy sheriffs handled 9,216 requests for assistance from disabled motorists.

Jefferson Parish Sheriff's Office

City of Gretna, Louisiana

Number of Officers
800 Full Time
200 Reserves
1,000 Total Officers

Minimum Training Hours Req.
860 Full Time
580 Reserves

The Jefferson Parish Sheriff's Office (Louisiana counties are referred to as "Parish") has a rather sophisticated approach to their reserve deputy sheriff program. The 200 reserves, who must serve at least 24 hours per month, are split among various internal sections including traffic, rescue, mounted and patrol.

Captain Tom Rushing, speaking from his office at the training academy, said the reserves get 580 hours of training on Tuesday, Wednesday and Friday evenings and half of the Saturdays for eight months. He indicated that a class is starting in June 1993 with

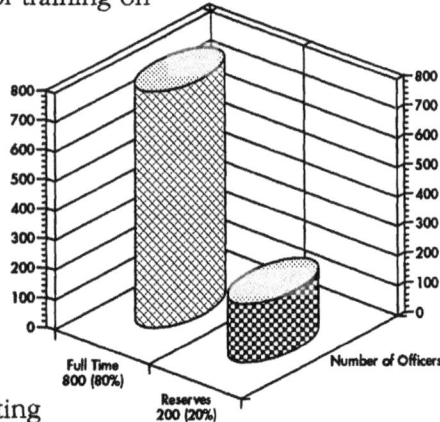

around 65 reserve hopefuls in it. The reserve field training officer (FTO) program goes for 144 hours. Full-time deputy sheriffs get 860 hours of training and a 960 hour FTO program.

Full Time 800 (80%)
Reserves 200 (20%)
Number of Officers

The reserves have full police powers and may carry their firearm off duty. The agency furnishes the Beretta 92F semi-automatic and reserves must qualify on the weapon once a year. In-service training is done four hours monthly.

Uniforms are also provided by the sheriff. They are identical to the salaried deputy garb in appearance except for the "R" collar insignia and "reserve" on the badge.

Reserves must be 21 at time of graduation from the academy (they may enroll at 20½).

They are tested for fitness to become a reserve with a background investigation, physical, drug screening, oral review board and a recently implemented polygraph.

Contact:

Captain Tom Rushing
Training Academy
Jefferson Parish Sheriff's Office
701 South Upland Street
River Ridge, LA 70123

504/465-1400

Laramie County Sheriff's Office

City of Cheyenne, Wyoming

Number of Officers
30 Full Time
20 Reserves
50 Total Officers

Minimum Training Hours Req.
410 Full Time
410 Reserve

Cheyenne ○

While most of the 20 reserve deputies serving with the Laramie County Sheriff's Office in Cheyenne work patrol, some of the fully certified officers fulfill assignments in detectives, crime lab or dispatch. The minimum service level is 60 hours a quarter, or 20 hours a month.

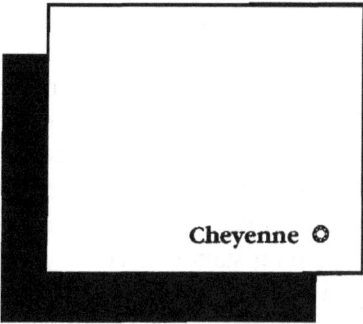

All officers undergo 410 hours of basic academy training and a 400 hour field training officer program. The academy for reserves is held two nights a week for a year and a half. Both the regulars and the reserves qualify on their agency furnished firearm four times a year. The department pays for the firearm and uniform which is identical for all deputies.

Applicants 21 and older have to pass a written test, physical, interview, polygraph, psychological and background.

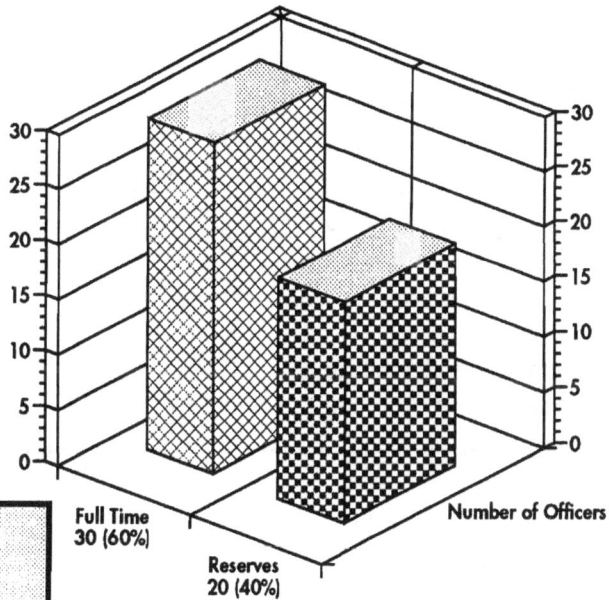

Full Time
30 (60%)

Reserves
20 (40%)

Number of Officers

Contact:

Sergeant Bob Bomar
Personnel Office
Laramie County Sheriff's Office
1910 Pioneer Avenue
Cheyenne, WY 82001

307/778-3700

Las Vegas Police Department

City of Las Vegas, Nevada

Number of Officers
1,105 Full Time
   12 Reserves (Commissioned)
   40 Reserves (Search & Rescue)
1,157 Total Officers

Minimum Training Hours Req.
680 Full Time
680 Reserve (Commissioned)
200 Reserve (Search & Rescue)

In the old days, reserve officers serving with the Las Vegas Metropolitan Police Department only had to meet the then stated Nevada POST requirement of 220 hours. Nowadays, however, Lt. Dwight E. Mahan, who oversees the reserves, the 12 commissioned reserves are expected to meet all training standards set for full-time officers under the "like job, like training" concept. Las Vegas' police academy is set at 680 hours and all commissioned officers far exceed the POST minimum of 24 hours of annual in-service training. The mandatory training covers many areas including PR-24, driving and an eight hour cultural awareness course.

The sworn reserve officers, minimum age of 21, are required to serve 16 hours per month and they work primarily in the field services division. They must pass the same obstacles as a regular officer including written test, physical, agility test, psychological and polygraph. Las Vegas provides both the firearm and the uniform, which is the same except that the badge has "reserve" on it.

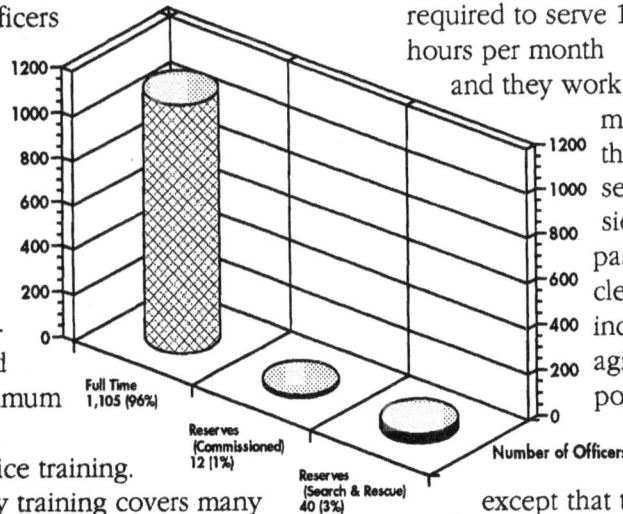

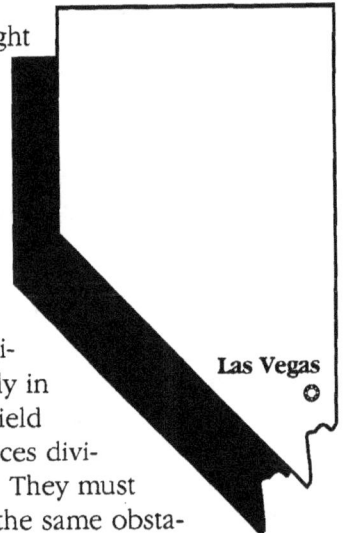

Mahan said the metropolitan agency, which merged with the Clark County Sheriff's Office some years ago and now covers 8,000 square miles with 75% of Nevada's population, also utilizes 40 unarmed, non-commissioned reserves in a Search & Rescue section. Divided into two branches, Search & Rescue has 25 in Mountain Rescue and the Aero Squad numbers 15.

Las Vegas

Number of Officers

Full Time
1,105 (96%)

Reserves
(Commissioned)
12 (1%)

Reserves
(Search & Rescue)
40 (3%)

Contact:

Lt. Dwight E. Mahan
Las Vegas Metropolitan Police Dept.
4810 Las Vegas Boulevard South
Las Vegas, NV 89119

702/729-3567

The volunteers, who must be 21 or older, wear a green fatigue utility uniform and last year donated 1,427 operational hours and 3,461 training hours. The department pays for the uniform and the Search & Rescue reservist purchases around $300 worth of personal gear such as harnesses and the like. They receive 200 hours of mission oriented training. In-service training takes place at a rate of four days a month for four hours. Two reserves were recently sent to Colorado for an ice climbing course.

Mahan said that he prefers people who are experienced climbers for mountain rescue, whereas trained emergency medical personnel may be less experienced climbers. Among the health professionals are three trauma nurses, as well as paramedics and emergency medical technicians (EMTs). Applications are accepted two times a year and 130 people competed for three open slots last year.

Los Angeles County Sheriff's Office

City of Los Angeles, California

Number of Officers
8,000 Full Time
963 Reserves
8,963 Total Officers

Minimum Training Hours Req.
840 Full Time
391 Level I. Non-des. Reserve
249 Level II. Reserve

The Los Angeles County Sheriff's Office's 963 reserve deputy sheriffs donated 290,000 hours last year working in 40 different reserve units including assignments such as patrol stations, mounted posse, mountain rescue unit, medical company,

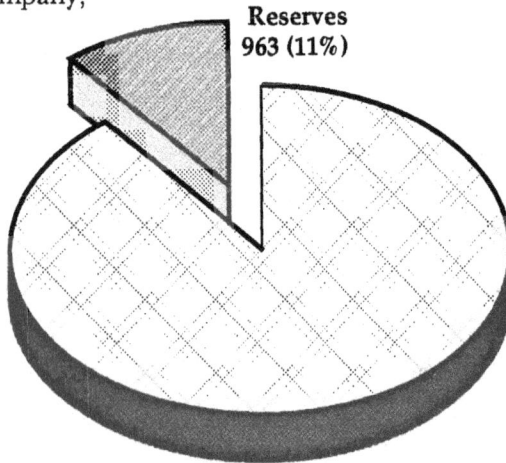

Reserves
963 (11%)

Full Time
8,000 (89%)

weapons training platoon and motorcycle unit. Police motorcycles are purchased by the reserve deputy sheriff and

leased to the County for $1.00 per year. The lease agreement provides for insurance coverage, as well as maintenance by the County of Los Angeles.

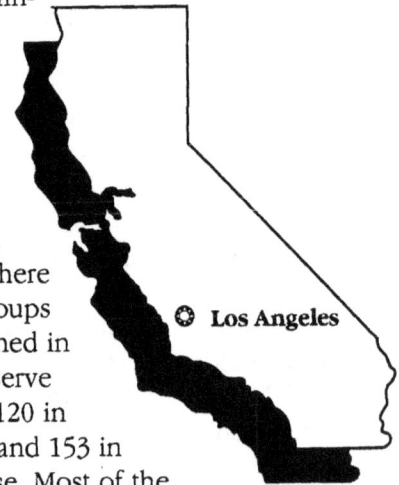

◉ Los Angeles

The Reserve Forces Bureau's Sergeant Frank G. Decker said that there are three main groups and 690 are assigned in the uniformed reserve component with 120 in mountain rescue and 153 in the mounted posse. Most of the mountain rescue and mounted posse reserves are Level II. certified, although a few hold dual status as Non-designated Level I. patrol reserves. Reserves must serve at least 20 hours a month.

Contact:

Sgt. Frank G. Decker
Reserve Forces Bureau
Los Angeles County Sheriff's Office
11515 South Colima Road
Whittier, CA 90604

310/946-7871

The department's reserve program, founded in 1941, pays each reservist $1.00 per year (initially to cover them under workman's comp.) and utilizes California POST certified Non-designated Level I.s and Level II.s, although five or six Level III.s are holdovers from earlier years.

L.A. County exceeds state certification minimums. Non-designated Level I.s go through 391 hours at the police academy and complete a 200 hour field training officer (FTO) program. Level II.s attend for 249 hours. The academy runs on Sundays (ten hours), Tuesdays (four hours) and Thursdays (four hours) for 12 to 13 weeks for Level II. reserves and 20 weeks for Non-designated Level I. reserves.

The 8,000 full-time deputy sheriff's attend an 840 hour academy and a 960 hour FTO program. "All full-time personnel go into custody (detention services) before they go into field operations," explained Decker. "Under our decentralized process, reserves apply directly to their unit of choice and are processed and assigned to that unit. They can transfer elsewhere later."

Applicants for the position of reserve deputy must be between 20 and 54 and ½ years of age and undergo a rigorous background investigation.

Decker said the reserves are issued identical uniforms and equipment as the regulars including the helmet, vest and Beretta 92F firearm which they must qualify on every four months.

Los Angeles County Sheriff's Reserve Academy Curriculum

Class	Module	Hours
Criminal Justice System	A	2
Constitutional Rights Law	A	2
Ethics and Professionalism	A	2
Discretionary Decision Making	A	2
Criminal Law	A	6
Search and Seizure	A	6
Laws of Arrest	A	3
Preliminary Investigations	A	3
Concepts of Evidence	A	2
Legal/Moral Aspects of Force and Firearm	A	4
Weapons Training	A/B	60
Laser Village	A	8
Community Relations - Role of a Reserve	A	2
Interpersonal Communications	A	2
Searching and Handcuffing	A	10
Field Interviews	A	2
Interrogations	A	1
Note Taking for Reports	A	2
Defensive Tactics	A	8

Class	Module	Hours
Physical Training	A	3
Physical Training Test #1	A	1.5
Physical Agility Test #1	A	1.5
Examinations	A	5
Command Time	A	4
History of Law Enforcement	B	1
Burglary, Theft, RSP Laws	B	3
Miscellaneous Crimes	B	2
Violent Crimes	B	2
Dangerous Weapons Laws	B	2
Report Writing	B	8
Telephone Demeanor	B	1
Vehicle Operations (Lecture)	B	4
Driver Training	B	8
Patrol Procedures	B	4
Vehicle Stop Tactics	B	6
Vehicle Stop Field Problems	B	5
Radio Procedures	B	2
Crimes in Progress - Tactics	B	5

Class	Module	Hours
Officer Survival	B	4
Hazardous Occurrences	B	2
First Aid	B	8
Sudden Infant Death Syndrome	B	2
C.P.R.	B	7
Introduction to Traffic	B	3
Traffic Direction	B	1
Custody Orientation	B	2
Baton Training	B	9
Crowd and Riot Control	B	1
Physical Training	B	3
Physical Training Test #2	B	1.5
Physical Agility Test #2	B	1.5
Examinations	B	3
Command Time	B	4
Career Influences	C	1
Related Law Enforcement Agencies	C	1
Crime Prevention	C	1
Stress Management	C	1
Crimes Against Children - Child Abuse Invest.	C	4
Public Nuisance Laws	C	1
Robbery and Homicide Laws	C	2
Sex Crimes - Sexual Assault Investigations	C	4
Narcotics and Dangerous Drugs	C	6
ABC Laws - Juvenile Alcohol Laws	C	1
Juvenile Laws	C	4
Rules of Evidence	C	2
Field Show-ups	C	1
Vehicle Search	C	1
Missing Persons Reports	C	2
Prowler Calls	C	1
Crimes in Progress - Building Search	C	5
Crimes in Progress - Field Problems	C	5
Handling Disputes/Disturbances	C	4
Handling Animals	C	1
Handling Mentally Ill Persons	C	2
Fire Conditions	C	1
Hostage/Barricaded Suspects	C	1
Domestic Violence	C	8

Class	Module	Hours
Vehicle Code Violations	C	3
Driving Under the Influence	C	4
Auto Theft Investigations	C	2
Traffic Accident Investigations	C	2
Identification and Collection of Evidence	C	3
Courtroom Demeanor	C	1
Proposition 115	C	2
Officer Survival	C	8
Field Assignments	C	32
Physical Training	C	3
Physical Training Test #3	C	1.5
Physical Agility Test #3	C	1.5
Examinations	C	3
Graduation Practice/Family Day	C	10
Graduation	C	3
Command Time	C	3

Module A - 144 Hours
Module B - 105 Hours
Module C - 142 Hours
Total   - 391 Hours

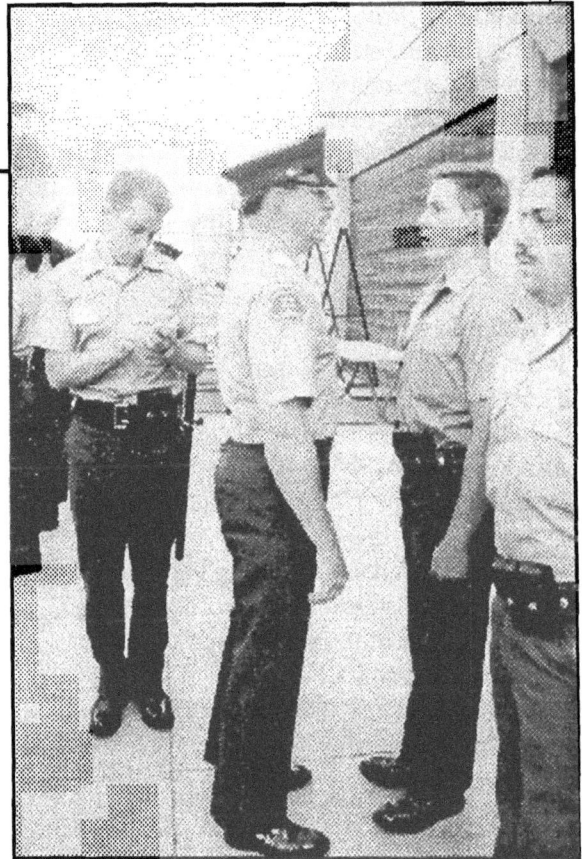

Outside Assignments:

Laser Village	- 8 Hours
Driver Training	- 8 Hours
Assistant Jailer	- 8 Hours
Patrol Rides	- 24 Hours

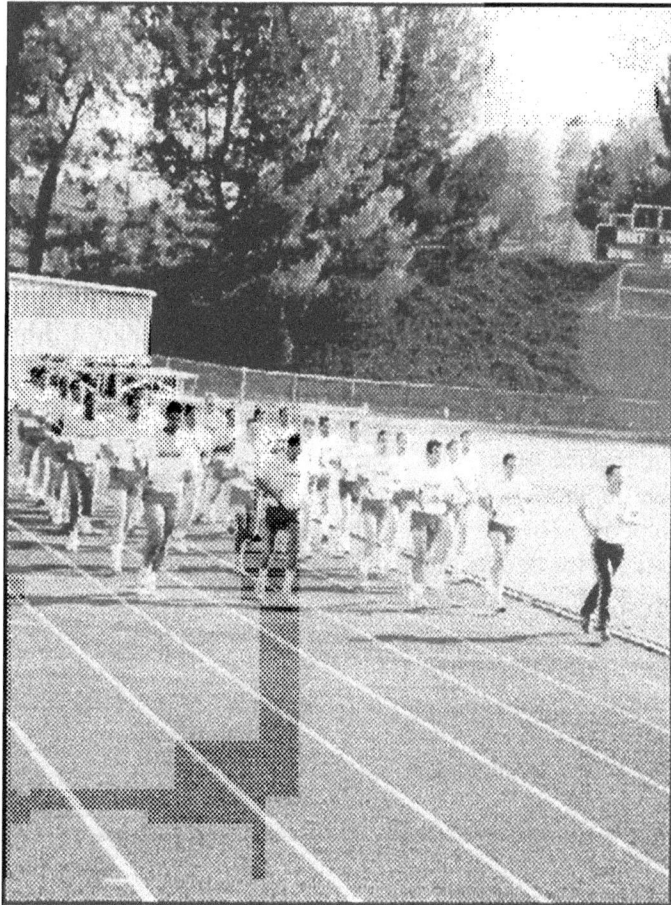

Los Angeles Police Department

City of Los Angeles, California

Total Number of Officers	
7,700	Full Time
325	Level I. Reserves
325	III. Reserves
8,350	**Total Officers**

Minimum Training Hours Req.	
720	Full Time
720	Level I. Reserve
267	Level III. Reserve

The Los Angeles Police Reserve Corps., under the attentive eyes of reserve officer in charge James C. Lombardi, who also serves as the president of the California Reserve Peace Officers Association (CRPOA), serves as a model reserve program for other agencies in the country such the Metro Dade County, FL, Police Department. Reserves in Los Angeles are uniformed identically as the regular officers at the department's expense. The famous LAPD oval badge has an "R" before the serial number on the badge and the ID card states "Reserve Corps."

The 7,700 full-time officer department uses 650 reserves who are certified, at the Los Angeles Police Academy, beyond the California POST certified Level I. designated (560 hours) or Level III. (64 hours) classifications. The department's Level I.'s get 720 hours of training two nights a week and every other weekend (Saturday and Sunday), whereas the Level III.'s receive 267 hours of training following the same schedule. The 325 Level I.'s, or "line reserves," work general law enforcement solo. The 325 Level III. reserves are called "technical reserves" and work specialized non-law enforcement functions such as the Drug Recognition Expert (DRE) program.

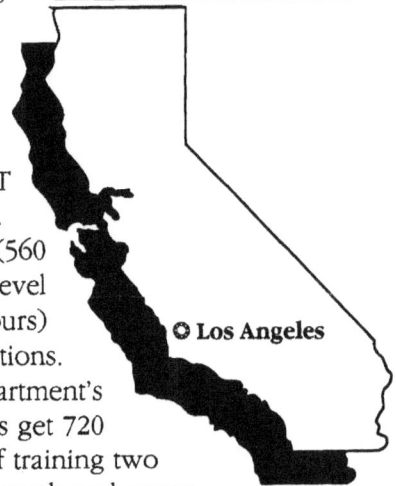

Level I. Designated reserve officers have a 200 hour field training officer (FTO) program, whereas the full-timers complete a 2,080 hour FTO program.

Both line reserves and technical reserves must meet the same basic entry requirements, however Level I.'s must be age 21 or older and Level III.'s have to be at least 18 years of age. In addition to a high school diploma or G.E.D., applicants must be 5'0" to 6'8" in

Contact:

James C. Lombardi
Reserve Officer in Charge
Reserve Coordination Section
Los Angeles Police Department
1880 North Academy Drive
Los Angeles, CA 90012

○ Los Angeles

height with weight proportionate to height. Normal color vision and depth perception is required and vision must be 20/40 with both eyes correctable to 20/30. Examinations include oral interview and written test, physical agility test, medical examination, personality inventory evaluation, and background interview and investigation.

Los Angeles' reserves, once graduated from the academy, are required to work a minimum of two eight hour shifts per month and attend each monthly meeting.

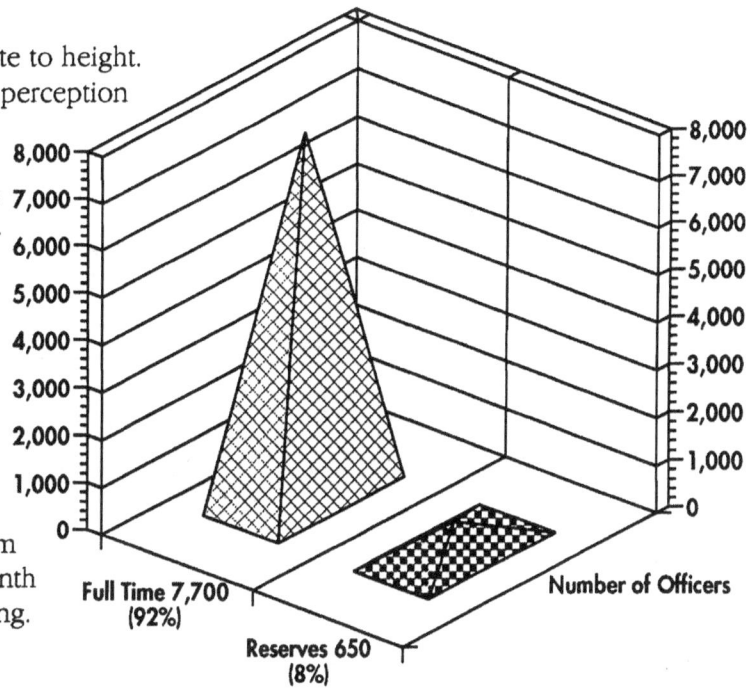

Full Time 7,700 (92%)

Reserves 650 (8%)

Number of Officers

Maplewood
Police Department

City of Maplewood, New Jersey

Number of Officers	
56	Full Time
27	Auxiliaries
83	Total Officers

Minimum Training Hours Req.	
669	Full Time
117	Auxiliary

Maplewood's 27 volunteer auxiliary officers, who have become known by the label "reserve," donated 7,000 hours last year patrolling with another auxiliary and handling special events. One third of the department's 56 full-time officers carried a gun and a badge as an auxiliary at one time.

Acting Auxiliary Chief Joseph D. Kelly, Jr., who recently took over the top volunteer cop slot from Joseph Frieman, said that the auxiliary officers have a total of 117 hours of training prior to serving the community. The training is broken up into two components: a 77 hour county auxiliary police academy and a 40 hour firearms course.

Auxiliary officers attend the Essex County Auxiliary Police Academy at the Essex County Police Academy in Cedar Grove. The 77 hour course is held on Tuesday and Thursday nights for three months. It exceeds the 42 hour minimum guidelines set by the New Jersey State Police/Office of Emergency Management, the governmental body which oversees auxiliary officer standards in the Garden State. Following academy graduation, the officers are then immersed in a 40 hour basic firearms course according to regulations set up by the New Jersey Police Training Commission (PTC).

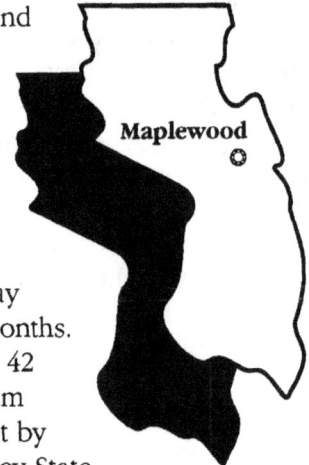

Full-time officers in New Jersey get 669 average hours of training. Maplewood's salaried officers get an additional 480 hours in a field training officer (FTO) program. The auxiliaries must ride with all six superior reserve officers for three months.

Qualification on the agency furnished .38 revolvers is

Contact:

Acting Auxiliary Chief Josepph D. Kelly, Jr.
Maplewood Police Department
125 Dunnell Road
Maplewood, NJ 07040

201/762-3400

twice a year on day and night fire. The auxiliary officers must work 14 hours a month, which exceeds the minimum of eight hours a month to retain state certification. The figure includes two hours of monthly in-service training. Day and night fire qualification happens twice a year.

Kelly indicated that reserves patrol with another reserve and handle special event details. The reserves worked 7,000 hours last year.

The police department supplies the .38 revolver and the uniform. The badge and shoulder patch says "reserve" and the shirts are light blue. Shirts for the full-time officers are navy blue.

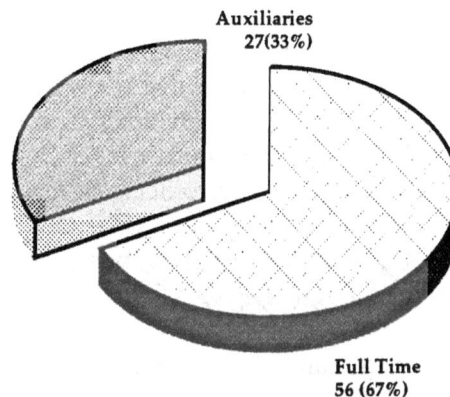

Auxiliaries
27(33%)

Full Time
56 (67%)

Maricopa County Sheriff's Office

City of Phoenix, Arizona

Number of Officers
460 Full Time
80 Reserves
540 Total Officers

Minimum Training Hours Req.
680 Full Time
440 Reserve

Maricopa County's reserve program takes less than 50% of those that apply to become reserve deputy sheriffs. The active reserve component is comprised of 61 individuals. The 12 member retired reserve is made up of former full-time law enforcement officers. Seven reserves are completing the basic academy. The department utilizes the same standards as those applied to full-time deputies.

Applicants go through a written exam, oral board interview by regular deputy sheriffs, background investigation, psychological, polygraph, agility test and medical. Vision must be corrected to 20/20 and cannot be in excess of 20/80 in either eye uncorrected if glasses or hard contacts are used. If corrected by soft contact lenses, uncorrected acuity must be 20/200 or better. Uncorrected hearing with no loss greater than 25 decibels in the 500, 1,000, 2,000, 3,000 hertz frequencies as measured by an audiometer.

Applicants must be at least 21 years of age and have a high school diploma or G.E.D. Applicants may be 20 years of age, as long as their 21st birthday occurs prior to academy graduation. The department prefers those who are older than 21 at entry into the academy.

Phoenix ⊙

The 440 hour Arizona Law Enforcement Officers Advisory Council (ALEOAC) certification is achieved by attending the academy at either Mesa or Glendale Community College. Reserves pay the tuition out of their own pockets. New classes begin in January and August and those that complete the program are awarded 26 college credit hours.

Full-time law enforcement deputies complete a 680 hour academy and a 400 hour field training officer (FTO) program. Reserves go through a 320 hour FTO program which leads to "car commander" status or solo qualification. A three hour in-service training meeting must be attended each month. Firearms qualification is four times annually.

Last year, the reserves worked approximately 20,000 hours. Some work beats in

Contact:

Judy Reznik
Reserve Secretary
Maricopa County Sheriff's Office
3325 West Durango
Phoenix, AZ 85009

602/256-1895

the districts as car commanders, while others ride with another reserve or regular deputy sheriff. They also work lake patrol, transportation, records and I.D., communications, detention, warrants and detectives. The monthly minimum requirement is 16 hours.

Reserve deputies furnish their own uniforms and equipment which are the same as the full-timers. Two complete uniforms and an authorized service weapon cost about $1,000. Reserves, who have 24 hour carry privileges as state certified law enforcement officers, may carry a 9mm, .45 or any revolver (.38 and up). They are also authorized to carry a .380 as a back up weapon.

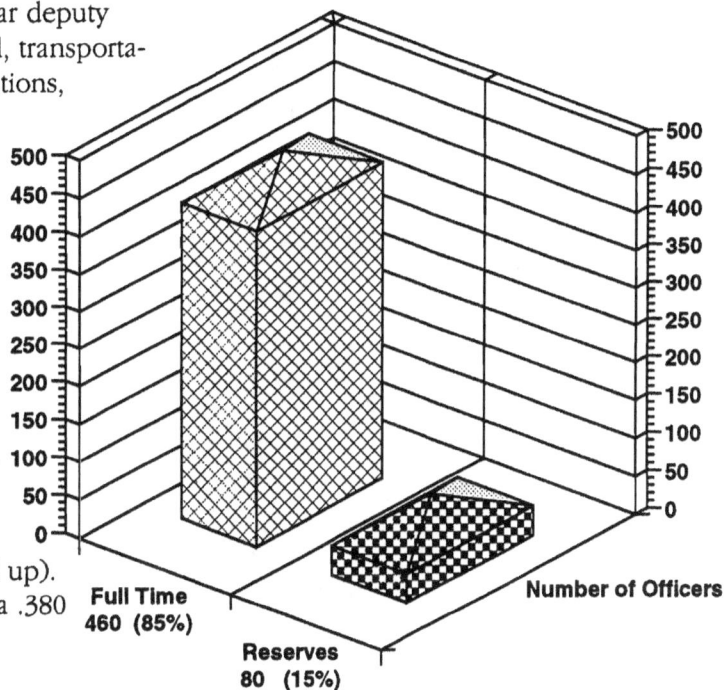

Full Time
460 (85%)

Reserves
80 (15%)

Number of Officers

Middletown Police Department

City of Middletown, Ohio

Number of Officers	
72	Full Time
20	Reserves
92	Total Officers

Minimum Training Hours Req.	
450	Full Time
450	Reserve

Middletown's reserve officers, because they are fully trained and certified officers under Ohio law, are like many other Ohio reserves in that they have full police powers and carry a firearm 24 hours a day, seven days a week. Middletown's 72 full-timers and 20 reserves exceed the Ohio Peace Officers Training Academy minimum of 420 hours with their 450 hours.

The intensive reserve academy schedule has the trainee attending school Monday through Thursday nights and all day Saturday for three months. Reserves go through an additional 216 hour field training officer (FTO) program, regular officers complete an FTO stint of 960 hours.

The uniform and Smith & Wesson 9mm firearm, on which officers must qualify twice a year, is provided by the agency. The badge and cap shield says "reserve."

The screening process for applicants 21 and older involves a background investigation, oral interview, psychological, polygraph and physical.

The Middletown police reserve unit donated 4,380 hours last

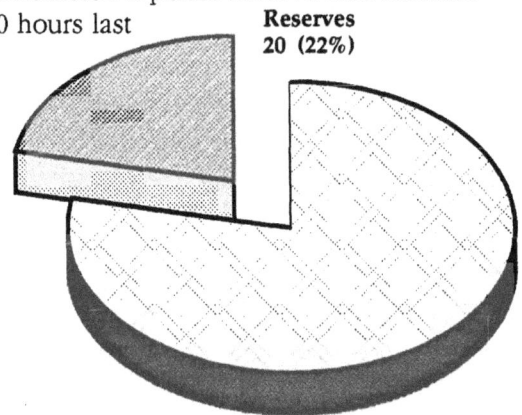

Reserves
20 (22%)

Full Time
72 (78%)

Contact:

Res. Capt. John D. Webster
Reserve Commander
Middletown Police Dept.
1 City Center
Middletown, OH 45042

513/425-7756

year patrolling as second officer, conducting jail transports and working special events such as parades and foot races. Reservists must serve at least 18 hours a month and receive three hours of monthly in-service training.

Mobile
Police Department

City of Mobile, Alabama

Number of Officers	
472	Full Time
20	Reserves
492	Total Officers

Minimum Training Hours Req.	
680	Full Time
280	Reserve

Mobile's reserves are trained to the state certified officer level of 280 hours in-house, though the reserve liaison, Lieutenant George H. Goodwin, explained that the police department does accept them if they have previously received certification on their own through a college. The department's academy ran Tuesday and Thursday nights for four hours and some Saturdays for nine months.

The 14 reserves assist the 472 full-time officers, trained for 680 hours with a 480 hour field training officer (FTO) program, on patrol. A few work in narcotics, traffic and the training section. Age 21 or older, they work for at least eight hours per month and have four hours of in-service training each month.

Reserve police officers go through a back

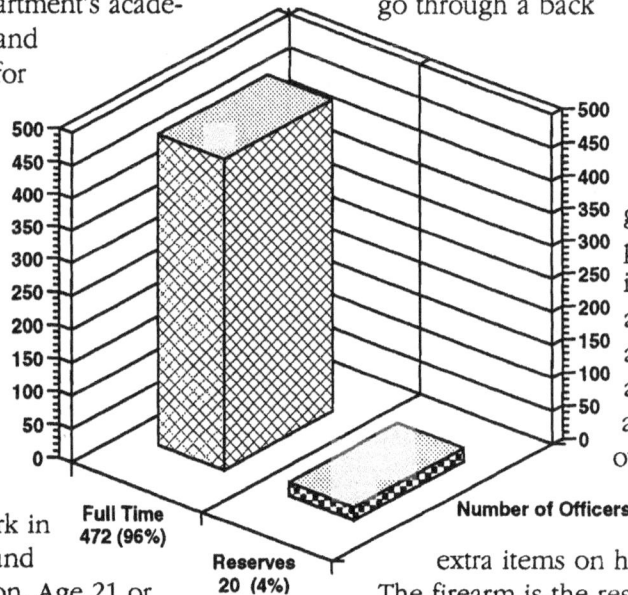

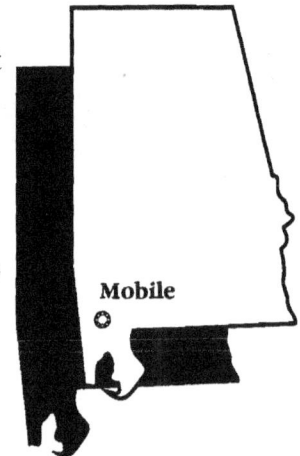

Mobile

Full Time 472 (96%)

Reserves 20 (4%)

Number of Officers

ground investigation, polygraph, drug screening, physical agility test and interview and wear an identical uniform with a "reserve" badge. They are supposed to buy their own uniform and equipment, but Goodwin said the department often has extra items on hand that they give them. The firearm is the responsibility of the reserve and they may use a revolver or semi-automatic, though the agency is leaning towards the use of 9mm firearms. Qualification is once a year and the reserves carry off-duty on a permit.

Contact:

**Lieutenant George H. Goodwin
Reserve Liaison
Mobile Police Department
2460 Government Boulevard
Mobile, AL 36606**

205/434-7791

Multnomah County Sheriff's Office

City of Portland, Oregon

Number of Officers	
56	Full Time
63	Reserves
119	Total Officers

Minimum Training Hours Req.	
328	Full Time
328	Reserve

D ue to annexations by the City of Portland and other municipalities, the once 300 strong full-time deputy agency has gone down to 56 regulars and 63 reserves. Police departments with responsibility for the newly annexed territories picked up the extra law enforcement officers needed from the Multnomah County Sheriff's Office.

The reserve commander, reserve captain Ernest H. Winterton, said that both the full-timers and the reserves complete 328 hours of police training. The agency has a three phase, 18 month probationary period for their new reserve deputy sheriffs. Phase I. consists of six months riding with a field training officer (FTO), during the six month phase II., the reserve rides with a senior reserve, with the remaining six month phase III. involving riding with any other deputy. Full-timers have a 960 hour FTO program.

In order to keep their certification, reserve deputy sheriffs must serve 260 hours per year, which comes out to 21.66 hours per month. Last year, 24,837 hours were donated. In-service training is held once a month for nine months out of the year.

Reserves, minimum age of 21, are responsible for acquiring their own firearm and may use a Smith and Wesson .357 Model 66 revolver, or choose a 9mm Sig Saur 226 or Glock Model 17 or 19. Reserves qualify twice a year and are supplied with 100 rounds of practice ammo each month.

The agency buys the uniform, but the reserve purchases the leather and equipment. The tan and brown reserve uniforms differ from those worn by the green regular deputy, but Winterton indicated that the reserves will soon switch over to the same green outfit. Salaried deputy badges are gold and reserve badges are silver and say "reserve."

Reserve deputies work in two man district units and are paired up with either a regular or a fellow reserve. They work in every area of the department including marine and park units in the summer, as well as plainclothes decoy work. Civic functions

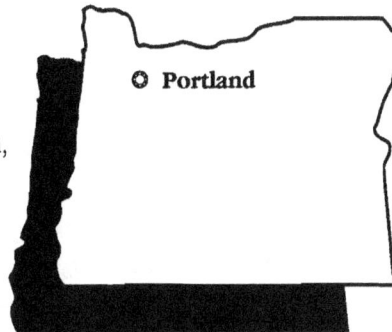

Contact:

Reserve Captain Ernest H. Winterton
Reserve Commander
Multnomah County Sheriff's Office
12240 N.E. Glisan Street
Portland, OR 97223

503/255-3600, Ext. 315

such as parades and runs are also handled for crowd control and traffic control purposes.

Individuals interested in becoming a reserve deputy fill out a preliminary information form, a longer four page application and go before a preliminary board, as well as a formal board comprised of senior reserves and regular officers. Candidates must also undergo a psychological and have their doctor fill out a medical form.

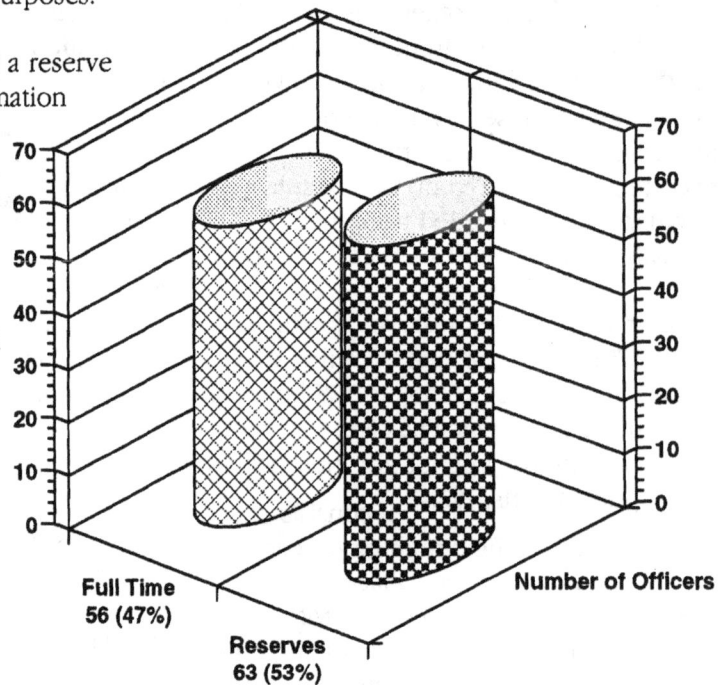

Full Time
56 (47%)

Reserves
63 (53%)

Number of Officers

New Orleans Police Department

City of New Orleans, Louisiana

Number of Officers
1,300 Full Time
175 Reserves
1,475 Total Officers

Minimum Training Hours Req.
500 Full Time
500 Reserves

New Orleans ○

W hen it comes to the 175 reserve officers with the New Orleans Police Department, equality is the word. Academy trained just like their 1,300 full-time counterparts, the reserves become fully Louisiana POST-certified through their 500 hour academy which takes place over the course of eight months. Sergeant Ronald Horst, assistant commander of the agency's reserve division, said the volunteers attend the police academy Tuesday and Thursday nights and all day on Saturdays. The field training officer (FTO) program also mirrors the full-time FTO process and comes in at just over 300 hours.

Reserve officers, who have a rank structure, perform the same duties as regulars officers and must donate a minimum of 24 hours a month. The uniforms are the same with the badge stating "RES." on it. Reservists, who must serve a monthly minimum of 24 hours, pay around $1,000 for their own firearm and uniform. They do receive a $300 uniform allowance if they serve 288 hours or more during the previous year (24 hours X 12 months).

The screening process is tough and 41 are set to graduate soon from an initial application field of 500 aspiring reserve officers. Utilizing the same procedures as the regular officers, the reserve hopefuls, minimum age of 21, must pass a battery of tests including a polygraph, urinalysis, MPI, CPI, physical, and agility test.

Contact:

Sergeant Ronald Horst
Assistant Commander
Reserve Division
New Orleans Police Department
1700 Moss Street, Room 103A
New Orleans, LA 70119

504/827-3274

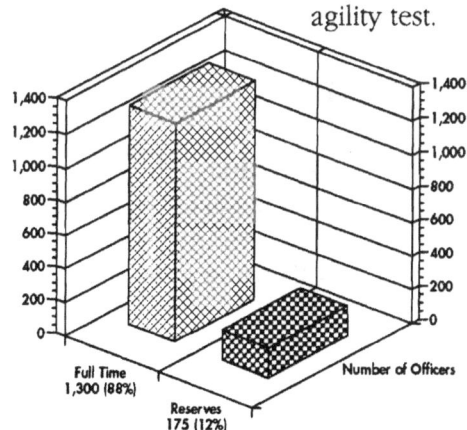

New York City Police Department

City of New York, New York

Number of Officers	
27,157	Full Time
4,402	Auxiliary
31,559	Total Officers

Minimum Training Hours	
640	Full Time
54	Auxiliary

The largest police department in the world, with 27,157 full-time officers, New York City has the largest auxiliary force with 4,402 volunteer officers. The officers, who are unarmed, are uniformed the same as the regular officers except for a seven point star badge which says "auxiliary" and a shoulder patch which also includes the designation.

Upon entering the program, auxiliary officers are issued uniforms by headquarters' police equipment section

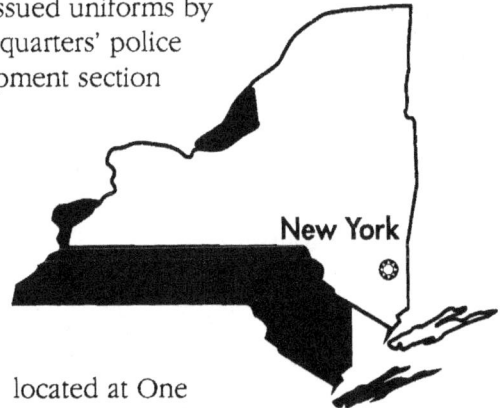

New York

located at One Police Plaza in Manhattan. Volunteers who meet the four hour a week or 16 hour a month minimum service requirement, are given a $115 uniform allowance once a year.

Trained, for 54 hours one night a week for for 16

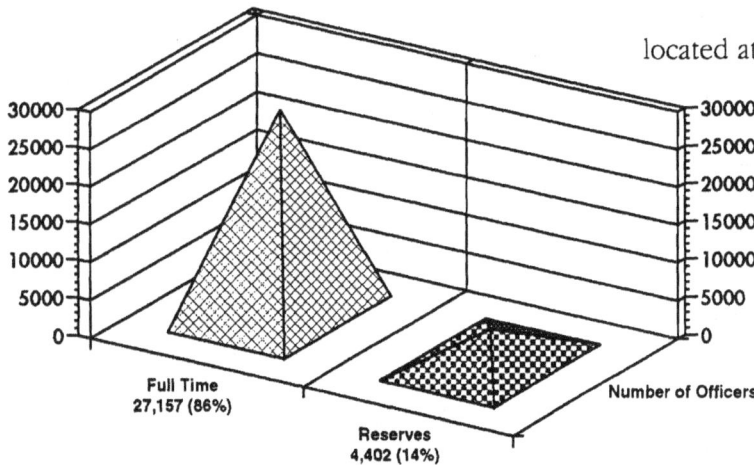

Full Time
27,157 (86%)

Reserves
4,402 (14%)

Number of Officers

Contact:

**Auxiliary Police Section
New York City Police Department
120-55 Queens Boulevard
Kew Gardens, NY 11424**

212/289-1000

task that is hard given the fact that crime more often than not finds the volunteer officers during the four hours each week minimum they are obligated to serve. While the majority of officers can be found on foot patrol and radio motor patrol (RMP) duty, a number of them are on horseback, on harbor boats and on emergency service units (ESU).

Individuals interested in joining the program which was founded on December 17, 1950 must be between the ages of 17 and 60 and live or work in New York City.

weeks on such topics as handling of the nightstick, community relations, first aid, radio procedures, patrol tactics, and subway operations, the auxiliary officers in the Big Apple are told to remain the eyes and ears of the police. It is a

Newark Police Department

City of Newark, New Jersey

Number of Officers
825 Full Time
170 Auxiliaries
995 Total Officers

Minimum Training Hours Req.
669 Full Time
77 Auxiliary

According to Ralph Palazzi, the auxiliary deputy chief who commands the auxiliary officer program in New Jersey's largest city, 70 of the 170 volunteers on the books are active and put in the minimum eight hours per month or more. The remaining 100 are available if an emergency of some magnitude arises.

The program is undergoing some changes. Officers have been traveling to the Essex County Auxiliary Police Academy, which at 77 hours exceeds the 42 hour New Jersey State Police/Office of Emergency Management minimum, located at the Essex County Police Academy in Cedar Grove. Plans are in the works to move the basic auxiliary officer training to the City of Newark's Police Academy. In-service training comes in at two hours per month.

The 825 full-time police officers in the city get their 669 PTC average hours of basic training at the Newark Police Academy or at another PTC certified academy.

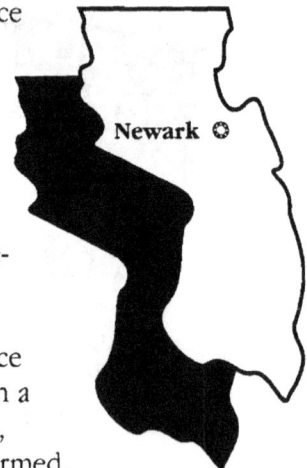

Newark auxiliary police officers are outfitted in a city provided uniform, however they are unarmed. The badge and patch says "auxiliary." The auxiliary patrolmen's shirts are powder blue, while the regular patrolmen wear navy blue. Superior officers have white shirts.

Palazzi said his people donated over 11,000 hours last year on patrols with another auxiliary officer. Special event details and emergency situations provided the remaining activity for the officers.

Interested residents fill out a nine page application which is submitted to field operations. A background investigation is conducted, as is an oral interview.

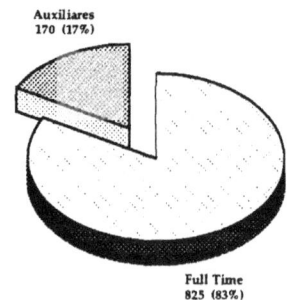

Contact:

Auxiliary Deputy Chief Ralph Palazzi
Newark Police Department
1 Lincoln Avenue
Newark, NJ 07104

201/733-6306

Auxiliares
170 (17%)

Full Time
825 (83%)

Norfolk
Police Department

City of Norfolk, Virginia

Number of Officers
687 Full Time
14 Auxilaries
701 Total Officers

Minimum Training Hours Req.
840 Full Time
560 Auxiliary

Norfolk's much anticipated program has taken off in its first year. Modeled on identical lines to the full-timers, Norfolk's volunteer auxiliary officers are utilized in all aspects of the city's police service mission.

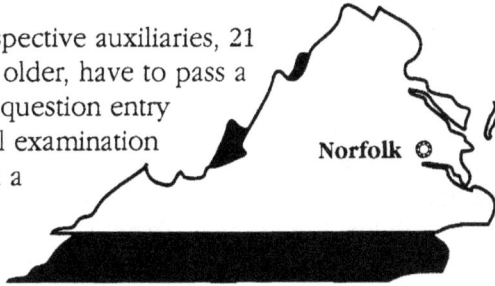

In an unusual setup, Norfolk's Department of Human Resources handles all public safety applicants. Investigator J.J. Rawlings said that they're shooting for an auxiliary force of 60 armed officers. He detailed the rather elaborate entry process which mirrors that used for full-time officer candidates.

Prospective auxiliaries, 21 and older, have to pass a 100 question entry level examination with a minimum passing score of 70%. They also have to pass a four event physical agility test, polygraph, background, physical, drug screen, psychological and oral review board.

According to the police department's Lieutenant W.O. Carrow, based in the training division, auxiliary officers complete a 560 hour basic police academy and a 520 hour field training officer (FTO) program. Full-time police officers take an 840 hour academy curriculum and a 1,920 hour FTO program. All officers, paid and unpaid, are required to have 40 hours of in-service training every two years and qualify on their agency provided Smith

Contact:

Lieutenant W.O. Carrow
Training Division
Norfolk Police Department
7665 Sewells Point Road
Norfolk, VA 23505

804/441-1778

Investigator J.J. Rawlings
Department of Human Resources
City of Norfolk
Norfolk City Hall, Room 100
Norfolk, VA 23505

804/441-2584

and Wesson 6906 9mm semi-automatic four times each year.

The auxiliary officer's badge and uniform, which is the same in appearance as the salaried officers' gear, is provided by the Norfolk Police Department. The auxiliary officers don the uniform for at least 24 hours per month during which time they ride solo or with a regular officer, among other duties.

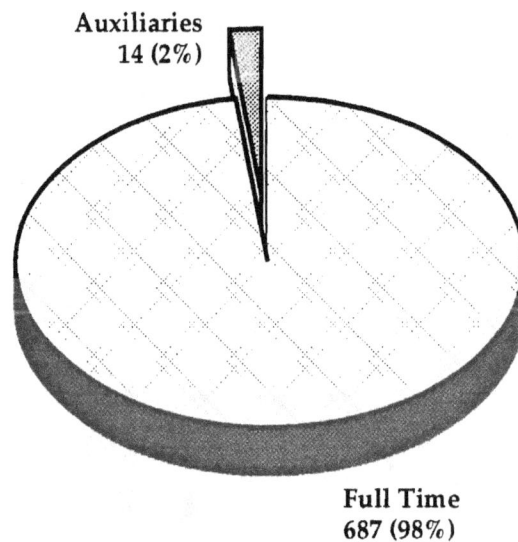

Auxiliaries
14 (2%)

Full Time
687 (98%)

Oklahoma County Sheriff's Office

City of Oklahoma City, Oklahoma

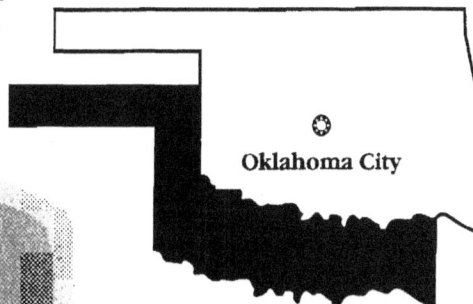

Based out of Oklahoma City and covering a metropolitan population of 1,000,000 people, the Oklahoma County Sheriff's Office divides their 300 reserve deputies into several main divisions, with the patrol division having higher training and service minimums. All of the reserves are training past the 120 hour state minimum for 160 hours. The academy is held two nights a week and several Saturdays and Sundays for three months.

The 80 full-time deputies train for 300 hours with a 160 hour field training officer (FTO) period.

In-service training for all personnel is around four hours per month.

Uniforms are identical to those worn by the regulars and are purchased at the expense of the reserve deputy sheriff.

The 40 patrol division reserves, who work solo patrol, take 30 hours of extra academy training for a total of 190 hours. They do a minimum of 60 shifts (480 hours) with an FTO and must serve at least 24 hours a month. Qualification occurs twice a year and Major Bill Kerr, the chief of the reserves, said all reserves have their choice of using their own firearm, "except for weapons such as a Taurus."

Reserves in other areas are required to serve only eight hours a month and qualify only once a year. The Mounted Patrol reserves supply their own horse. The Field Division provides reserves, mostly on foot, for parades and horse shows. The Courthouse Division includes reserves in communications, who must be

Contact:

Major Bill Kerr
Chief of Reserves
Oklahoma County Sheriff's Office
201 North Shartel
Oklahoma City, OK 73102

405/236-1717

state certified through a 911 course, as well as civil, court and records.

Kerr said he is particularly proud of the Sheriff's Bomb Squad. Started in 1981, the unit is made up of 80% reserve deputies who are called out to assist throughout the county, as well as other departments.

Kerr said he has 60 more reserves coming out of a 160 hour academy class soon and that the reserves donated in excess of 40,000 hours last year. The screening for applicants 21 and older includes a background check, MMPI, interview board and physical standards assessment.

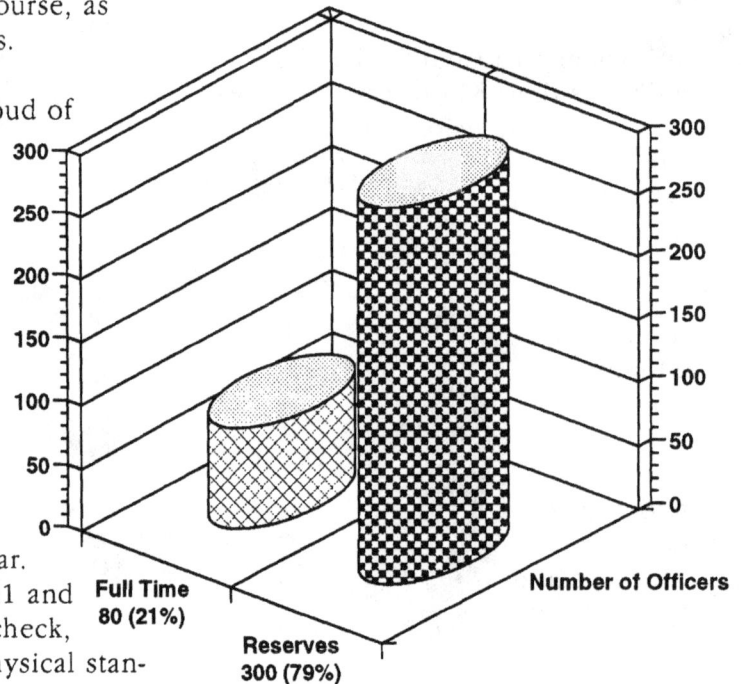

Full Time
80 (21%)

Reserves
300 (79%)

Number of Officers

Olympia Police Department

City of Olympia, Washington

Number of Officers	
68	Full Time
25	Reserves
93	Total Officers

Minimum Training Hours Req.	
480	Full Time
175	Reserve

Lieutenant Tor Bjornstad, the Olympia Police Department's reserve coordinator, who recently took over the program from former Los Angeles County, CA reserve deputy sheriff Cappy Gagnon who left the agency, said that his reserve police officers have more than their share of work at demonstrations and the like. "Being the capital city, we have quite a few demonstrations," said Bjornstad.

The 25 reserve officers, who serve a minimum of 16 hours per month and donated around 6,000 hours last year, also find themselves at special events such as parades, as well as on patrol with another reserve or regular officer.

The reserve officers, minimum age of 21, earn their Washington Criminal Justice Training Commission reserve certification through a 175 hour county wide course. The school is held Tuesday and Thursday nights from 7:00 PM to 10:00 PM and a few Saturdays for the six month period of January through June. In-service training is held for about two hours a month.

The 68 full-time officers go through a 480 hour basic academy. Newly minted police officers, who are not laterally transferring from another Washington agency, also have a 480 hour field training officer (FTO) program.

Olympia pays for the uniform, except for the shoes, which is the same in appearance. The badge says "reserve" in small letters. The department also furnishes the Smith and Wesson 5903 9mm firearm and qualification on the weapon is scheduled four times a year.

The department used to use a three tiered system for their reserves. Level I. reserves were in the academy and could patrol

Contact:

**Lieutenant Tor Bjornstad
Reserve Coordinator
Olympia Police Department
900 Plum Street
Olympia, WA 98501**

206/753-8300

unarmed with an academy certified officer. Level II. reserve officers were academy graduates who were armed and
patrolled only with a regular officer. To
progress to Level III. solo patrol status,
the reserve had to apply and show that
the necessary experience was possessed.

Last year, Olympia's program took ten out
of the 80 reserve hopefuls who applied.
The components of the screening process
include background investigation, psychological, polygraph and an oral board
made up of a mixture of full-time and
reserve personnel.

Olympia'a armed reserves today receive
their academy training pre-service and
patrol only with another reserve or regular officer. They may carry their firearm
off-duty provided that they have a concealed weapons permit. Bjornstad indicated

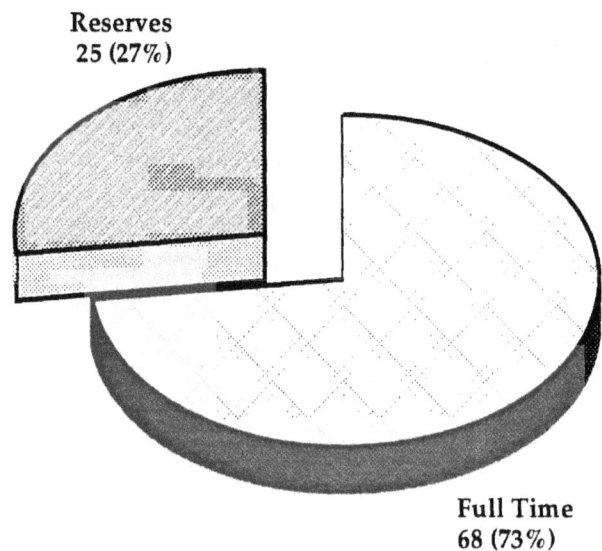

**Reserves
25 (27%)**

**Full Time
68 (73%)**

that is was fairly easy for reserve police officers to secure the permit.

Orange County Sheriff's Office

City of Santa Ana, California

Number of Officers	
1,300	Full Time
28	Level I. Reserves
130	Level II. Reserves
94	Level III. Reserves
1,552	**Total Officers**

Minimum Training Hours Req.	
888	Full Time
180	Level I. Reserve
160	Level II. Reserve
64	Level III. Reserve

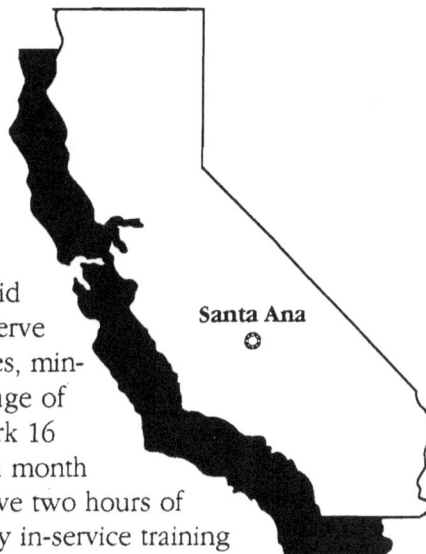

The Orange County Sheriff's Office divides their 252 armed reserve deputies among seven units with 66 in uniformed patrol and mounted, 61 in search and rescue, 14 in harbor, 15 in investigations, 58 in administrative unit, 39 in aero squadron and 19 in technical services unit. The Reserve Bureau's Sergeant Ray Karr indicated that 28 are 180 hour trained as Level I. reserves, 130 have their 160 hour Level II. certification and 64 hour Level III.s number 94 people.

Training is received three nights a week at the department's affiliate, Irvine, CA-based Rancho Santiago College. It takes ten months to complete Level I. training. Level I.s also have to complete the same 480 hour field training officer (FTO) program as the full-timers. Some top level certified Level I. Designated reserves, who have completed a regular academy and FTO program, have been included in the Level I. figure. The regular academy for the 1,300 paid deputies is 888 hours long.

Karr said the reserve deputies, minimum age of 18, work 16 hours a month and have two hours of monthly in-service training for a total of 18 hours monthly minimum service. Department furnished uniforms are identical to the regular garb, except that the badge has an "R" on it and the state seal in the center is not painted.

If available, the agency also supplies the revolver, but reserves may purchase the Smith and Wesson 9 mm 5904 semi-automatic if they want to. Qualification for reserves in patrol, search and rescue, harbor and investigations, who have been dubbed the "operational reserves," is monthly. The remaining "non-operational reserves" (administrative, technical, etc.) qualify with their weapon on a quarterly basis.

The screening for entry into the agency's

Contact:

Sergeant Ray Karr
Reserve Bureau
Orange County Sheriff's Office
550 North Flower Street
Santa Ana, CA 92702

714/538-3718

reserve program includes written and spelling tests, as well as physical agility, oral interview, background investigation and medical examination. Karr said the agency has an option to utilize polygraph examinations also.

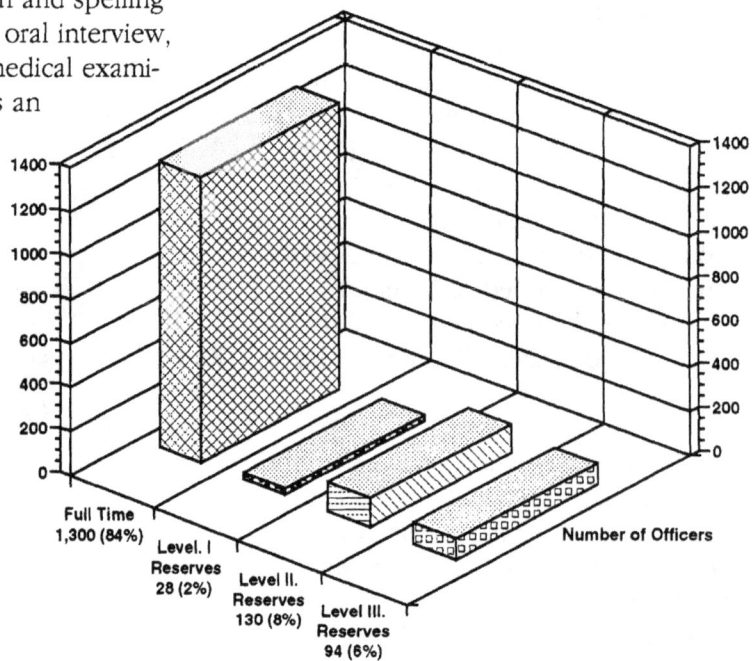

Full Time
1,300 (84%)

Level. I
Reserves
28 (2%)

Level II.
Reserves
130 (8%)

Level III.
Reserves
94 (6%)

Number of Officers

Orange County Sheriff's Office

City of Orlando, Florida

Number of Officers	
909	Full Time
80	Reserves
64	Auxiliaries
1,053	**Total Officers**

Minimum Training Hours Req.	
600	Full Time
600	Reserve
160	Auxiliary

The competition to become either a full-time or a volunteer Orange County deputy sheriff is fierce. Hundreds of applications await in the personnel office's files. The current pool of 80 certified reserves has been frozen because not enough field training officers (FTO) can be found, though the department indicated that they're working on enhancing the incentive for experienced deputies to serve as FTOs.

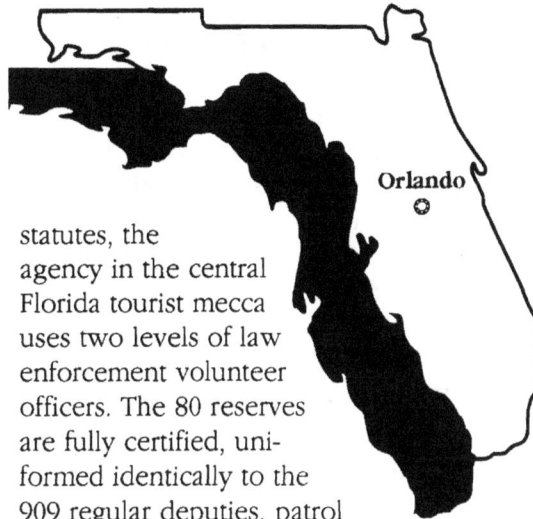

Mirroring the Sunshine State's statutes, the agency in the central Florida tourist mecca uses two levels of law enforcement volunteer officers. The 80 reserves are fully certified, uniformed identically to the 909 regular deputies, patrol alone in zone cars, and have full police powers. Full-timers and reserves have a 560 hour field training officer (FTO) program which must be completed within one year or they are terminated. Auxiliary deputy sheriffs, of which there are 64, have authority only while on duty and must serve as a second deputy in the patrol unit.

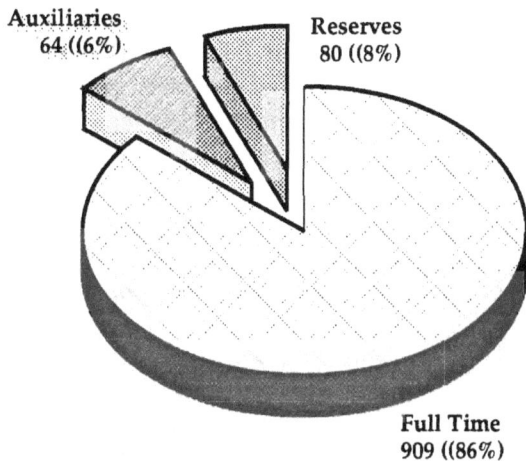

Auxiliaries
64 ((6%)

Reserves
80 ((8%)

Full Time
909 ((86%)

All deputy candidates acquire their training through outside organizations and local community colleges such as the Central Florida Criminal Justice Center, Kissimmee Police Academy, Mid Florida Tech and Seminole Community College. The curriculum for certified officers (volunteer reserve and paid full-time) runs 600 hours and the volunteer auxiliary course goes for 160 hours. They exceed the state minimums as the state requires 520 and 97 hours respectively.

Contact:

Lieutenant Clarence Cain
Orange County Sheriff's Office
475 West Story Road
Ocoee, FL 32761

407/889-4100

Reserves must serve at least 20 hours per month with auxiliaries responsible for the minimum of ten monthly hours. A four hour monthly in-service training meeting must also be attended. Qualification on the sidearm is scheduled four times a year. Reserves have their firearm provided by the sheriff's office while auxiliaries purchase their own. Issued guns are Smith and Wesson .357 Model 66 revolvers and the volunteer deputies have the option to carry a 9mm provided they complete transitional training.

Uniforms are provided by the department with the exception of the shoes and belt. Reserve attire is identical to the full-timers right down to the five pointed star which does not differentiate reserve from regular. Auxiliary deputies have a six pointed star badge that says "auxiliary" on it.

A great amount of attention has been paid to the federal Americans with Disabilities Act (ADA). Full-time, reserve and auxiliary personnel are put through the same screening process. In general, the Orange County Sheriff's Office rules out people who have had more than three moving violations in the last year or who have not been drug free for at least one year.

Following satisfactory completion of a pre-screening questionnaire, application, physical agility test, writing skills test, interview with a recruiter and background investigation, reserve and auxiliary deputy candidates are offered a slot contingent on their performance in a psychological, polygraph, medical and panel interview with three full-time lieutenants. Aspiring reserves must also pass a swim test.

Palm Beach County Sheriff's Office

Number of Officers	
850	Full Time
20	Reserve I.s
15	Reserve II.s (Auxiliary)
985	Total Officers

Minimum Training Hours Req.	
740	Full Time
740	Reserve I.s
200	Reserve II.s (Auxiliary)

City of West Palm Beach, Florida

The Palm Beach County Sheriff's Office, like many Florida law enforcement agencies, have dubbed their two tiered reserve and auxiliary volunteer deputy program with the titles "Reserve I." and "Reserve II." The 20 Reserve I.s, who may carry their firearm off duty, and 850 full-time deputies exceed the 520 hour state mini

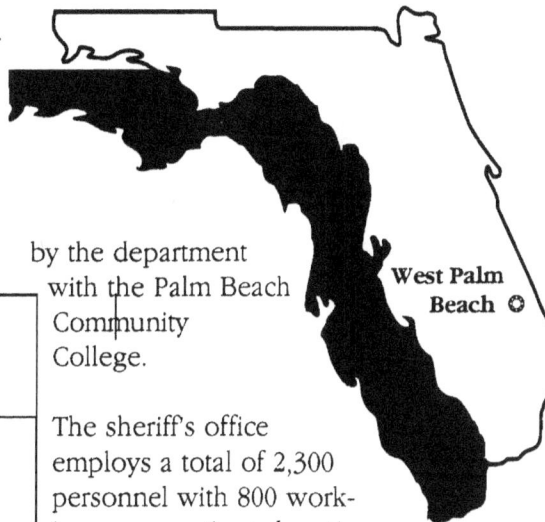

by the department with the Palm Beach Community College.

West Palm Beach ○

The sheriff's office employs a total of 2,300 personnel with 800 working as corrections deputies and 850 as law enforcement deputies. A 400 hour filed training officer program must be completed by road deputies and Reserve I. volunteers. The monthly minimum for Reserve I. and II. personnel is 20 hours, not counting at least one hour of in-service training.

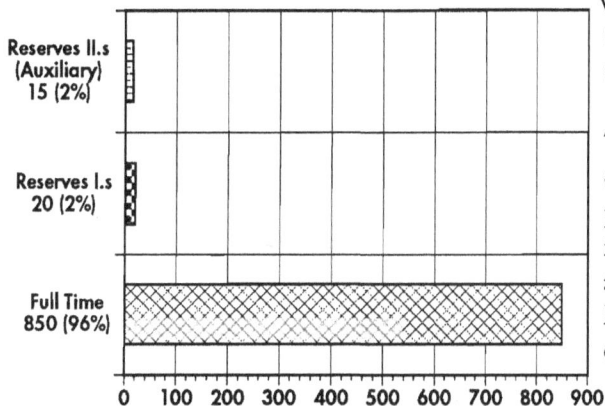

mum by having 740 hours of police academy training. The 15 Reserve II.s go beyond the 97 hour auxiliary curriculum with 200 hours of training. Volunteer officer training is sponsored

The agency supplies the uniforms, except for the shoes, which are identical to those worn by full-time deputy sheriffs. The one difference is that "reserve officer" appears under the deputy's name on the nametag. Reserves must supply the .38, .357 or 9mm firearm with which they must qualify once a year.

In Palm Beach County, reserve deputy sheriffs ride on patrol with full-timers. They also serve in specialized assignments which

Contact:

Captain Fred Mascaro
Reserve Liaison
Palm Beach County Sheriff's Office
3228 Gun Club Road
West Palm Beach, FL 33406

407/688-3000

are approved on an individual basis. Those areas include community relations, the environmental section and the tax squad.

The screening process utilized by the agency involves a preliminary interview, written application to personnel, oral review board, polygraph, physical, psychological and oral interview with the captain and executive lieutenant.

Phoenix
Police Department

City of Phoenix, Arizona

Number of Officers
2,100 Full Time
  26 Reserves
2,126 Total Officers

Minimum Training Hours Req.
620 Full Time
480 Reserve

S ergeant Larry Jacobs, the 2,100-full-time officer Phoenix Police Department's reserve coordinator, said his 26 reserve officers are required to serve 100 hours a quarter which translates to 400 hours a year or 33.3 hours per month. They donated 14,629 hours last year.

Regular officers are trained for 620 hours with a 2,080 hour field training officer (FTO) program. Prior to engaging in a 500 hour FTO

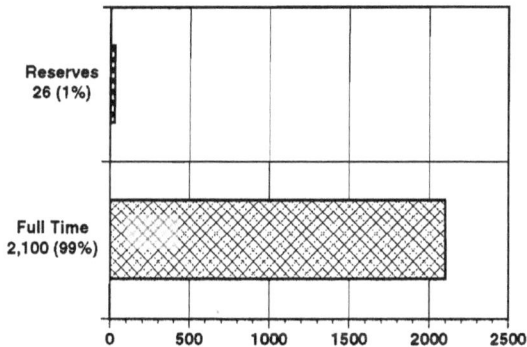

program, the reserves receive 480 hours of academy training through either Glendale Community College or Mesa Community

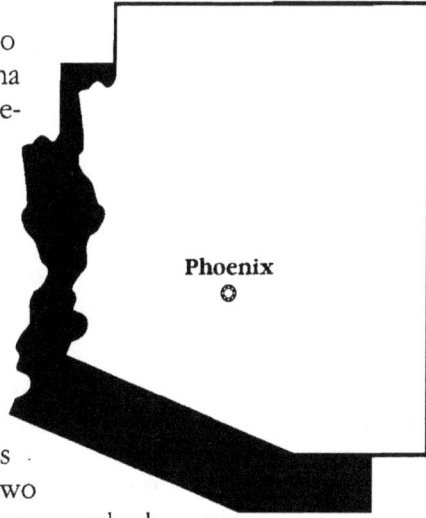

College, two local Arizona Law Enforcement Officer Advisory Council (ALEOAC)-certified community college academies. Jacobs said it is a two semester program scheduled on Tuesday and Thursday nights and all day on Sunday. In accordance with state mandates, in-service training for all officers tallies in at a minimum of 24 hours annually.

"We've tightened up our reserve program," said Jacobs. "Six or seven years ago, we had 200 reserves who were not as well screened or trained." The much more equal training has given the reserve police officers the option to

Contact:

Sergeant Larry Jacobs
Reserve Coordinator
Patrol Administration
Phoenix Police Dept.
620 West Washington
Phoenix, AZ 85003

602/262-7288

patrol districts throughout the city's six precincts on a solo basis answering all types of calls for police service. One reserve is active in the DUI program.

The Glock 9mm Model 17 or 19 firearm is provided by the Phoenix Police Department and the reserve officers qualify on it four times a year including one outdoor shoot.

The uniforms, identical except for the badge which says "reserve," are provided by the department if the reserve puts in 1,000 or more hours. At the 500 to 999 hours of service level, the city pays for 75% of the uniform cost. The reimbursement rate drops to the 50% mark for serving 200 to 499 hours.

Among the incentives Jacobs said his department proudly offers their reserves is coverage under industrial insurance and a free bus pass. Reserves are also reimbursed for up to $450 for a ballistic vest. In an unusual move, Phoenix allows their reserve officers to work off duty jobs and also pays them if they to count on official police business.

Reserve hopefuls are processed through the agency's employment services office and have to take a written exam, polygraph, psychological and drug screening.

Portland
Police Bureau

City of Portland, Oregon

Number of Officers	
858	Full Time
52	Reserves
910	Total Officers

Minimum Training Hours Req.	
850	Full Time
280	Reserve

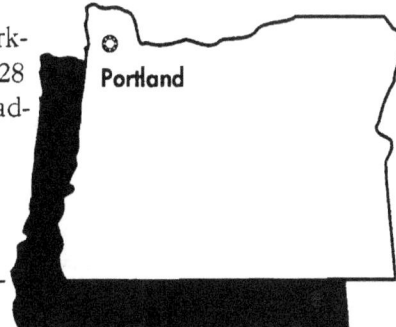

Portland's 52 reserve officers, who have a ranking system, served the 850 member police organization for 17,000 hours in 1992. Officer Haven Baxter, the reserve coordinator, said the reserves receive 280 hours of training two nights week and eight hours on Saturday for five months. In addition to the 52 reservists currently working, another 28 are in the academy.

The reserve officers wear the same uniform and firearm, a Glock .45 or 9mm, which they must qualify on quarterly. The Portland Police Bureau recently started paying for the uniform and sidearm. The shoulder patch and badge designate the officers' reserve status during their minimum 16 hours of monthly duty.

The background investigation is thorough. Reserves, who must be at least 21, take a written exam, physical, and undergo a half hour taped oral interview.

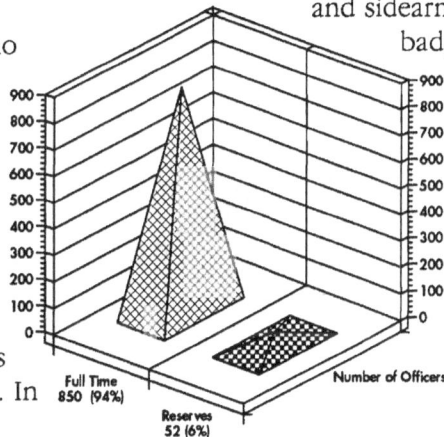

Contact:

Officer Haven Baxter
Reserve Coordinator
Portland Police Bureau

503/796-3179

Pulaski County Sheriff's Office

City of Little Rock, Arkansas

Number of Officers
136 Full Time
75 Auxiliaries
211 Total Officers

Minimum Training Hours Req.
320 Full Time
102 Auxiliary

Based in Little Rock, the Pulaski County Sheriff's Office has 25 auxiliary deputies in mounted and 50 in other areas such as patrol. All auxiliaries must have 102 hours of training which takes place three nights a week and some Saturdays.

The full-time liaison to the auxiliary, Lieutenant Ronnie Tamburo, said that a background check is done for people wishing to enter the 102 hour training course. He explained that they must successfully complete the course and a more intensive background, along with psychological, oral board, physical, drug screening, in order to become an auxiliary deputy. "I had 42 people in the course in November. Out of that, 32 graduated and we picked up nine," said Tamburo.

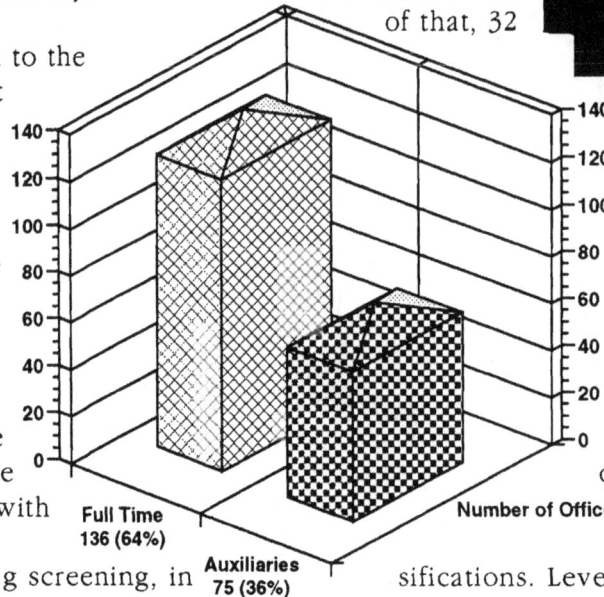

Auxiliary Major Lester Gauntt, the auxiliary program coordinator, said their field training officer (FTO) program was divided up into three classifications. Level III. auxiliaries must

Little Rock

Full Time
136 (64%)

Auxiliaries
75 (36%)

Number of Officers

Contact:

Lieutenant Ronnie Tamburo
Auxiliary Liaison
Pulaski County Sheriff's Office
2900 South Woodrow
Little Rock, AR 72204

501/661-1520

Auxiliary Major Lester Gauntt
Auxiliary Program Coordinator
Pulaski County Sheriff's Office
2900 South Woodrow
Little Rock, AR 72204

501/661-1520

work in the company of a full-time deputy for 960 hours before being elevated to Level II. status. Level II. auxiliaries serve with a higher positioned Level I. auxiliary deputy sheriff for 48 hours. The volunteer can then progress to Level I. and patrol alone provided that a year's probation has also been completed.

The 136 enforcement deputies get 320 hours of training and have a 320 hour FTO program. The agency also has 130 correctional deputies.

The auxiliary deputies have the same badge, patch and uniform as the salaried officers and

must personally purchase the uniform and the .38 or .357 revolver. Qualification is scheduled four times a year and in-service training sessions meet the first Tuesday of every month for two hours.

The Pulaski County auxiliaries are required to serve 16 hours a month in such areas as patrol, criminal investigations division (CID), warrants, corrections, records and communications. The mounted auxiliary deputies worked 3,130 hours last year while the remaining volunteers served 12,975 for a total auxiliary time donation of 16,105 hours.

Ramsey County Sheriff's Office

City of St. Paul, Minnesota

Number of Officers
280 Full Time
40 Reserves (Licensed)
30 Reserves (Non-licensed)
350 Total Officers

Minimum Training Hours Req.
400 Full Time
400 Reserve (Licensed)
36 Reserve (Non-licensed)

The Ramsey County Sheriff's Office's reserve deputies are mostly comprised of criminal justice college students who are using the program as a stepping stone into a full-time career. 40 of the 70 total reserves have achieved their Minnesota state license as police officers and carry a Glock 9mm Model 17 firearm following 400 hours of training.

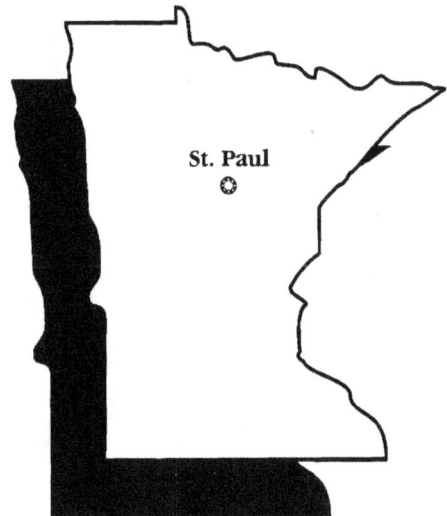

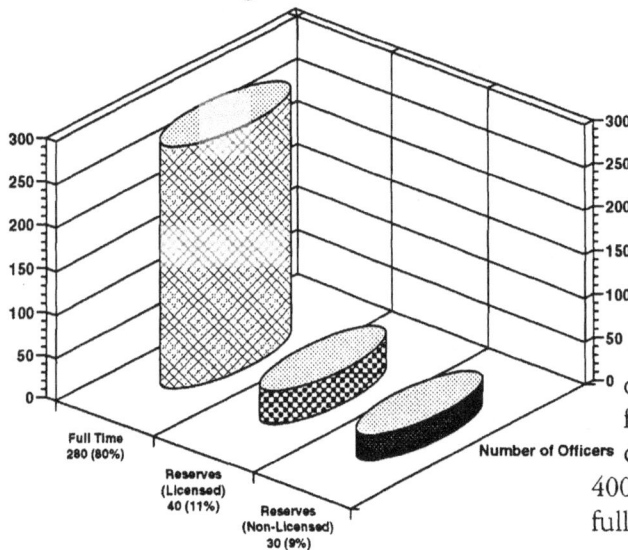

St. Paul

New reserves must have 36 hours of preservice training and are allowed to patrol unarmed with a licensed officer. The block of instruction is held every Wednesday night for four hours. The agency has 30 in this category who each month chip away at the 400 hours they need to be licensed. The 280 full-time deputy sheriffs have 400 hours of preservice training.

The reserve deputies must be 21 or older and must work at least 10 hours per month. They were in uniform for around 23,000 hours last year patrolling the county parks and waterways, as well as handling civic events such as dances.

The reserves pay for their own Glock and for the uniform which has "reserve" on the badge and patch. A uniform allowance of

Contact:

Sergeant G. Gary
Reserve Advisor
Ramsey County Sheriff's Office
655 West County Road E
Shoreview, MN 55126

612/481-1312

$75.00 is disbursed annually by the St. Paul-headquartered department which provides contract law enforcement services to six municipalities, as well as to the county.

Entry into the non-licensed ranks is achieved by passing an oral board and background investigation. When the newly minted 400 hour trained reserve deputy is ready to be considered for licensing by Minnesota, a more thorough process takes place which includes MMPI psychological and drug screening.

Reno
Police Department

City of Reno, Nevada

Total Number of Officers
285 Full Time
70 Reserves
355 Total Officers

Minimum Training Hours Req.
600 Full Time
480/600 Reserve

Out of the 70 total reserve officers with the City of Reno Police Department, an amazing 45, more than half, have taken 15 weeks off from their full-time occupations to attend the 600 hour regular officer academy. The academy is held at a local community college and the $1,500 tuition is picked up by the department. The remaining 25 secured their minimum 480 hours of training in a reserve academy held one day a week on Saturdays.

○ Reno

Both the reserve officers, who must be a U.S. citizen and reside in the Reno area, and the 285 full-time officers go through a 560 hour field training officer (FTO) program. The screening process for the candidate, who must be 21 or older, involves a background investigation and physical.

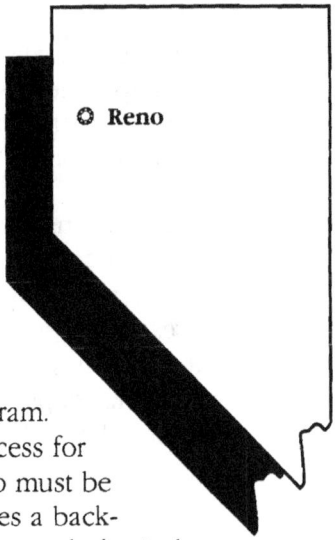

The department furnished uniform for the reserves are identical to the regulars' attire except for "reserve" on the badge. The reserve police officer must provide his own firearm which may be a semi-automatic or revolver, although the city is phasing the revolvers out and 90% carry semi-automatics. The approved 9mm or .45 are Beretta, Glock, Sig Saur and Smith and

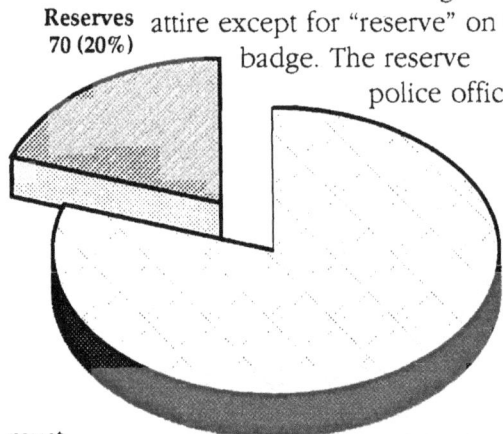

Reserves
70 (20%)

Full Time
285 (80%)

Contact:

Officer Don Ernhot
Reserve Coordinator
Reno Police Dept.
P.O. Box 1900
Reno, NV 89505

702/334-3873

Wesson and the sanctioned wheel guns are Colt, Ruger and Smith and Wesson in .38 or .357. Reserves qualify on their firearms four times annually.

The reserves must work ten hours a month on patrol duties with two hours a month spent in a training meeting for a total of 12 minimum hours monthly. Last year, 16,000 hours were donated on such duties as augmenting patrol as a second officer. They also worked at special events assignments such as parades and conducted phone surveys.

Rockland County Sheriff's Office

City of New City, New York

According to Sheriff James Kralik, Rockland County's part-time deputy sheriff program precedes the hiring of full-timers. Conceived in 1962, the department did not hire full-time personnel until 1966. He said the program was strong due to its long history in the suburban New York City county.

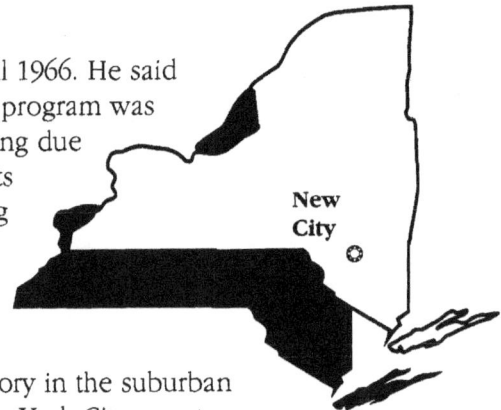

New City

The Sheriff, said his 250 full-time and 50 part-time deputy sheriffs are fully certified law enforcement officers who exceed the 445 hour New York State Bureau of Municipal Police minimum requirement with their 550 hours of basic police academy training. The 550 hour academy is held by Rockland County on Monday, Tuesday and Wednesday nights from 7:00 PM to 11:00 PM and on Saturdays from 8:00 AM to 4:00 PM for a period of six months. Part-time deputy sheriffs have full police powers and carry their firearm off duty.

The field training officer (FTO) program comes in at 480 hours for all officers. Full-time deputies complete the FTO program in 12 straight weeks. In-service training is conducted for 40 hours each year. Firearms qualification, on the agency furnished Glock 9mm semi-automatics, is scheduled twice a year.

The sheriff's office pays for all uniforms which have identical color schemes and

Contact:

Chief Harry Stewart
or
Sergeant Buddy Gibson
Rockland County Sheriff's Office
55 New Hempstead Road
New City, NY 10956

914/638-5400

shoulder patches. The badges for the part-timers state "Deputy sheriff," like the full-time officers. The only difference is that the part-time deputies have six pointed stars and the regulars wear seven pointed star badges.

The agency has 50 part-time deputy sheriffs and 250 total full-time deputies. The patrol division has 70 law enforcement deputies with the remaining 180 used in corrections and other areas.

"The public can't tell the difference," said Sheriff Kralik. "There is no differentiation such as 'part-time' on the uniform. Differentiation subjects the deputy to danger and abuse."

The Sheriff, who started as a member of the mounted unit, said the department utilizes the part-timers, technically called "relief officers," in five areas. He said that 14 work in court security, 10 work in transportation, eight work in patrol support services, seven are in the com-

munity support unit, and the mounted unit has 11 members.

Patrol support services deputies work where additional manpower is needed and on the desk. The community support unit provides traffic and crowd control for events such as the Haitian Soccer Tournament. They also staff programs such as "CAT: Combat Auto Theft." The Sheriff does not allow the mounted unit to be used as merely a parade unit. Instead, he has them patrolling shopping malls and villages.

Sheriff Kralik is a big proponent of hiring former full-time police officers and has many working 20 hour weeks in prisoner transport and court security.

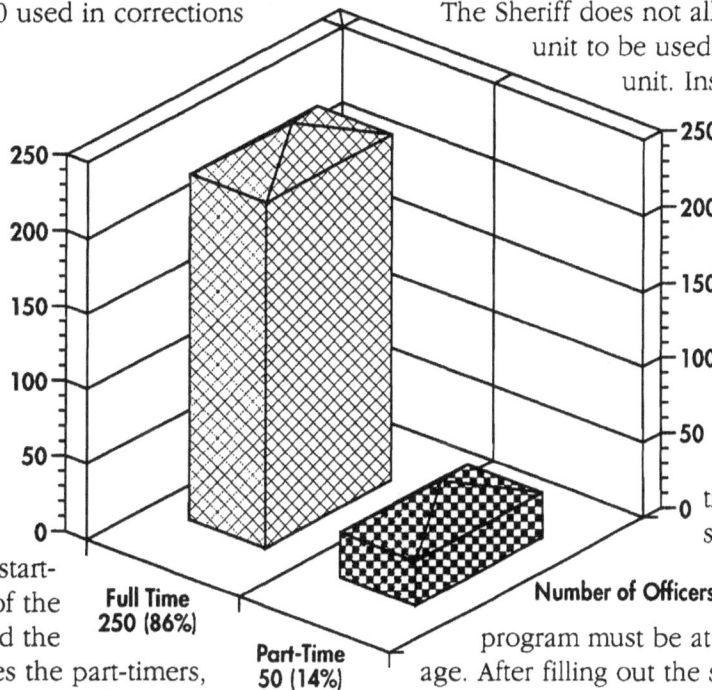

Applicants to the program must be at least 21 years of age. After filling out the same ten page application as full-time candidates, aspring part-time deputies go through a background investigation and screening board.

Full Time
250 (86%)

Part-Time
50 (14%)

Number of Officers

Frank Shanahan, a retired New York City Police Sergeant, works for Sheriff Kralik as a part-time deputy sheriff in Rockland County.

Wayne Tripp (left), a 550 hour trained and fully certified part-time Rockland County, NY, deputy sheriff, confers with Sheriff James L. Kralik in the Sheriff's office.

Sacramento
Police Department

City of Sacramento, California

Number of Officers	
597	Full Time
93	Reserves
690	Total Officers

Minimum Training Hours Req.	
720	Full Time
214	Level I. Reserve
146	Level II. Reserve
64	Level III. Reserve

The Sacramento Police Department utilizes California POST certified Level I. (214 hours), Level II. (146 hours) and Level III. (64 hours) reserve officers, although they now only accept applications from previously trained Level I. reserves. Sergeant Thomas Sweeney, the director of the

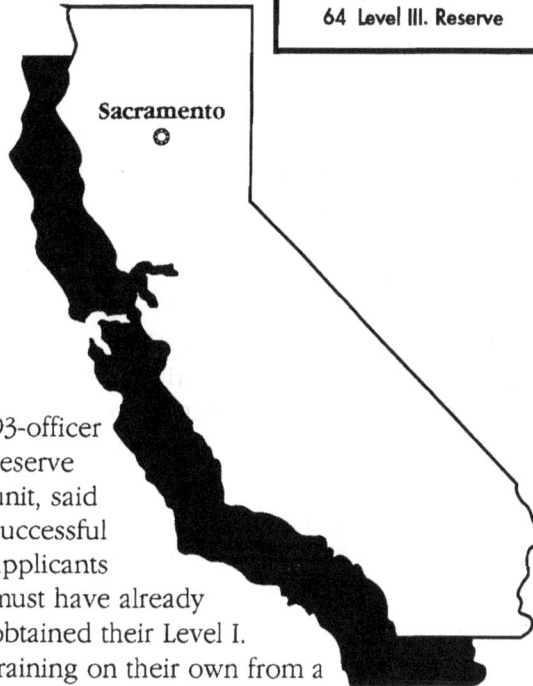

Sacramento

93-officer reserve unit, said successful applicants must have already obtained their Level I. training on their own from a local community college.

Sergeant Betty Parker, who handles the application process, said the same methods are used to screen the reserves as are utilized for the 597 full-time officers. "We spend at least 40 hours on each background investigation," explained Parker who added that a CBI credit check, agility test, oral board, polygraph, psychological, medical evaluation and written examination are also conducted. Minimum age is 21, although 18 year olds were accepted for a short time as part of a failed experiment.

Reserve officers go through a 192 hour field training officer (FTO) program and the full-timers complete an FTO program of 1,040 hours. The reserves used to have a three

Contact:

Sgt. Thomas Sweeney
Director of Reserve Unit
Sacramento Police Dept.
5303 Franklin Boulevard
Sacramento, CA 95820

916/277-6058

hour monthly training meeting, but the sessions have been temporarily halted since November 1992. They work a minimum of 16 hours a month and may not exceed 20 hours per week.

The agency provides one set of the uniform which differs from the navy blue full-time officers' attire. Reserve officers have a light blue shirt with a stripe down the pants. "Reserve" is stated on the badge. A Smith & Wesson Model 15 revolver is also furnished by the city. The officers qualify twice a year on their sidearm and once annually on a shotgun. Some acquire CCW permits to carry a gun off duty.

The reserve police officers, who worked 46,167 during calendar year 1992, conduct some car patrol, but mostly handle crowd and traffic control, parks patrol, boat patrol, and work furlough and hospital prisoner supervision.

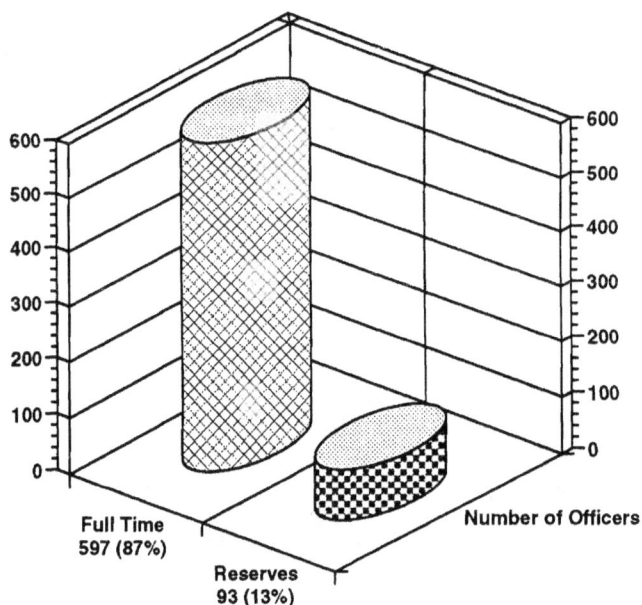

Full Time
597 (87%)

Reserves
93 (13%)

Number of Officers

Salt Lake City Police Department

City of Salt Lake City, Utah

Number of Officers	
330	Full Time
16	Reserves
346	Total Officers

Minimum Training Hours Req.	
400	Full Time
200	Reserve

Persons interested in becoming a reserve police officer in Salt Lake City have to present their 160 hour Category II. officer certificate before they can even apply for the post. Lieutenant John Schroen, the reserve coordinator, said after they are accepted, an additional 40 hours of agency academy training is given for a total of 200 hours. The 40 extra hours are given two nights a week and all day Saturday.

Salt Lake City

The 16 reserves get their Category II. training on their own at night and on weekends at local institutions such as Salt Lake Community College and Weaver State College. Schroen indicated that people can also put themselves through the state academy, which held during the day, for Category II. and that they "can also do right up to Category I." (fully certified officer). The 330 full-time officers are 400 hour Category I.s and they have a 440 hour field training officer (FTO) program.

The reserves, minimum age of 21, are used as a second patrol officer and must serve 24 hours a month or more. They donated hours last year were 2,200 for the reserves who are identical except for their patch which says "reserve." Uniforms are bought by the agency and the reserve is responsible for obtaining the leather, as well as any

Contact:

Lieutenant John Schroen
Reserve Coordinator
Salt Lake City Police Department
315 East 200 South
Salt Lake City, UT 84111

801/799-3301

one of a number of approved guns. Qualification happens once a year and 40 hours of in-service training is held annually.

Prospective reservists go through the same screening process as a regular except for the written examination. They must pass a background investigation, agility test, physical exam, polygraph and interview.

Reserves 16 (5%)

Full Time 330 (95%)

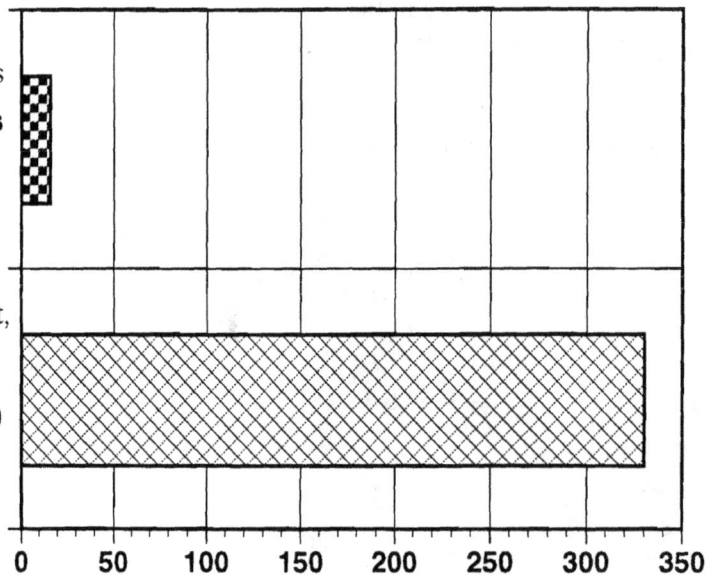

| 0 | 50 | 100 | 150 | 200 | 250 | 300 | 350 |

San Bernardino County Sheriff's Office

City of San Bernardino, California

Number of Officers	
980	Full Time
1,091	Reserves
2,071	Total Officers

Minimum Training Hours Req.	
1,200	Full Time
254	Level I. Reserve
156	Level II. Reserve
66	Level III. Reserve

Because their beat covers the largest geographical county in the United States (mostly desert stretching from Los Angeles County to the Arizona and Nevada borders), the San Bernardino County Sheriff's Office divides their 1,091 armed, California POST certified reserve deputies into three

main areas encompassing 102 units.

The 392 Level I. and 276 Level II. reserves engage in field patrol with the higher trained reserves allowed to do so on a solo basis following completion of a 400 hour field training officer (FTO) program. Level II. reserve deputies patrol as a second officer and have an FTO program of 200 hours. The 980 full-time deputies complete a 1,200 hour academy, which includes an 80 hour jail school, and a 400 hour FTO program. The sheriff's office has 1,900 total employees including civilians.

The 392 Level III. reserve deputy sheriffs are utilized in Search and Rescue, Mounted Posse and a section called Administrative support which includes underwater search and recovery and recruiting. They must have 66 hours of training. The county has a POST certified search and rescue academy which goes an additional 32 hours and covers basic search and rescue techniques such as rope tying and compass reading.

Contact:

Deputy Sheriff John G. Plasencia
Coordinator
Sheriff's Volunteer Forces
San Bernardino County Sheriff's Office
655 East 3rd Street
San Bernardino, CA 92415

909/356-3939

All individuals applying to the program must have already attained at their own expense at least their POST certified Level III. certificate. Many local community colleges, such as Rio Hondo and Chapman College, offer the program. With a minimum age of 21, San Bernardino screens their reserve applicants as they would an aspiring full-time deputy sheriff. They must take an agility test, polygraph, psychological, medical, and oral interview.

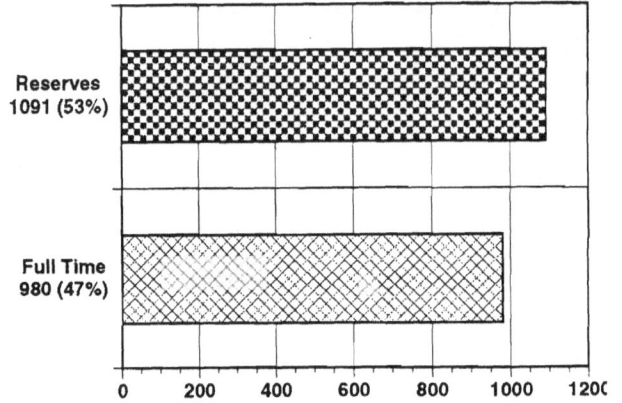

Reserves 1091 (53%)

Full Time 980 (47%)

Level I. and II. reserves, who donated

134,732 hours last year engaged in field patrol, narcotics investigation, arson investigation and other similar law enforcement line duties, must serve at least 20 hours per month, not counting any in-service training prescribed for the full-timers. Level III. reserves work eight hours per month with an additional eight hours spent each month in training. The Level III.s in Search and rescue and Mounted Posse served 74,846 hours last year, while those in Administrative donated 160,386 hours. The reserve forces total hours donated was 369,964 hours.

All reserves qualify on their personally purchased revolver or semi-automatic firearm four times a year and must also take a quarterly use of force course, just like the salaried deputies. Uniforms, also bought by the individual reserve deputy, is the same as the regular, except that the badge has an "R" before the serial number. Level II. badges are in the 2,000 series and Level I. badges are in the 1,000 series.

San Diego County Sheriff's Office

City of San Diego, California

Total Number of Officers	
1,528	Full Time
325	Level I & III Reserves
1,853	Total Officers

Minimum Training Hours Req.	
712	Full Time
565	Reserve

The 325 reserve deputies of the San Diego Sheriff's Office, under the administration of Sheriff Jim Roache, wear identical uniforms, patches, and weapons as the regular deputies during their 16 hours of minimum service. The reserves pay around $600 for the uniform and also pay for the sidearm.

The 4,200 mile, 2.5 million population county's three different reserve divisions offer a variety of different duties. The support services bureau, staffed fully by reserves, consists of a personnel branch, an underwater search and recovery unit, video team, and weapons training instructors. The search and rescue bureau, with California's only 119 hour search and rescue academy, subjects its volunteers to emergency callouts at all hours of the day and night.

The law enforcement bureau utilizes California POST-certified non-designated Level I. reserves, but exceeds the 214 hour state

Contact:

Lieutenant David Wm. Herbert
Reserve Support Detail
San Diego County Sheriff's Office
9621 Ridgehaven Court
San Diego, CA 92123

619/974/2160

Sheriff Jim Roache

minimum by bringing them in at a whopping 565 hours. They then go through a 400 hour FTO program similiar to the regular deputies' 480 hours. Reserve Lieutenant Randy Dick said potential reserves, minimum age of 21, must undergo the same background investigation as the 1,528 sworn full-timers who get 712 academic hours of training..

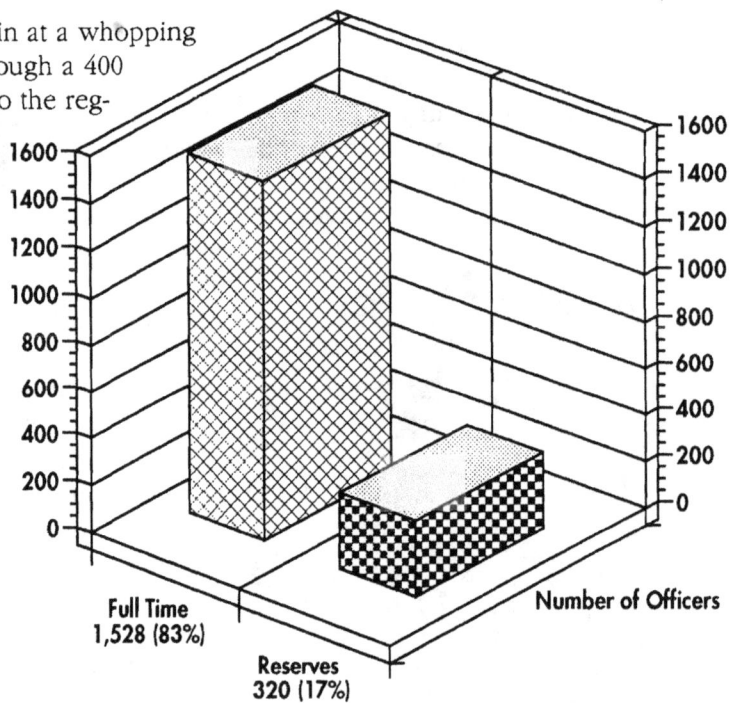

1600

1400

1200

1000

800

600

400

200

0

1600

1400

1200

1000

800

600

400

200

0

Full Time
1,528 (83%)

Reserves
320 (17%)

Number of Officers

San Diego
Police Department

City of San Diego, California

Both the 100 reserve officers and 1,990 full-time officers with the San Diego Police Department go through a 200 hour field training officer (FTO) program. The reserves are California POST certified at

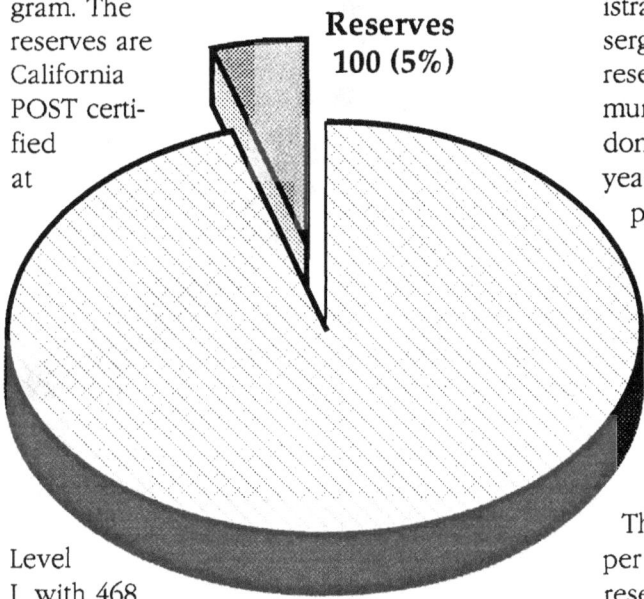

**Reserves
100 (5%)**

**Full Time
1,990 (95%)**

Level I. with 468 hours and the regulars are certified with 944 hours of academy training.

Sergeant Mary Cornicelli, the reserve administration sergeant, said the reserves, minimum age of 21, donated 34,657 last year and work in patrol with "a few in domestic violence units." The usual polygraph, psychological and other tests are used to examine officer candidates.

San Diego

Reserves apply for CCW permits if they wish to carry their 9mm Ruger off duty. The gun, which must be qualified four times per year, is supplied by the agency unless the reserve prefers to carry a personally owned weapon.

Minimum service has been set at 24 hours a month and the city reimburses the reserve's uniform expenses if he or she serves 288 hours a year (24 X 12 months). The uniform looks the same except that the badge says "reserve" and is silver. The regular officers' badges are gold.

Contact:

**Sergeant Mary Cornicelli
Reserve Administration Sergeant
San Diego Police Dept.
1401 Broadway
San Diego, CA 92103**

619/531-2240

San Francisco
Police Department

City of San Francisco, California

Number of Officers	
1,400	Full Time
37	Reserves
1,437	Total Officers

Minimum Training Hours Req.	
900	Full Time
146	Level II. Reserve
64	Level III. Reserve

San Francisco has a few Level III. (64 hour) California POST-certified

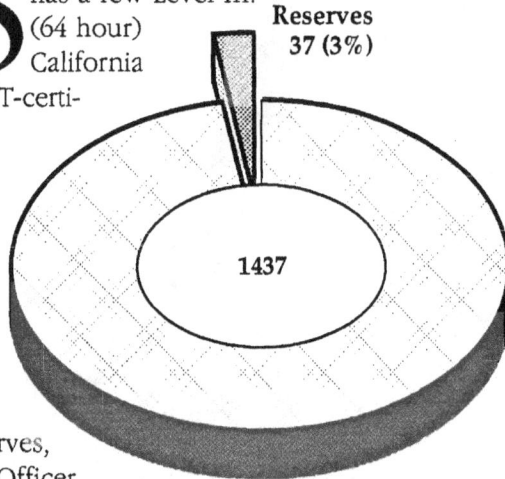

Reserves
37 (3%)

1437

Full Time
1,400 (97%)

reserves, but Officer Les Adams indicated that most of the 37 reserve officers are Level II.s (146 hour certified). "We won't even look at them if they don't have their Level II.," he said of those that come forth to apply.

Before they begin the process to become part of the San Francisco Police Department's

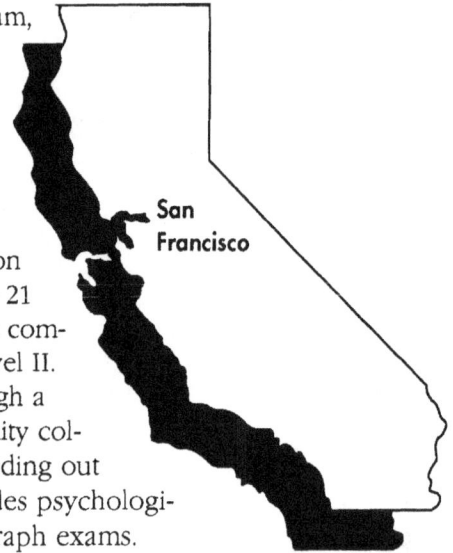

San Francisco

reserve program, aspiring reservists, who must be residents of the 46 square mile city (26 square miles on land) and age 21 or older, must complete their Level II. training through a local community college. The weeding out process includes psychological and polygraph exams.

The 1,400 full-time officers for the 800,000 population city, are trained for 900 hours and complete a 480 hour field training officer (FTO) program.

Contact:

Officer Les Adams
Field Operations Bureau
San Francisco Police Dept.
85 Bryant Street
San Francisco, CA 94103

415/553-1527

The program, which is currently being revamped, finds San Francisco reserves assisting at Candlestick Park ballgames and on patrol posts. No minimum monthly service hours have been established as of yet, though Adams indicated that the retooling of the program should rectify that situation.

The volunteer officers wear the same agency provided uniform as the regular officers, except that the patch is light blue with a "reserve" rocker above it. The reserves buy the Smith & Wesson or Colt .357 or .38 revolver and must qualify with their weapon three times per year.

Seattle Police Department

City of Seattle, Washington

Number of Officers	
1,250	Full Time
50	Reserves
1,300	Total Officers

Minimum Training Hours Req.	
440	Full Time
260	Volunteer Reserve

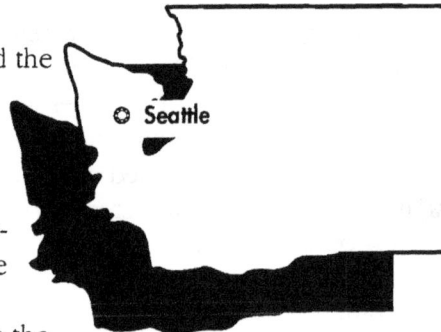

Much like the Los Angeles Police Department's Reserve Corps., Seattle's reserves eschew ranks in favor of administrative titles. All officers in the 500,000 population, 83 square mile city, from the reserve chief Richard Ostbye on down, wear the same silver badge, thereby minimizing the public's confusion concerning reserve and full-time ranking status.

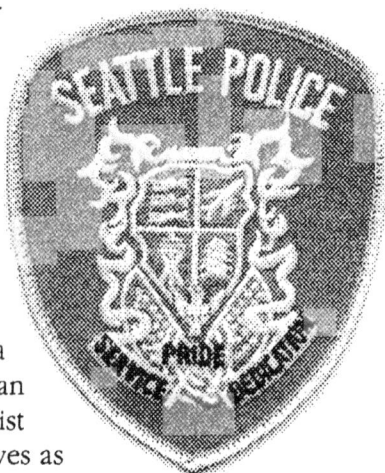

Terry Lattin, a 23 year veteran Seattle reservist who also serves as president of the Washington State Reserve Law Enforcement Association, said all reserves are armed and uniformed the same as the regular officers with the exception of the badge which has the word "reserve" in small letters at the bottom. The uniforms are supplied through the department's quartermaster system.

The Seattle P.D. also issues a Smith & Wesson .38 revolver. The department went to semi-automatics within the last year and a half. With three years reserve time, reserves can request transitional training and qualify to carry one of seven different semi-auto models approved by the dept.

Contact:

Lieutenant Dave Malinowski
Commander
Special Activities Section
Seattle Police Department
305 South Harrison Street
Seattle, WA 98109

206/684-7376

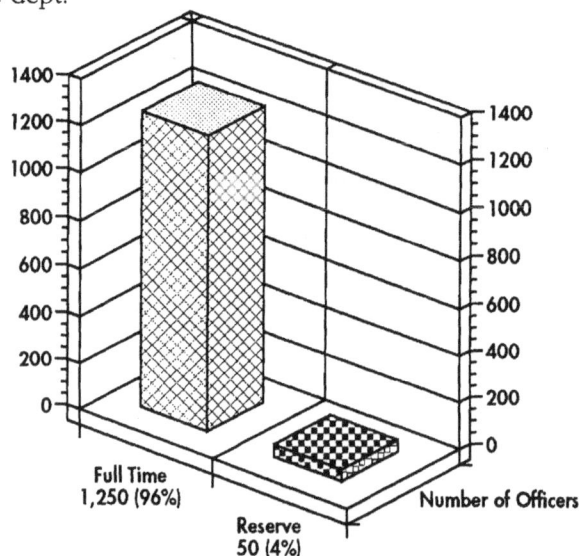

Lieutenant Dave Malinowski, commander of the Special Activities Section, which oversees the reserves, said the 1,250 full-time officer department's 50 volunteer officers, minimum of age of 21, must serve 16 hours in uniform. The 16 hours does not include four hours of monthly in-service training. There is a one year, 192 hour probationary/ field training officer (FTO) period.

Reserves in Seattle, who donated 17,000 hours in 1991, are able to ride with a regular officer or they may go solo for some duties (prisoner transport, foot beats in Seattle center). Once they've fulfilled their 16 hour a month in uniform obligation, Malinowski said they may also work with detective units on followup. Other details include the harbor unit and the mounted horseback unit. Two reserve officers even work with the gang unit 150 hours a month.

Malinowski said the reserves undergo 260 hours of training for two nights a week and some Saturdays for driving and firearms over the course of six months. Full-timers are trained for 440 hours and have a 600 hour FTO program.

Pictured above are a few of Seattle's 50 reserve police officers. Reserve Officer Terry Lattin, president of the Washington State Reserve Law Enforcement Association, can be spotted on the left side of the second to last row.

Shelby County Sheriff's Office

City of Columbiana, Alabama

Number of Officers	
58	Full Time
27	Reserves
85	Total Officers

Minimum Training Hours Req.	
280	Full Time
280	Reserve

Shelby County Sheriff's Reserve Captain Mark Neeley, who also serves as president of the Alabama Sheriffs Reserve Association, explained that his volunteer reserve deputies have several options they may take to acquire their 280 hour Alabama Peace Officers Standards Commission certification. "They can go three days a month on weekends for a year (a Saturday, Sunday, Saturday type of scenario) at Jefferson State College in Birmingham or at the University of Alabama at Tuscaloosa," the full-time personnel director

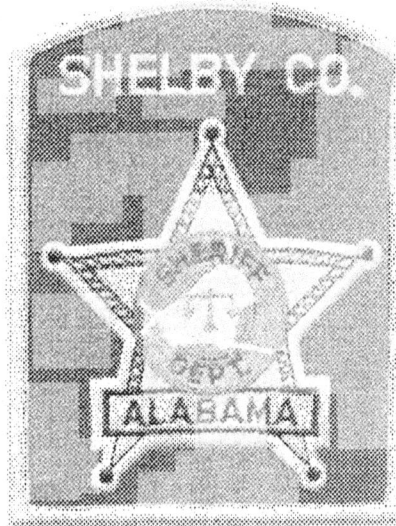

for a steel company explained. "They could also go to the regular day academy for seven straight weeks in Tuscaloosa."

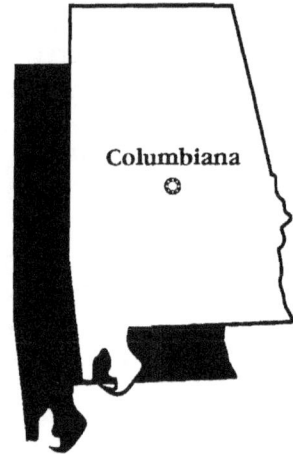

Columbiana

The 27 reserve deputy sheriffs are 280 hour trained just like the 58 full-timers. The reserves have a 40 hour field training officer (FTO) program and the full-timers have a 160 hour FTO program. Three hours a month of in-service training is slated.

Reserves pay for all uniforms, equipment and firearms, which are identical to those utilized by the regulars. The Glock 9mm or .40 caliber firearm must be qualified on twice a year.

Contact:

**Reserve Captain Mark Neeley
Shelby County Sheriff's Office
104 Depot Street, P.O. Box 1095
Columbiana, AL 35051-1095**

205/669-4181

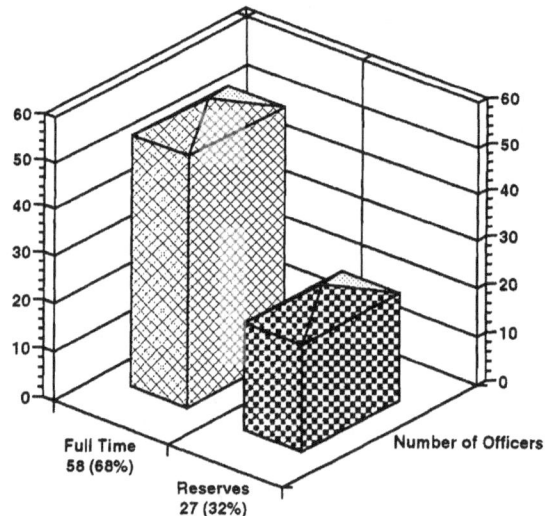

Full Time
58 (68%)

Reserves
27 (32%)

Number of Officers

The slight uniform difference is manifested in the five point star badge which is gold for full-time deputies and silver for the reserves.

Neeley said the Shelby County program, under the watch of Sheriff James Jones and Captain Chris Curry, has gained much ground. The reserves put in at least 16 hours per month and last year donated 10,000 hours riding with another reserve or with a salaried deputy. Five reserves take home fully marked and equipped patrol units to keep cruisers strategically deployed throughout the county.

Reserve deputy sheriff applicants, who must be 21 or older, have to run through a gauntlet comprised of an in-house panel interview, driving record and criminal history check, academic records and background check with interviews.

Shelby County Sheriff's Office

City of Memphis, Tennessee

Number of Officers
800 Full Time
280 Reserves
1,080 Total Officers

Minimum Training Hours Req.
430 Full Time
430 Reserve

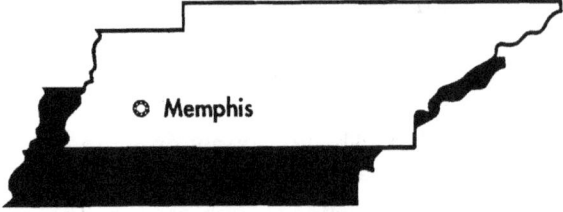

Administrators of the Shelby County Sheriff's Office's reserve deputy program view themselves as early pioneers of the equal status reserve concept. All deputies, paid and volunteer, are identical from their training right down to their ID cards and have full police powers and carry a firearm 24 hours a day. The 800 full-time and 280 reserve deputy sheriffs go through the same 430 hour basic police curriculum.

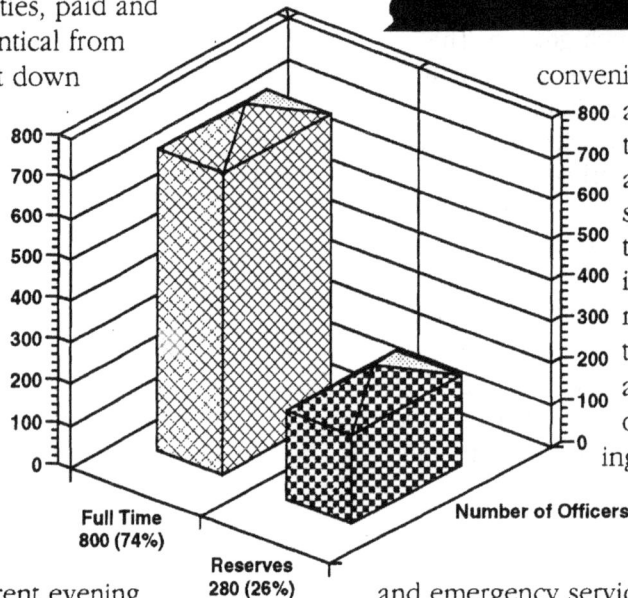

In fact, in the current evening academy class designed for reserves, 16 of the students are full-timer officers who like the convenient scheduling. The academy is held Tuesday through Thursday nights and all day Saturday for seven months. An additional 192 hour field training officer (FTO) component, dubbed preceptor training, is also taken by all officers, as is 40 hours of annual in-service training.

○ Memphis

Full Time
800 (74%)

Reserves
280 (26%)

Number of Officers

Chief B.J. Patterson, the director of the reserves and emergency services, said that uniforms are identical and the initial cost is borne by the reservists with a yearly uniform allotment pegged at $125.00. The firearm may be a revolver or semi-automatic (most choose semi-automatic) and the reserve officer may use one of the agency supplied guns or purchase his own. Qualification takes place two to three times a year depending on the firearm carried.

The reserve deputies, who serve at least 32 hours per month, are paid $1.00 per year to make

Contact:

Chief B. J. Patterson
Director of Reserves and Emergency Services
Shelby County Sheriff's Office
5735 Shelby Oaks Drive
Memphis, TN 38134

901/373-1780

them employees of the 800 square mile county with a population of a little more than 1,000,000 people. The $1.00 payment makes the reserves eligible for hospitalization. Reserves are utilized in every section of the department which covers unincorporated areas of the county along with seven municipalities, although they must initially serve for six months in patrol before going to a specialized unit. Some of the challenges the reservists take on include solo patrol, patrol as a second officer, traffic (including motorcycle), civil process, fugitives, interstate drug interdiction patrol, crime scene investigations, general and narcotics investigations and undercover detective work.

The reserves, who donated 85,758 hours last year, do not regularly work in the county jail, with it's population of a little over 2,400, but come in when law enforcement deputies are called on to conduct sweeps. The department has 2,000 total personnel including the jail deputies.

As with full-timers, applicants for the volunteer commissioned slots go through an elaborate process. Over 200 already processed and approved applications are in the files just waiting for an opening in the evening academy. Following the initial application, a background investigation is conducted by the Shelby County Sheriff's internal affairs bureau (IAB). A physical agility test must then be passed with a minimum score of 70%. A 500 question MMPI and psychological is taken, as is a physical and drug screening. An interview by a team of two to three senior reserves along with a review by the sheriff caps the long road to becoming a reserve deputy.

In addition to doctors, lawyers, and a few multimillionaires, many of the reserves serve in the U.S. Marines or the Navy. The minimum age to join is 21, although Patterson indicated that the median age is 30.

The sheriff's department also has 141 civilian emergency medical search and rescue volunteer personnel made up of paramedics and emergency medical technicians (EMTs), some of whom serve dually as commissioned law enforcement reserve deputies.

St. Louis Police Department

City of St. Louis, Missouri

Number of Officers	
1,550	Full Time
56	Reserves
1,606	Total Officers

Minimum Training Hours Req.	
680	Full Time
240	Reserve

Reserve officers in St. Louis used to wear a reserve patch but eschewed it sometime ago in favor of the patch-less style sported by the 1,550 full-time officers. The 56 reserves wear the

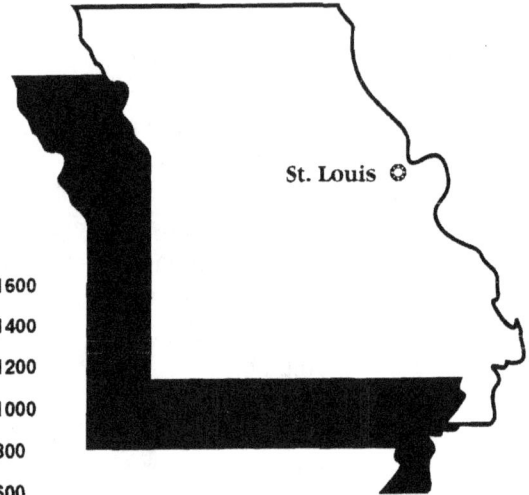

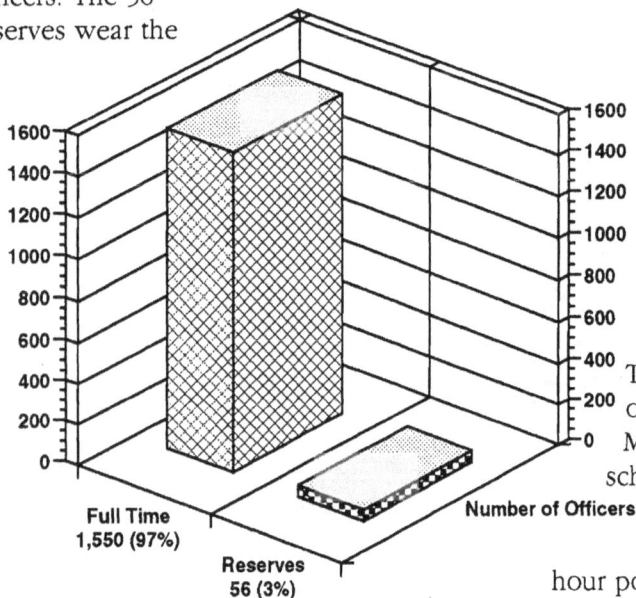

Full Time
1,550 (97%)

Reserves
56 (3%)

Number of Officers

same agency supplied uniform as the regulars, except for the "R" which is placed before the badge number.

The reserve officers undergo 240 hours of training for four hours a night on a Monday through Thursday evening schedule. The 13 week training stint also includes some eight hour Saturday sessions. Full-time officers complete a 680 hour police academy.

In-service training is conducted four hours each month and reserves must qualify on their agency purchased Smith and Wesson .38 revolver two times a year. Reserves must serve a minimum of 240 hours a year (20 hours a month) working patrol, as well as events such as baseball games and parades. Detectives are allowed to utilize reserve officers on cases as long as they remain in uniform.

Applicants to the program must be 21 years old and pass a battery of tests including psychological, physical and oral board.

Contact:

Sergeant Darrel Battle
Commander of Police Reserve Unit
St. Louis Police Department
1200 Clark
St. Louis, MO 63103

314/444-5640

Tampa
Police Department

City of Tampa, Florida

Number of Officers
800 Full Time
25 Reserves
55 Auxiliaries
880 Total Officers

Minimum Training Hours Req.
570 Full Time
570 Reserve
132 Auxiliary

The 80 volunteer officers in Tampa's reserve forces bureau are divided into the 55 auxiliaries, with 132 hours of basic police training, and the 25, 570 hour police academy trained reserves. As detailed in Florida statutes, auxiliary officers are armed and have police powers while on duty and under the supervision of a certified officer. Reserves go through the same training as full-time officers, 570 hours in Tampa, and have the same authority as they are fully certified.

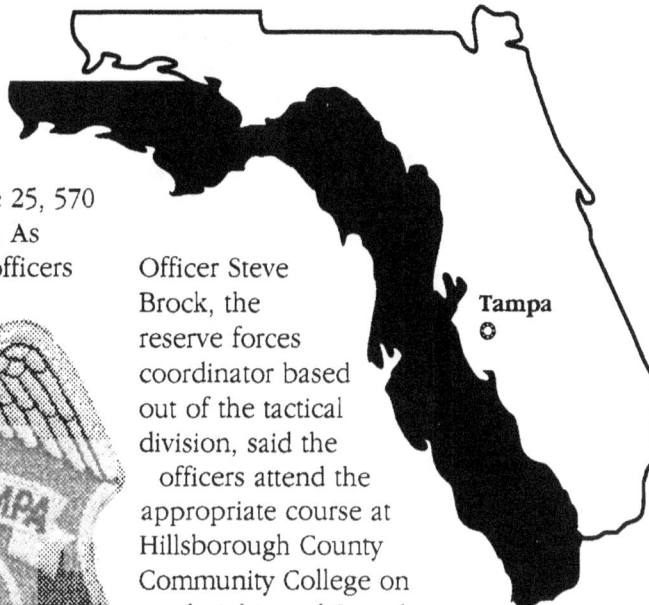

Officer Steve Brock, the reserve forces coordinator based out of the tactical division, said the officers attend the appropriate course at Hillsborough County Community College on weeknights and Saturdays.

The auxiliary officers have an additional 132 hour field training officer (FTO) program, while reserve officers and salaried officers have a 640 hour FTO program.

Auxiliary officers are used with a certified officer on patrol. Reserve officers are serving as detectives and on patrol. Brock said many of the reserves are former full-time Tampa police officers.

Reserves and auxiliaries must serve one eight hour shift and one four hour in-service training meeting for a total commitment of 12 hours monthly. Brock said 1,800 assignments were completed in 1992 for a total hourly donation of 17,623 hours and "a savings to the city of $600,000."

Contact:

Officer Steve Brock
Reserve Forces Coordinator
Tampa Police Department
1710 North Tampa Street
Tampa, FL 33602

813/932-1555

All three categories (regular, reserve and auxiliary) of officers' uniforms are identical, except that auxiliary officers are identified as such on their shoulder patch in small letters under the city seal. In order to minimize the confusion due to the volunteer officers' rank structure, the white shirts worn by the regular supervisors were jettisoned in favor of the patrol officers' blue shirt. Gold rank insignia is still worn by volunteer supervisors.

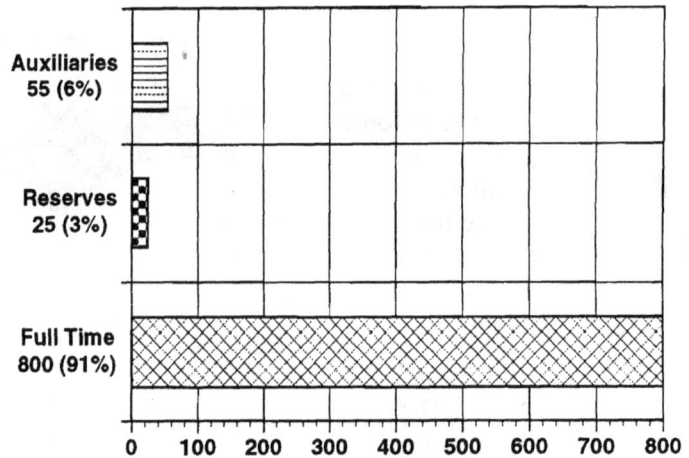

The agency pays for all uniforms, equipment and the Glock 9 mm firearm. Officers qualify once a year on the weapon.

With a minimum age of 21, reserve or auxiliary officer candidates go through the same weeding out process as full-timers. The entry gauntlet includes preliminary interview, application, interview, polygraph, background investigation, psychological and physical fitness test.

Auxiliaries 55 (6%)

Reserves 25 (3%)

Full Time 800 (91%)

0   100   200   300   400   500   600   700   800

Trenton
Police Department

City of Trenton, New Jersey

In the Garden State's capital city, former Trenton Police detective and bomb squad member Charles R. Betz oversees a force of 29 auxiliary police officers. Betz, the 25 year law enforcement veteran and director of municipal disaster control bunkered deep within Trenton Police Headquarters, has had quite a few auxiliaries make the transition from volunteer to full-time status.

Unlike many other New Jersey municipal auxiliary police officers, such as Bloomfield and Maplewood, the 29 auxiliaries are unarmed. They are Monadnock PR-24 certified and carry sidehandle police batons. Uniforms and equipment are provided by the city. The badge and patch says "auxiliary."

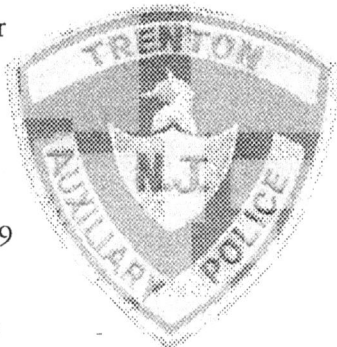

Because Mercer County does not have an auxiliary academy, Trenton's people have to travel up Route 1 North to attend the 87 hour Middlesex County Auxiliary Police Academy held at the Middlesex County Police Academy in Edison. Betz said in-service training is held two hours a month.

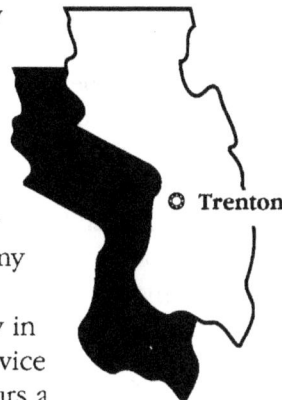

Trenton follows the minimum eight monthly hours required by the New Jersey State Police/Office of Emergency Management, however most of the Trenton auxiliaries far exceed it. Last year, Betz said his officers donated 2,928 hours on special events and handling disasters and emergencies such as crowd and traffic control at fires.

With a minimum age of 18, auxiliary police officers for the City of Trenton fill out the same 12-page application as full-time officers. They must also undergo a background check, medical exam and oral interview.

Contact:

Charles R. Betz
Director
Municipal Disaster Control
Trenton Police Headquarters
225 North Clinton Avenue
Trenton, NJ 08609

609/989-3630

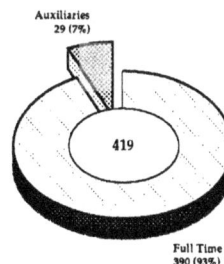

Auxiliaries
29 (7%)

419

Full Time
390 (93%)

Tucson
Police Department

City of Tucson, Arizona

Number of Officers
776 Full Time
26 Reserves
26 Limited Reserves
828 Total Officers

Minimum Training Hours Req.
440 Full Time
500 Reserve
365 Limited Reserve

The Tucson Police Department's Officer Jeff Todd, based at the 776 full-time officer agency's training center, said the organization groups its reserve officers in two categories with the distinction determined by the amount of training received. The 26 limited reserves, who ride as a second officer, have 365 hours of academy training and have yet to complete a 560 hour field training officer (FTO) program and an additional training period for a total academy hour tally of 500 hours. A solo qualified, top level reserve, of which Tucson has 26, has fulfilled all of the requirements as stated. Ten of the 26 are former full-time officers.

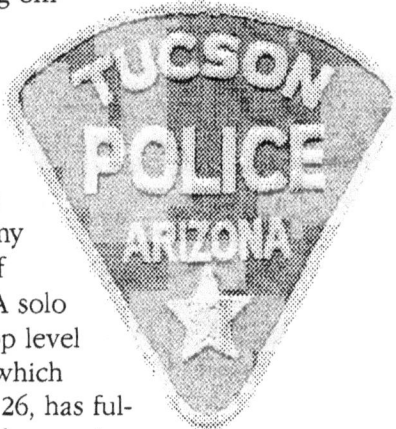

Founded in 1976, The reserve program's training is conducted Tuesday and Thursday nights for four hours and on eight hour Saturdays for a little more than six months. Although the Arizona Law Enforcement Officer Advisory Council (ALEOAC) requires that all certified officers undergo eight hours of training every three years, Tucson has its regular and reserve officers do so on an annual basis. Firearms qualification takes place two times a year.

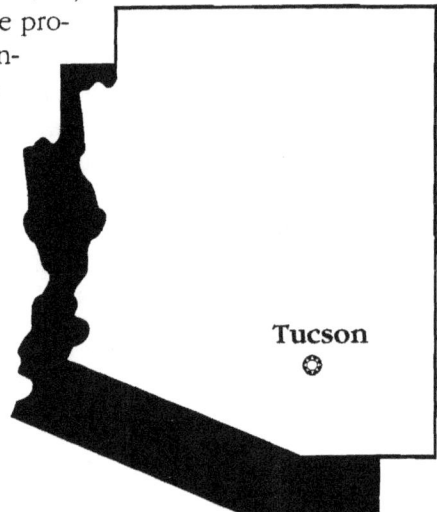

As with the salaried officers, reservists, mini-

Contact:

Officer Jeff Todd
Training Center
Tucson Police Department
3200 North Silverbell
Tucson, AZ 85745

602/791-4464

Sergeant John Heiden
Reserve Coordinator
Tucson Police Department
P.O. Box 1071
Tucson, AZ 85702-1071

602/791-4404

mum age of 21, are given a revolver by the department with the option to acquire a semi-automatic on their own. Uniform costs are borne by the reserve, but Todd indicated that surplus usually has extras that they give to them. Other than the word "reserve" on the badge, the uniforms are identical.

Sergeant John Heiden, the reserve coordinator, said that his 52 reserves (he has another 27 in the police academy) donated 28,491 hours in calendar year 1992. Around 18,000 of those hours were spent in patrol and 10,000 were spent on special events and training. They are required to serve two ten hour shifts a month and one four hour monthly training meeting for a total of 24 hours. "The average reserve worked 440 hours last year. Some reserves give 1,000 hours annually."

Heiden said the main focus of the reserves is patrol, but that they also work as narcotics and fraud detectives and as pilots in air support, as well as in community resources.

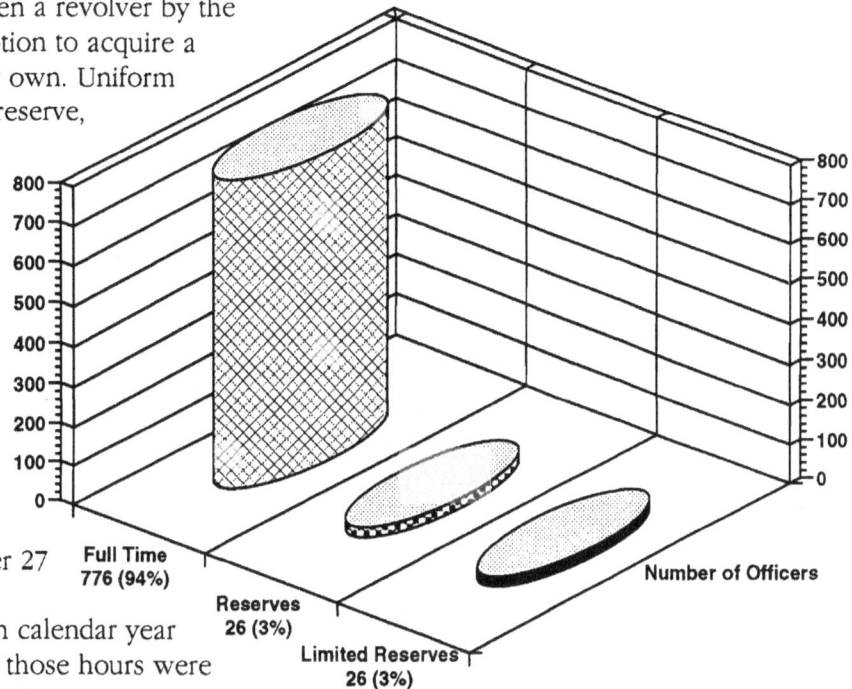

Full Time
776 (94%)

Reserves
26 (3%)

Limited Reserves
26 (3%)

Number of Officers

Vineland Police Department

City of Vineland, New Jersey

In the City of Vineland, the 30 member special law enforcement officer (SLEO) force is comprised of five Class II. specials and 25 Class I. specials. Sergeant Harvey Shaw, the coordinator of the program, explained that, pursuant to state statutes, Class II.s carry firearms and Class I. special officers do not.

The department primarily sends their Class II. specials to two county academies, though the state certification, which averages 452 hours, may be earned elsewhere. One of the two academies utilized is the 600+ hour SLEO II. academy at the Gloucester County Police Academy in Deptford Township which takes place over the course of nine months. The other route is the Cape May County Police Academy. Their intensive session runs six very long days a week for seven weeks straight for a total of over 300 hours.

The Class I. special officers, which get an average of 78 hours of training, according to the New Jersey Police Training Commission (PTC), normally attend the Gloucester County Police Academy.

The 113 full-timers, who get an average of 669 hours of training, go to many different academies including the Atlantic City Police Academy and the Gloucester County Police Academy. The full-time officer field training officer (FTO) program is 480 hours.

The armed specials are issued Glock Model 17 9mm semi-automatics by the police department. Day and night fire qualification takes place two times a year. In-service training for the specials covers around 96 hours a year. The special officers pay for their own uniforms which indicate "special" on the badge and patch. Their shirt is medium blue, while the salaried officers have a light blue shirt.

Shaw said that the special officers worked in excess of 5,000 hours last year handling such assignments as courts, city facilities security, patrol of the city's 18 parks and foot patrol of the business and shopping districts.

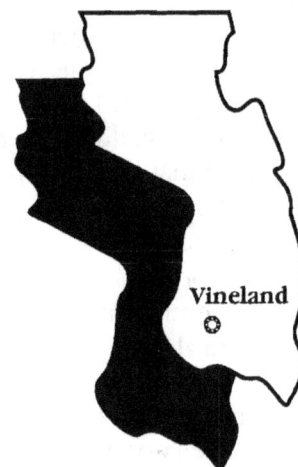

Contact:

Sergeant Harvey Shaw
Coordinator, Specials
Vineland Police Department
111 North 6th Street
Vineland, NJ 08360

609/794-4205

They also handle special events such as dances and sporting events, as well as emergencies the likes of civil disturbances.

Special police officers in the City of Vineland, minimum age of 21, have to fill out the same application as full-time officers. They also take a psychological exam, medical, background investigation and oral interview.

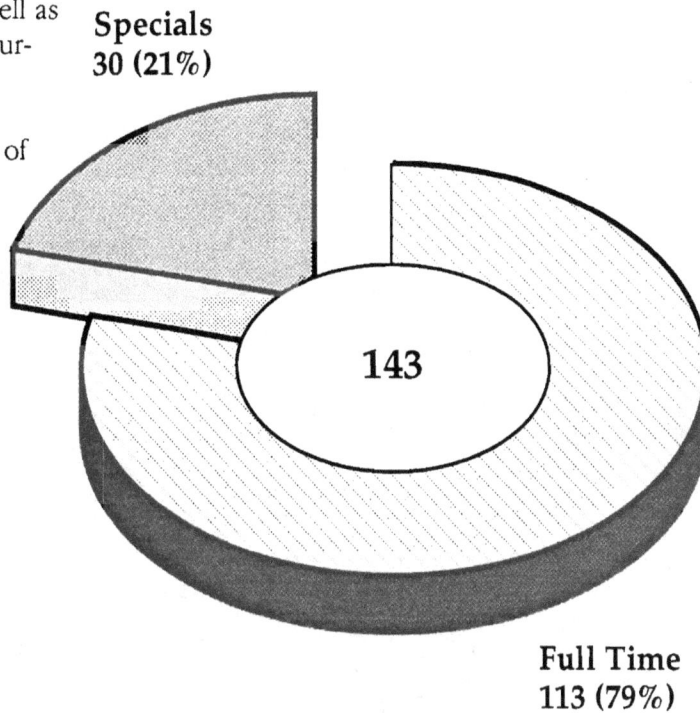

Specials
30 (21%)

143

Full Time
113 (79%)

Virginia Beach Police Department

City of Virginia Beach, Virginia

Number of Officers	
640	Full Time
60	Auxiliaries
700	Total Officers

Minimum Training Hours Req.	
520	Full Time
520	Auxiliary

The full-time officer who serves as the commanding officer over the auxiliary police program in Virginia Beach, Lieutenant J.W. Pritchard, said he expects to put 32 to 40 people (out of an applicant pool of 120 hopefuls) into an academy class soon adding to the 60 respected auxiliary volunteers already toting Smith and Wesson 6906 9mm firearms for the city.

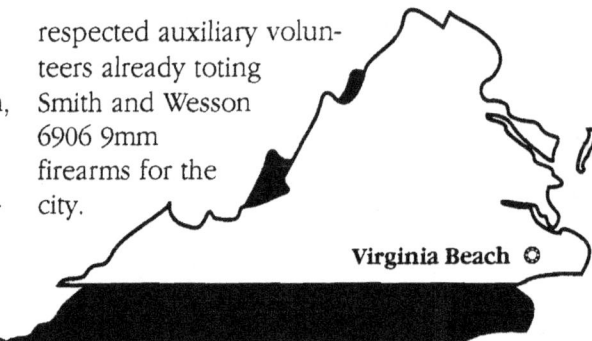

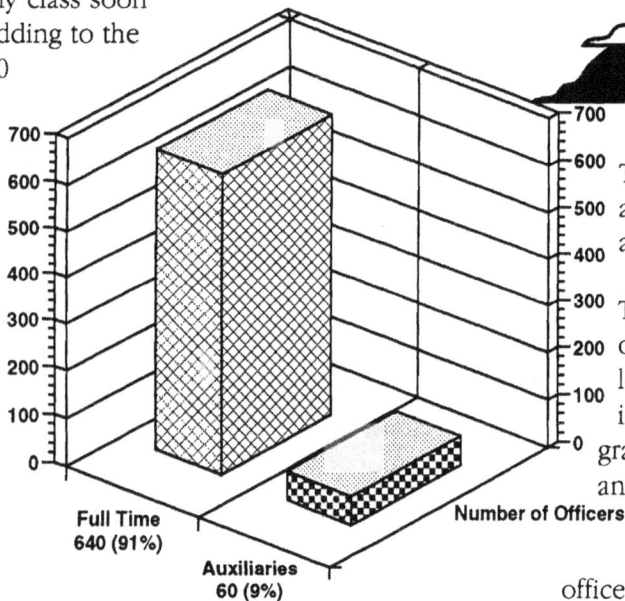

Virginia Beach ○

The class is held on Wednesday nights and all day on Saturday and Sunday for around 25 weeks.

The aspiring auxiliary officers must be 21 or older and have to pass the same gauntlet as salaried officers. The process involves background investigation, polygraph, psychological profile, aptitude test and oral board.

Full Time
640 (91%)

Auxiliaries
60 (9%)

Number of Officers

Virginia Beach has 640 full-time police officers and 60 auxiliaries with 520 hours of police academy training. Full-timers go through a 420 hour field training officer (FTO) program while reserves undergo 360 hours. Like the regulars, auxiliary police officers take 40 hours of in-service training in a two year block. Officers qualify twice a year on day and night fire for handgun and shotgun. Academy trained, FTO trained auxiliary officers, who according to Pritchard "are exactly the same right down to state certi-

Contact:

Lieutenant J.W. Pritchard
Commanding Officer, Auxiliary Police
Virginia Beach Police Department
Public Safety Building
Virginia Beach, VA 23456

804/427-4890

fication," may carry their agency provided 6906 firearm off duty.

Auxiliary officers are used in uniformed duties and each serve at least 20 hours a month. In fiscal year 1991-1992, the auxiliaries worked 28,895 hours. The department provides the identical gear (the badge and patch says "auxiliary").

The Virginia Beach program is divided into four levels. Level IV. auxiliaries are not trained or state certified. They work in the precinct on clerical duties. A Level III. auxiliary is a recruit in the police academy. Once they have graduated and are in the FTO program, the auxiliary progresses to Level II. status. At this level, they can't ride by themselves or carry their firearm off duty. A Level I. has completed the FTO program and has full police powers.

Washington, D.C. Police Department

Washington, D.C.

Number of Officers	
4,400	Full Time
180	Reserves
4,580	**Total Officers**

Minimum Training Hours Req.	
480	Full Time
160	Reserve

tributes to the crime fighting efforts in our nation's capitol. Special Operations Division Captain Bruce T. McDonald, who oversees the reserve corps., said the unarmed reserves are trained two nights a week for roughly six months for a total of 160 hours. Full-time officers get 480 hours in the academy along with a 240 hour field training officer (FTO) program.

Reserve officers in the District, who donated

With 180 men and women, the Washington, DC Metropolitan Police Reserve Corps. con-

38,616.5 hours in fiscal year 1992, ride as a second officer with a regular and generally do not drive patrol cruisers. They may also work a foot post with another reserve.

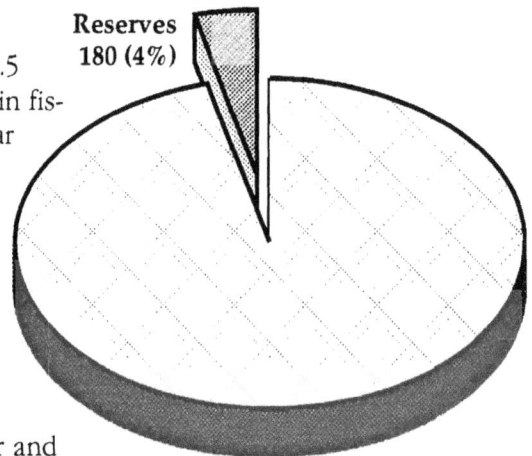

Reserves 180 (4%)

Full Time 4,400 (96%)

The reserves, who must be between the ages of 21 and 50, are uniformed the same, save for the badge which says "reserve." Aspiring reservists go through a background investigation, oral interview, fill out two questionaires and undergo a physical exam which includes a urinalysis.

Contact:

Capt. Bruce T. McDonald
Special Operations Division
Metropolitan Police
2301 L Street, N.W.
Washington, DC 20037

202/727-4627

Winston-Salem Police Department

City of Winston-Salem, North Carolina

Number of Officers
450 Full Time
16 Reserves
466 Total Officers

Minimum Training Hours Req.
432 Full Time
432 Reserve

Much like the Virginia Beach, VA, Police reserve program, Winston-Salem utilizes a level system for their 16 reservists. Following completion of a 432 hour police academy, which the 450 full-time officers also finish along with a 480 hour field training officer (FTO) program, reserves progress to Level I. and must work with another reserve or regular officer. Reserves attend local colleges, such as Forsyth County Technical College, Davidson Community College and Guilford County Technical College, for their 432 hour state certification.

After working 30 hours a month for six months with another officer and passing a written test, Level II. status is achieved. At Level II., the reserve officer may work alone on some assignments, but with another officer on others. At

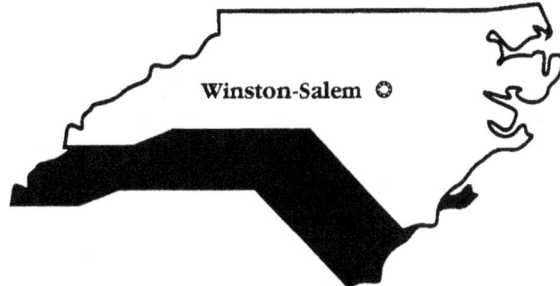

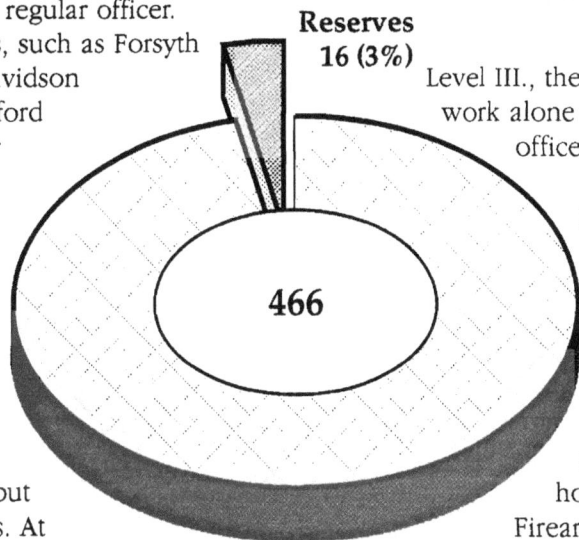

Winston-Salem ⊙

Reserves
16 (3%)

466

Full Time
450 (97%)

Level III., the reserve may work alone like a regular officer.

Reserves in Winston-Salem work at least 20 hours a month and have a monthly in-service training meeting two hours in length. Firearms qualification on the agency furnished Smith and Wesson 10mm firearm happens twice a year.

The department also pays for the uniform. It is identical except for the badge which says "reserve" in small letters.

The recruiting unit for the police department handles the processing of applicants who must be 21

Contact:

Reserve Major Tony Disher
Winston-Salem Police Department
P.O. Box 1707
Winston-Salem, NC 27102

919/773-7830

or older. The weeding out process includes a background investigation, basic agility test, psychological, interview and a physical with an option to conduct a drug urinalysis.

The reserve police officers assist the special operations division at special events such as runs, walks and demonstrations. They also work patrol assignments with the uniformed division.

Worcester
Police Department

City of Worcester, Massachusetts

```
Number of Officers
375  Full Time
 25  Auxiliaries
400  Total Officers

Minimum Training Hours Req.
720  Full Time
 96  Auxiliary
```

The 25 Worcester Police auxiliary officers, who patrol Massachusetts' second largest city, must be 96 hour reserve/intermittent Massachusetts Criminal Justice Training Council certified. Worcester trains 90% of their auxiliaries through an in-house 96 hour certification course, although some have gone elsewhere such as Mount Wachusett Community College's Central Massachusetts Training

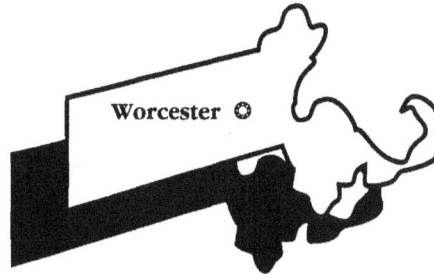

Academy based in Gardner, MA. The volunteer officers also have to take separate first responder, CPR and firearms courses.

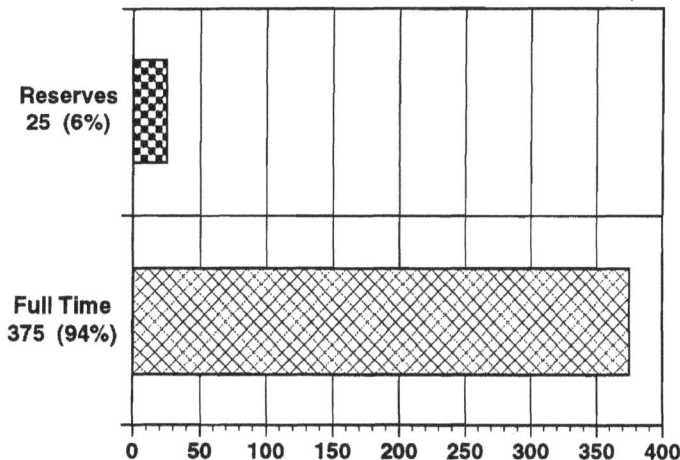

Full-time officers get a minimum of 720 hours (18 weeks) of academy training and complete a 480 hour field training officer (FTO) program.

The director of auxiliary operations, auxiliary sergeant Richard Courtemanche, said the officers' primary function is patrol of parks and city property. They also work civic functions such as parades. Auxiliaries generally ride with another auxiliary officer, those senior officers ride alone at the supervisor's discretion.

The auxiliary officers, who must be at least 18 years of age, work at least six hours on patrol with an additional three hours spent in in-service training. The total monthly minimum comes to nine hours. Courtemanche said the unit donated around 2,500 hours last year.

Auxiliary officers pay for their uni-

Reserves
25 (6%)

Full Time
375 (94%)

0   50   100   150   200   250   300   350   400

Contact:

Auxiliary Sergeant Richard Courtemanche
Director, Auxiliary Operations
c/o Training Division
Worcester Police Department
9-11 Lincoln Square
Worcester, MA 01608

508/799-8641

forms. They differ from the regulars' black shirts with their French blue shirts and badges and shoulder patches which state "auxiliary." The officers must also provide their own .38 or .357 revolver, but are issued .38 ammo by the Worcester Police Department. They qualify once a year on the gun and carry off-duty on a permit.

Aspiring auxiliaries must pass two background investigations conducted by the agency's internal affairs personnel and the auxiliary unit's board of review.

Yellowstone County Sheriff's Office

City of Billings, Montana

Number of Officers	
40	Full Time
35	Reserves
75	Total Officers

Minimum Training Hours Req.	
400	Full Time
180	Reserves

The 35 reserve deputy sheriffs with the Yellowstone County Sheriff's Office are uniformed the same as the 40 full-timers. Reserve Captain Don Wanner said the reserves are receiving 180 hours of training along with a 96 hour field training officer (FTO) program, whereas regulars undergo 400 hours of training. Reserves are released from the FTO program only after approval is obtained from all shift commanders and the sheriff.

Reserve deputies pay for the identical sheriff's department uniform, but the agency supplies the Glock 10mm semi-automatic firearm. Qualification for the Billings, MT,-based agency takes place three times a year with in-service training taking place four hours a month.

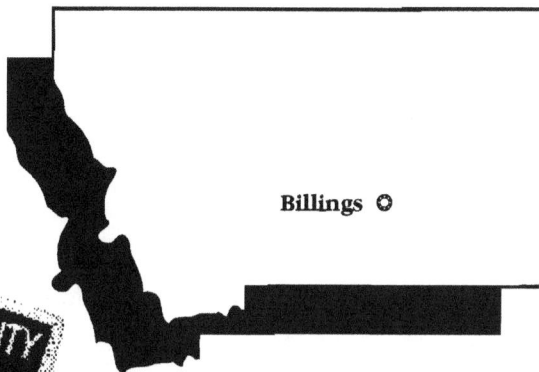

All reserves must be at least 21 years old, and serve at least eight hours a month. They contributed 12,000 hours last year patrolling alone or as a second deputy. They must complete an additional training program to become solo qualified.

Applicants to the volunteer program fill out an application and undergo a group of evaluation tests which include a background check, oral board, physical agility test, drug screening and polygraph.

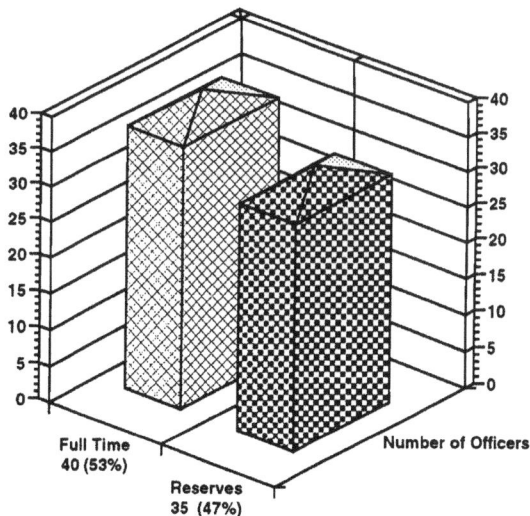

Contact:

Reserve Captain Don Wanner
Yellowstone County Sheriff's Office
Yellowstone County Courthouse
Billings, MT 59101

406/256-2929

SECTION
VII

Section VII.
State Police Highway Patrol: Overview

	Res.	Acad.	FT	FT Acad.	Monthly Min. Hrs.	Min. Age	Firearm
Alabama Highway Patrol	43	40	435	960	8	21	yes
Arizona Highway Patrol	45	440	495	440	20	21	yes
Connecticut State Police	271	207	980	960	16	18	yes
Florida Highway Patrol	589/12	97/520	1,644	800	11	19	yes
New Hampshire State Police	39	106	249	400	8	21	yes
New Mexico Mounted Patrol	300	200	N/A	N/A	16	21	yes
Ohio Highway Patrol	250	82	1,300	960	10	21	no
Vermont State Police	71	200	298	720	2.5	19	yes

SECTION VIII

Alabama Highway Patrol
Reserve Troopers

Number of Officers
435 Full Time
 43 Reserve Troopers
478 Total Officers

Minimum Training Hours Req.
960 Full Time
 40 Reserve Trooper

The 43 reserve troopers with the Alabama Highway Patrol bypass Alabama Peace Officers Standards and Training Commission (POST) 280 hour guidelines. They receive 40 hours of training and are not used as primary officers. Annual in-service training is pegged at 16 hours. They are used for event crowd management and as a second trooper in a patrol car during their eight hours a month of service.

"Reserve troopers must undergo the training and qualify with their .357 Model 19 firearm in school before they go out. They apply to their local troop and must pass backgrounds, be a resident of the state and over 21-years-of-age," said Captain James L. Fowler, assistant chief of the 435-trooper Highway Patrol agency.

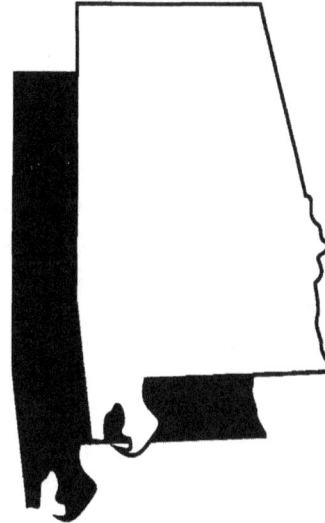

Contact:

Capt. James L. Fowler
Assistant Chief
Alabama Highway Patrol
P.O. Box 1511
Montgomery, AL 36102-1511

205/242-4383

Arizona DPS/Highway Patrol
Reserve Officers

Number of Officers	
495	Full Time
45	Reserve Officers
540	Total Officers

Minimum Training Hours Req.	
440	Full Time
440	Reserve Officers

Sergeant Iven T. Wooten, statewide reserve coordinator for the 45 reserve officers of the Arizona Department of Public Safety/Highway Patrol, said their volunteer troopers must go through the same 440 hour basic training mandated by the Arizona Law Enforcement Officer Advisory Council (ALEOAC) for full-time officers. Some ten academies are located across the state which offer the academy curriculum.

Screening for the volunteer officers is tough. They must pass all of the hurdles set for regular employees including medical, oral board and polygraph. The field training officer (FTO) program encompasses three shifts (24 hours) a week for a total of 320 hours.

Contact:

Sgt. Iven T. Wooten
Statewide Highway Patrol
Reserve Coordinator
Arizona Department of
Public Safety
2102 West Encanto Boulevard
P.O. Box 6638
Phoenix, AZ 85005-6638

602/223-2000

Connecticut State Police Auxiliary Troopers

Number of Officers
980 Full Time
271 Auxiliary Troopers
1,251 Total Officers

Minimum Training Hours Req.
960 Full Time
207 Auxiliary Trooper

Sergeant James J. Rodgers, auxiliary trooper coordinator with the Connecticut Department of Public Safety, Division of State Police, said the aura of the state police is a powerful drawing card. The individual who oversees standards for the 271 volunteer troopers said new policies are bringing the training level up to 207 hours with 24 hours devoted to firearms sessions. The program, in existence since 1941, used to mandate 100 hours of training one night a week for 26 weeks.

The 980 full-time troopers are trained for 960 hours and have a 960 hour (six month) field training officer (FTO) program.

Entry standards, outside of entry age restrictions, are the same as for paid troopers and include mandatory Connecticut residency. Auxiliary and full-time troopers must be at least 18 years of age.

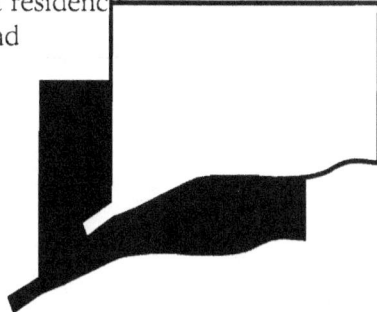

Auxiliary troopers, who donated 79,625 hours last year at 11 troops and at the range, pay for their own uniforms, equipment and Beretta 92F 9mm firearm. They qualify once a year and are given three opportunities to do so. Those that fail to qualify on one of their three tries, are given administrative duties (out of uniform and unarmed) until they can successfully qualify at the following year's scheduled range qualification day.

According to Mick Caruso, the auxiliary trooper who serves as the liaison in the State Police's Hartford headquarters, auxiliary troopers must serve at least 16 hours per month.

Contact:

Sgt. James J. Rodgers
Auxiliary Trooper Coordinator
Connecticut State Police
294 Colony Street
Meriden, CT 06450

203/238-6018

Auxiliary Trooper Mick Caruso
Auxiliary Trooper Liaison
Connecticut State Police
100 Washington Street
Hartford, CT 06106

203/566-2661

Florida Highway Patrol
Auxiliary Troopers/Reserve Troopers

Number of Officers	
1,644	Full Time
589	Auxiliary Troopers
12	Reserve Troopers
2,245	Total Officers

Minimum Training Hours Req.	
800	Full Time
97	Auxiliary Trooper
520	Reserve Trooper

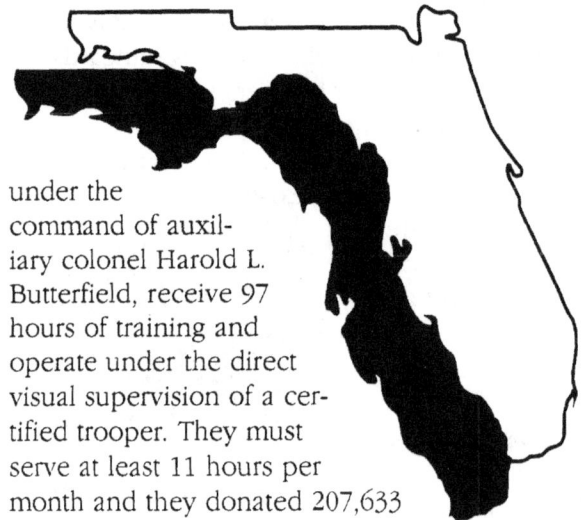

Reflective of the classifications codified in state statute, the Florida Highway Patrol has two distinct categories of volunteer troopers. Screening for both classifications is the same as for the 1,644 full-timer troopers and is conducted by the FHP investigators. The process includes polygraph and urinalysis.

The 589 armed auxiliary troopers, which serve under the command of auxiliary colonel Harold L. Butterfield, receive 97 hours of training and operate under the direct visual supervision of a certified trooper. They must serve at least 11 hours per month and they donated 207,633 hours in 1991. The 12 reserve troopers are fully trained and certified, just like the full-timers, for at least 520 hours. They have full police authority and discharge their duties on a solo basis.

Contact:

Aux. Col. Harold L. Butterfield
Florida Highway Patrol Auxiliary
c/o Indian River Appraisers, Inc.
2717 S.E. Morningside Boulevard
Port St. Lucie, FL 34952

407/335-9009

New Hampshire State Police Auxiliary Troopers

Number of Officers	
249	Full Time
39	Auxiliary Troopers
288	Total Officers

Minimum Training Hours Req.	
400	Full Time
106	Auxiliary Trooper

New Hampshire State Police Lieutenant Mark Furlone said the 39 auxiliary troopers in his agency go through an extensive background investigation similar to the 249 full-timers. The Granite State's auxiliary troopers, who carry Smith & Wesson 5906 9mm firearms during their 8 hour monthly minimum service, only have arrest powers while on duty. They must possess a valid New Hampshire driver's license, reside in one of the six field troops and be at least 21 years of age. The academy hours are pegged at 106.

The commander of the special services unit, which oversees the auxiliary program, said the State Police provide all equipment with the exception of the bulletproof vest. Auxiliary uniforms are identical, including the badge. The only difference manifests itself in the form of a rocker under the shoulder patch which says "auxiliary." The ID card states auxiliary as well.

Contact:

Lieutenant Mark Furlone
Commander, Special Services Unit
New Hampshire State Police
10 Hazen Drive
Concord, NH 03305

603/271-3793

New Mexico Mounted Patrol Troopers

Number of Officers	
xxx	Full Time
300	Auxiliary Troopers
xxx	Total Officers

Minimum Training Hours Req.	
xxx	Full Time
200	Auxiliary Trooper

In New Mexico, the state volunteers are the descendants of a mounted posse formed by the governor in the 1930s. No longer content with the sole qualifications of possessing a horse, saddle, and rifle, the modern day New Mexico State Police have established a demanding, symbiotic relationship with the 50 year old organization which, in an unusual statutory setup, is technically a separate state law enforcement agency.

Applicants, minimum age of 21, are subject to an oral review board, NCIC background check and random drug screening. Much like the Royal Canadian Mounted Police, New Mexico's Mounted Patrol is no longer confined to horseback and more often utilizes marked police cars.

"The name is a misnomer," NMSP Major Frank Taylor, the paid liaison, said. The agency has 300 armed volunteer officers who patrol in pairs in their own marked units or as a passenger in a regular cruiser with a full-time New Mexico State Police officer.

Members are allowed to use their own vehicles (free mounted patrol official license plates are furnished) provided the car meets inspection criteria involving emergency lights, siren, two way radio, first aid equipment and magnetic door signs. They still do sometimes ride horses for crowd control or search and rescue assignments. They have police powers while on duty and must work at least 16 hours per month.

New Mexico Mounted Patrol training first lieutenant Frank R. Kosciow explained

Contact:

**1st. Lt. Frank R. Kosciow,
Training Officer
New Mexico Mounted Patrol
District 5
2501 Carlisle, N.E.
Albuquerque, NM 87110**

academy certified police instructor added that they must pass a police officer proficiency exam (POPE) at the end of each stage and also go through a formal 100 hour field training officer (FTO) program.

that the volunteers undergo 200 hours of combined training made up of a pre-commission phase and a post-commission component.

"Pre-commission officers can work unarmed in cadet fatigues under the direct supervision of a mounted policeman or state police officer. When they are commissioned, they can carry and act as a mounted patrolman provided they complete the more advanced post-commission training within a year," Kosciow explained. The

Reserve Law Enforcement in the United States

New Mexico Mounted Patrol Statistics

The New Mexico Mounted Patrol, through their volunteer troopers, provided the equivalent of 50 full-time officers per year over the last three years (1989-1991). With an officer's salary pegged at $25,000 per annum, this amounts to a $1,241,667.00 savings. The NMMP also provided additional uniforms and equipment that amounted to $1,968,969.00 over the three year period. An extra 142 patrol cars for the last three years generated a cost savings of $3,541,667.00.

1991

EQUIPMENT/MATERIALS	Number	Value
Troop Owned:		
Patrol Units	16	$ 29,650.00
Radio Equipment	113	$ 69,600.00
Other Equipment		$ 39,866.00
Sub Total		$ 139,116.00
Trooper Owned:		
Patrol Units	117	$ 936,135.00
Radio Equipment	138	$ 82,270.00
Horse Units with Trans.	34	$ 88,470.00
Trooper Equipment		$ 347,456.00
Sub Total		$1,593,447.00
Total		**$1,593,447.00**

SERVICE (HOURS AND MILES)	HOURS	MILES
To New Mexico State Police	34,175	154,385
To Local Sheriff	3,843	22,825
To Local Police	3,363	12,456
To New Mexico State Fair	5,554	45,401
Other Events	2,570	41,240
Sub Total	39,505	276,207
Troop Administrative	5,157	31,247
Troop Meetings	4,036	29,842
Troop Training	11,564	30,330
Sub Total	20,757	91,419
Total	**93,834**	**367,626**

1990

EQUIPMENT/MATERIALS	Number	Value
Troop Owned:		
Patrol Units	11	$ 38,000.00
Radio Equipment	61	$ 55,300.00
Other Equipment		$ 147,400.00
Sub Total		$ 240,700.00
Trooper Owned:		
Patrol Units	137	$1,118,900.00
Radio Equipment	149	$ 156,100.00
Horse Units with Trans.	57	$ 259,800.00
Trooper Equipment		$ 489,000.00
Sub Total		$1,593,447.00
Total		**$2,023,800.00**

SERVICE (HOURS AND MILES)	HOURS	MILES
To New Mexico State Police	40,434	198,921
To Local Sheriff	2,226	12,459
To Local Police	3,027	20,095
To New Mexico State Fair	5,994	23,654
Other Events	4,298	53,171
Sub Total	56,024	308,300
Troop Administrative	20,153	48,803
Troop Meetings	8,521	47,122
Troop Training	31,720	103,124
Sub Total	60,394	199,049
Total	**116,418**	**507,349**

Reserve Law Enforcement in the United States

1989

EQUIPMENT/MATERIALS	Number	Value
Troop Owned:		
Patrol Units	11	$ 18,500.00
Radio Equipment	94	$ 86,400.00
Other Equipment		$ 221,317.00
Sub Total		$ 326,217.00
Trooper Owned:		
Patrol Units	133	$1,117,837.00
Radio Equipment	174	$ 215,615.00
Horse Units with Trans.	56	$ 389,290.00
Trooper Equipment		$ 484,502.00
Sub Total		$1,722,742.00
Total		**$2,048,959.00**

SERVICE (HOURS AND MILES)	HOURS	MILES
To New Mexico State Police	37,866	152,560
To Local Sheriff	2,986	9,617
To Local Police	3,126	7,686
To New Mexico State Fair	7,070	35,639
Other Events	3,983	40,779
Sub Total	**55,031**	**246,141**
Troop Administrative	12,353	20,715
Troop Meetings	5,614	5,614
Troop Training	26,777	106,207
Sub Total	**44,744**	**162,228**
Total	**99,775**	**324,456**

Source: 1993 New Mexico Mounted Patrol Annual Report, courtesy of First Lieutenant Frank R. Kosciow.

Ohio State Highway Patrol
Auxiliary Troopers

Number of Officers	
1,300	Full Time
250	Auxiliary Troopers
1,550	Total Officers

Minimum Training Hours Req.	
960	Full Time
82	Auxiliary Trooper

The 250 auxiliary troopers in Ohio have a newly upgraded training mandate of 82 hours with scheduling handled at the nine out of ten total districts which are involved in the program, which was founded in 1942.

The volunteers ride as a second trooper with the 1,300 strong full-time organization. With a minimum age of 21, they are required to serve 120 hours a year (10 hours a month) and they do not carry firearms.

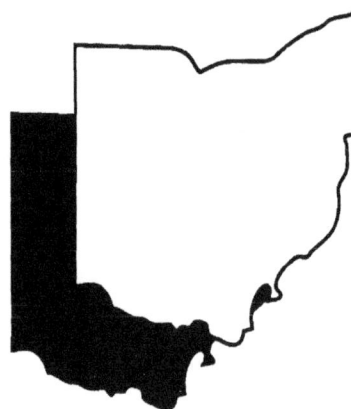

Contact:

Capt. Steven M. Raubenolt,
    Planning Services Section
Sgt. Mark R. Atkeson,
    Auxiliary Coordinator
Ohio State Highway Patrol
660 East Main Street
Columbus, OH 43205

614/466-2955

Vermont State Police
Auxiliary State Troopers

Number of Officers	
298	Full Time
71	Reserves
369	Total Officers

Minimum Training Hours Req.	
720	Full Time
200	Reserve

Sergeant Alan Buck, who oversees the auxiliary state trooper program for the Vermont State Police, said that his agency has a one year waiting list "assuming that the person gets through the screening process and that there is an opening." The department intends to bring on another 15 to 20 this year and stopped taking applications when 400 were amassed.

The 71 auxiliaries work mostly in the marine and snowmobile enforcement areas, but also sometimes work patrol. Buck said the 200 hours of training takes place at the State Police Academy in Williston, VT, on weekends for four to eight weeks. Two days are spent with the Coast Guard on marine issues. A 50 hour field training officer (FTO) program must be completed along with 30 hours of annual in-service training. The 298 full-time troopers take 720 hours of training and complete a 480 hour FTO program.

Buck explained that workman's comp., life insurance and per diem expenses are provided by the State Police, along with the Smith & Wesson 66-2 two and a half inch stainless .357

with .38 load. "The firearm is small because they work on boats and other cramped areas," said Buck. Qualification takes place twice annually in the spring and the fall. Because the auxiliary troopers are certified officers, they are allowed by state statute to carry their weapon off duty.

The uniform, also furnished by the agency, has an "auxiliary" rocker over the shoulder patch and the badge says "auxiliary state trooper."

Last year, in addition to some patrol rides with full-timers, Vermont's auxiliary state troopers, who must work at least 30 hours per year, worked 13,000 hours on marine patrol, 1,000 hours on snow mobile enforcement and 2,130 hours on training for a total of around 18,000 hours.

In order to become an auxiliary trooper, applicants age 19 or older are shepherded through the same elaborate process as full-time officers. A written exam is devised by the academy staff and given at different locations throughout the state. Among the hurdles to be passed are physical, polygraph, oral board, MMPI and a background investigation which covers motor vehicle records, NCIC, and employment and family interviews.

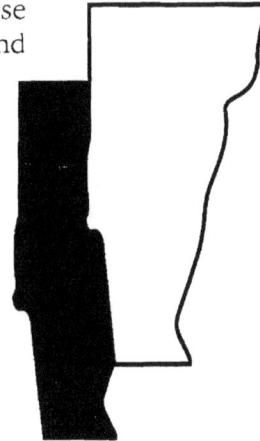

Contact:

Sgt. Alan Buck
Vermont State Police
565 St. George Road
Williston, VT 05495

802/828-0490

SECTION

IX

Alabama Sheriffs Reserve Association

The Alabama Sheriffs Reserve Association, under Shelby County Sheriff's reserve captain Mark Neeley, the president, has a membership of reserve deputies representing 25 county agencies from across the state. Membership is through employing agencies.

Started as insurance pool the group now has expanded mission concerning training. Two annual conferences are held. One is in the spring and the other is in the fall.

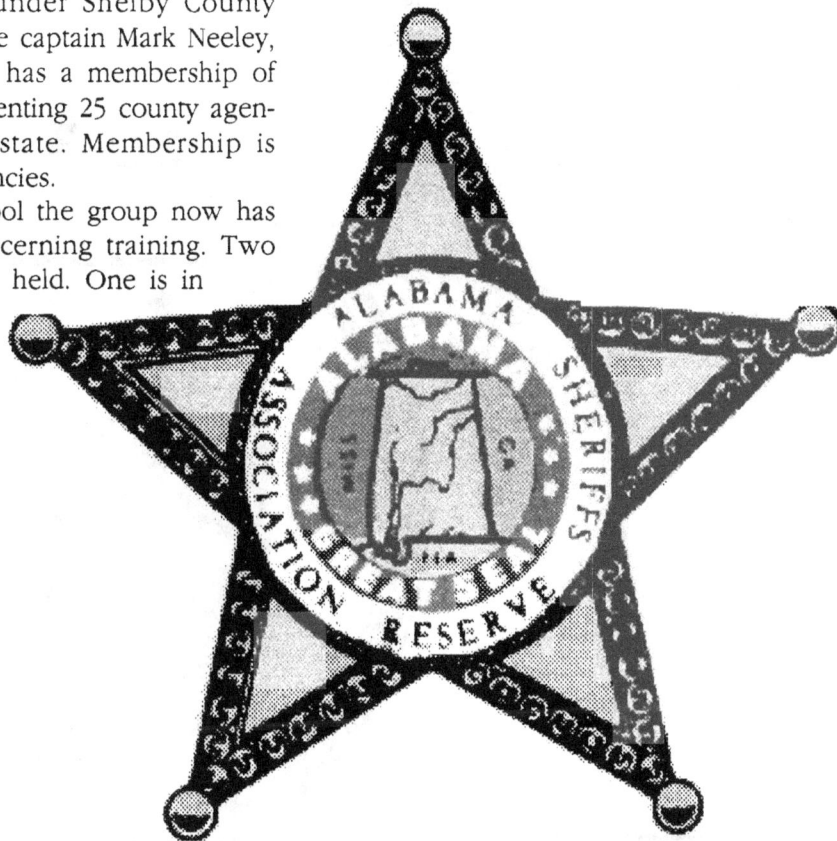

Contact:

Mark Neeley, President
Alabama Sheriffs Reserve
Association
2700 Royal Lane
Helena, AL 35080

California Reserve Peace Officers Association

Founded in 1974 by a group of reserve officers, the organization is currently headed by James C. Lombardi, the reserve officer in charge with the Los Angeles Police Reserve Corps. The group is very active with training and legislative agendas. CRPOA also publishes THE BACKUP magazine.

The 1992 Annual Reserve Peace Officers Conference (ARPOC) was hosted by the Sacramento County Sheriff's Office's reserves and was held at the end of September in Sacramento. More than 600 reserves representing 121 agencies were present.

Contact:

James C. Lombardi, President
California Reserve Peace
        Officers Association
P.O. Box 5622
San Jose, CA 95124

408/371-8239

Florida Police
Reserve Association

The group was founded in December 1991 by Jacksonville Sheriff's reserve Barry E. Newman. A private pilot, he works in the aviation unit. The group publishes the FLORIDA POLICE RESERVE OFFICER Magazine and is planning convention and training seminars.

Barry E. Newman

Contact:

Barry E. Newman, President
Florida Police Reserve Association
5030 Blanding Boulevard
Jacksonville, FL 32210

904/778-4501

Iowa State Reserve
Law Officer's Association

Annual training seminars are held in Iowa each August under the auspices of the 600 member Iowa State Reserve Law Officer's Association. Last year's seminar covered both defensive driving and child abuse. Daniel Brandt, the secretary/treasurer of the organization formed in 1973, said this August's seminar was a success.

Contact:

Daniel Brandt,
Secretary/Treasurer
Iowa State Reserve Law Officer's
Association
P.O. Box 26
Marshalltown, IA 50158

Massachusetts Reserve Law Enforcement Federation

Founded last year by Spencer, MA, auxiliary officer Erick Hoffman, the organization is working on an annual convention and will be publishing its magazine shortly.

Contact:

Erick Hoffman, President
Massachusetts Reserve Law
Enforcement Federation
430 Franklin Village Drive,
Suite 306
Franklin, MA 02038

Missouri Reserve Peace Officers Association

The Missouri Reserve Peace Officers Association was formed by David Blodgett, a Maryland Heights, MO, reserve police officer, as a spinoff of the Missouri Auxiliary & Reserve Police Association. Blodgett had served as president of that organization.

The new group focuses more intensely on training and legislative concerns.

Contact:

David Blodgett, President
Misouri Reserve Peace
Officers Association
550 Blazewood Drive
Ballwin, MO 63021

New Jersey Auxiliary Police Officers Association

Representing the interests of the state's auxiliary and special law enforcement officers, the New Jersey Auxiliary Police Officers Association serves as a networking and information base for its members, a source of advice for administrators and a tool to promote the concept of auxiliary and special polcie to the public.

Members of the organization, under president Richard B. Weinblatt, an auxiliary lieutenant with the South Brunswick Township, NJ, Police Department, receive the Association magazine, THE SHIELD, which is also sent to all police chiefs and sheriffs in the Garden State. The NJAPOA also holds a variety of in-service courses taught by full-time police officers on a range of topics including PR-24, PR-24 Instructor, Cap Stun, Use of Force, Domestic Violence, Stop/Frisk Narcotic Enforcement, Vehicle Stops and Approaches, Night Vehicle Stops and Approaches, Police Ethics and Professionalism and Traffic Direction.

Contact:

Richard B. Weinblatt, President
New Jersey Auxiliary Police
          Officers Association
7 Deer Park Drive
Building 2, Suite A2
Monmouth Jct., NJ 08852-9689

908/329-8924

Ohio Volunteer Peace Officers Association

Pat Feighery, first vice president of the Ohio Volunteer Peace Officers Association, said his 600-member organization looks out for the well-being of volunteer and part-time police by keeping in tune with legislation and working to further officer training. The reserve lieutenant with the Middletown, OH, Police Department explained that the group, which was founded in 1984, provides a networking foundation for those looking to see what ideas have worked elsewhere.

Quarterly meetings are held and the Association is planning a publication to upgrade their newsletter.

Contact:

Pat Feighery, First Vice President
Ohio Volunteer Peace Officers
    Association
P.O. Box 32481
Columbus, OH 43232-3481

614/443-7664

Oregon Reserve Peace Officers Association

Founded by John S. O'Brien, a reserve officer with the City of Sisters, OR, Police Department, the organization positions itself as a resource for Oregon reserve law enforcement. O'Brien, the president, served as a reserve polcie officer in Burbank, CA, and was present during the early days of the California Reserve Peace Officers Association.

Contact:

John S. O'Brien, President
Oregon Reserve Peace
    Officers Association
903 N.W. 95th Street
Redmond, OR 97756

Texas Reserve
Law Officers Association

The Texas Reserve Law Officers Association's president, former Dallas reservist Bill Martin, said the Lone Star state's reserve convention, complete with training opportunities for the 3,200 member organization, was attended by 150 volunteer police officers, deputy sheriffs and deputy constables. The group also publishes a newspaper for its members.

Contact:

Bill Martin, President
Texas Reserve Law
**   Officers Association**
P.O. Box 270407
Dallas, TX 75227

214/321-4300

Washington State Reserve Law Enforcement Association

The 350 members of the Washington State Reserve Law Enforcement Association welcome the annual convention that has been held for five years running. Terry Lattin, president of the group based in the Pacific Northwest and a 23 year veteran Seattle Police reserve officer, said training topics like firearms, gangs and drug updates have proven interesting the 250 attendees at the late summer conventions.

Contact:

Terry Lattin, President
Washington State Reserve Law
   Enforcement Association
P.O. Box 5432
Kennewick, WA 99336-0432

ANSWERS

In this book, find out...

What local department has their reserve officers police academy trained for 768 hours?
Dallas Police Department

What local county department's individual reserves donate an average of 43 hours each month ?
Harris County Sheriff's Office in the City of Houston, TX

What state has a minimum training requirement of only ten hours for their auxiliary officers?
State of New York

What state has 589 armed auxiliary state troopers?
Florida Highway Patrol

What local reserve unit donated $13,220,900 in equipment and manpower last year?
Fulton County Sheriff's Office in Atlanta, GA

What state does not have any minimum standards set for their full-time, part-time and volunteer law enforcement officers?
State of Hawaii

What local police department's reserve officers worked 40,000 hours last year?
Honolulu Police Department in Hawaii

What state has more then twice as many part-timers than full-timers?
State of Vermont

What state can part-time officers receive state certification through a correspondance course?
State of North Dakota

What state abolished their volunteer police in 1988?
State of Delaware

What state does a citizen have a 50% chance, depending on the time and day of week, of having a reserve officer respond to their call for police service?
State of California

What state changed their minimum academy training standards in one shot from zero to 400 hours in July of 1992?
State of Kentucky

What local city has the most volunteer officers with 4,402 uniforms hitting the streets?
New York City Police Department

What local agency's field training officer (FTO) program consists of 15 stints on each of the three shifts (within two years) for a total of 360 hours?
Broward County Sheriff's Office in Fort Lauderdale, FL

"Reserves in the U.S. save taxpayers millions of dollars and this book should give counties that don't have them the information they need to start a reserve program."

Res. Off. Barry E. Newman
President
Florida Police Reserve Association
Jacksonville, FL

"Rich Weinblatt's book is a long overdue reference for reserve and auxiliary policing in the United States. This is the first real attempt at gathering statistics on reserve and auxiliary programs."

Aux. Off. Erick Hoffman
President
Massachusetts Reserve Law Enforcement Federation
Franklin, MA

"Training is important. It is important for auxiliary police officers so they can provide professional backup and support to regular officers."

E.F. Maybanks, OBE, QPM
Chief Commandant
Metropolitan Special Constabulary
London, England

For additional copies of this book or if you require additional information, please contact

Richard B. Weinblatt, President
Center for Reserve Law Enforcement, Inc.
New Jersey Auxiliary Police Officers Association, Inc.
7 Deer Park Drive
Building 2, Suite A2
Monmouth Jct., NJ 08852-9689

TEL: 908/329-8924
FAX: 908/329-0479

"Richard has been an asset to this department as an auxiliary lieutenant and to the rest of the law enforcement community as an expert on reserves. We are very proud of the work he has done with *Reserve Law Enforcement in the United States*. The book underscores the need for and existence of professionalism within the volunteer officer ranks."

Captain Frederick A. Thompson
South Brunswick Township Police Department
Monmouth Jct., NJ

"Mr. Weinblatt's book reassures us that volunteer and part-time policing is the norm, embraced by the whole country, and does not only exist in a few states. His book points out that more people are dependent on volunteer police for service than we ever imagined."

Res. Lt. Pat Feighery
First Vice President
Ohio Volunteer Peace Officers Association

"We have had a highly effective, cost-efficient reserve program in Fulton County and commend Richard for his work brining reserves out of the closet and into the forefront. Reserve Law Enforcement in the United States is well written and points out the good work that reserves do."

Major Richard H. Davis
Chief Deputy of Reserves
Fulton County Sheriff's Office

"Through Richard Weinblatt's "Reserve Reports" column for our magazine, reserves are getting the attention and press they have long been denied. This useful book continues his work serving the information needs of reserves across the country."

Bruce W. Cameron
Editorial Director
LAW and ORDER Magazine
Wilmette, IL

"As commander of the nation's largest state highway patrol auxiliary, whose 589 auxiliary troopers donated a quarter of a million hours last year, I have long felt the need for a reference of this type for training and evaluation purposes. An FHP trooper has never lost his life while in the company of an auxiliary trooper."

Aux. Col. Harold L. Butterfield
Auxiliary Commander
Florida Highway Patrol
Port St. Lucie, FL

"As a reserve for many years, I always wanted to know where auxiliary and special officers in New Jersey stood in relation to each other, as well as to other reserves across the country. The book Richard wrote answers these questions and helps reserve administrators make educated judgements concerning what we need to do. As a NJAPOA board member, I am pleased to have been a part of the mechanism that has made such a useful reference source available."

Res. Lt. Frank Rizzo
Paramus Police Department
Paramus, NJ